The American Crisis Series
Books on the Civil War Era
Steven E. Woodworth, Associate Professor
Texas Christian University
SERIES EDITOR

∼ The Civil War was the crisis of the Republic's first century —the test, in Abraham Lincoln's words, of whether any free government could long endure. It touched with fire the hearts of a generation, and its story has fired the imaginations of every generation since. This series offers to students of the Civil War, either those continuing or those just beginning their exciting journey into the past, concise overviews of important persons, events, and themes in that remarkable period of America's history.

Volumes Published

James L. Abrahamson. *The Men of Secession and Civil War, 1859–1861* (2000). Cloth ISBN 0-8420-2818-8   Paper ISBN 0-8420-2819-6

Robert G. Tanner. *Retreat to Victory? Confederate Strategy Reconsidered* (2001). Cloth ISBN 0-8420-2881-1   Paper ISBN 0-8420-2882-X

Stephen Davis. *Atlanta Will Fall: Sherman, Joe Johnston, and the Yankee Heavy Battalions* (2001). Cloth ISBN 0-8420-2787-4
Paper ISBN 0-8420-2788-2

Paul Ashdown and Edward Caudill. *The Mosby Myth: A Confederate Hero in Life and Legend* (2002). Cloth ISBN 0-8420-2928-1
Paper ISBN 0-8420-2929-X

Spencer C. Tucker. *A Short History of the Civil War at Sea* (2002). Cloth ISBN 0-8420-2867-6   Paper ISBN 0-8420-2868-4

Richard Bruce Winders. *Crisis in the Southwest: The United States, Mexico, and the Struggle over Texas* (2002). Cloth ISBN 0-8420-2800-5   Paper ISBN 0-8420-2801-3

Ethan S. Rafuse. *A Single Grand Victory: The First Campaign and Battle of Manassas* (2002). Cloth ISBN 0-8420-2875-7
Paper ISBN 0-8420-2876-5

John G. Selby. *Virginians at War: The Civil War Experiences of Seven Young Confederates* (2002). Cloth ISBN 0-8420-5054-X
Paper ISBN 0-8420-5055-8

Edward K. Spann. *Gotham at War: New York City, 1860–1865* (2002).
Cloth ISBN 0-8420-5056-6 Paper ISBN 0-8420-5057-4

Anne J. Bailey. *War and Ruin: William T. Sherman and the Savannah Campaign* (2002). Cloth ISBN 0-8420-2850-1
Paper ISBN 0-8420-2851-X

Gary Dillard Joiner. *One Damn Blunder from Beginning to End: The Red River Campaign of 1864* (2003). Cloth ISBN 0-8420-2936-2 Paper ISBN 0-8420-2937-0

Steven E. Woodworth. *Beneath a Northern Sky: A Short History of the Gettysburg Campaign* (2003). Cloth ISBN 0-8420-2932-X
Paper ISBN 0-8420-2933-8

John C. Waugh. *On the Brink of Civil War: The Compromise of 1850 and How It Changed the Course of American History* (2003).
Cloth ISBN 0-8420-2944-3 Paper ISBN 0-8420-2945-1

Eric H. Walther. *The Shattering of the Union: America in the 1850s* (2004). Cloth ISBN 0-8420-2798-X Paper ISBN 0-8420-2799-8

Mark Thornton and Robert B. Ekelund Jr. *Tariffs, Blockades, and Inflation: The Economics of the Civil War* (2004).
Cloth ISBN 0-8420-2960-5 Paper ISBN 0-8420-2961-3

Paul Ashdown and Edward Caudill. *The Myth of Nathan Bedford Forrest* (2004). Cloth ISBN 0-8420-5066-3 Paper ISBN 0-8420-5067-1

The Shattering
of the Union

The Shattering of
the Union
America in the 1850s

The American Crisis Series
BOOKS ON THE CIVIL WAR ERA
NO. 14

Eric H. Walther

A Scholarly Resources Inc. Imprint
Wilmington, Delaware

Scholarly Resources Inc.
104 Greenhill Avenue
Wilmington, DE 19805-1897
www.scholarly.com

Cover

Top (*left to right*): Abraham Lincoln by Samuel Montague Fassett, National Portrait Gallery, Smithsonian Institution; John Brown by James Wallace Black, National Portrait Gallery, Smithsonian Institution; "Union Is Strength," Library of Congress; Frederick Douglass, unidentified artist, National Portrait Gallery, Smithsonian Institution.

Bottom (*left to right*): Harriet Elizabeth Beecher Stowe, unidentified artist, National Portrait Gallery, Smithsonian Institution; "Auction Sale," Library of Congress; Jefferson Davis, U.S. Senate Historical Office; William Lloyd Garrison, Wichita State University.

Library of Congress Cataloging-in-Publication Data

Walther, Eric H., 1960–
    The shattering of the Union : America in the 1850s / Eric H. Walther.
        p. cm. — (The American crisis series ; no. 14)
    ISBN 0-8420-2798-X (alk. paper) — ISBN 0-8420-2799-8 (pbk. : alk. paper)
        1. United States—History—1849–1877. 2. United States—Politics and government—1849–1861. I. Title. II. Series.
E415.7 .W35 2003
973.7'11—dc21

                                                                2003009146

For Travis Dennington

ABOUT THE AUTHOR

Eric H. Walther, an associate professor of history at the University of Houston, received a B.A. in history and American studies from California State University, Fullerton, and a Ph.D. from Louisiana State University. Walther served as an editorial assistant for *The Papers of Jefferson Davis*, is the author of *The Fire-Eaters* (1992), and is director of the Texas Slavery Project. He is currently completing a comprehensive biography of secessionist William Lowndes Yancey.

CONTENTS

It was said more than eighteen hundred years ago that a house divided against itself cannot stand, and the truth of the saying is written on every page of history, antecedent and subsequent. It is not unlikely that the history of our own country may furnish fresh and pregnant examples, by which philosophy may teach the same truth to future ages.

—Edmund Quincy, abolitionist, March 25, 1852
Quoted from Allen Nevins, *The Ordeal of the Union:*
A House Dividing, 1852–1857

When one section wars upon another, the contest must, *ex necessitate rei*, be a sectional contest. Nothing can be truer—not even that other great truth, that a house divided against itself cannot stand.

—William Lowndes Yancey, secessionist, June 21, 1855
Montgomery (Alabama) Advertiser and State Gazette

"A house divided against itself cannot stand." I believe this government cannot endure, permanently half *slave* and half *free*. I do not expect the Union to be *dissolved*—I do not expect the house to *fall*—but I *do* expect it will cease to be divided. It will become *all* one thing, or *all* the other.

—Abraham Lincoln, June 16, 1858
Roy P. Basler et al., eds., *The Collected Works of Abraham Lincoln*

PREFACE

IN 1997 MY FRIEND and colleague Steven Woodworth approached
me at the Southern Historical Association meeting in Atlanta with
a tantalizing and somewhat ominous proposal. He referred to
David M. Potter's renowned, brilliantly written monograph, *The
Impending Crisis, 1848–1861*, published in 1976 (completed and edited by Don E. Fehrenbacher). We agreed that Potter's remains the
best single-volume coverage for the political chain of events that led
to the American Civil War, but we also agreed that its sheer size—
638 pages—renders it impractical for use in most college and university courses, especially introductory-level ones. Plus, an explosion
of scholarship in this field over the quarter-century since the first
printing of Potter's book called for a synthesis of these works, an
opportunity to reevaluate some conventional wisdom and to bring
more up-to-date information to a new generation of readers, within
academia and beyond it. We further agreed that Bruce Levine's *Half
Slave and Half Free: The Roots of the Civil War* (1992) came the closest
to what Professor Woodworth desired, but that this fine book covered a much broader chronological period than Potter's and, at
nearly 300 pages, still did not fill the niche that he was after. So he
asked me if I wanted to try my hand at some sort of revised version
of Potter, synthesizing in all the current literature that I could, doing so in no more than about 45,000 to 55,000 words—roughly 200
pages in print. Excited by the challenge, confident that I knew my
own research and teaching fields well enough, and lacking common sense, I enthusiastically accepted his offer to make this contribution to his *American Crisis Series: Books on the Civil War Era*.

Two fascinating things happened as I began my effort. When I
created my own working bibliography to guide me, and then as I
began to write, it struck me that I simply could not use David
Potter's book as a model. The scholarly writing of political history
had changed too much for me to do that—too much for me even to
fall back on my own previous research and writings. The notion of
"politics" had already begun its transformation within the professional discipline of history as Potter and Fehrenbacher completed
their work, and it has flowered ever since then. Most historians
now conceptualize politics and political processes quite differently

than they used to. Although political historians, perhaps especially those who wrote about the coming of the Civil War, have rarely confined their study strictly to elected politicians, those who aspired to gain public offices, and national political institutions—grassroots abolitionists and secessionists, for instance, have seldom failed to appear in older studies—traditionally, multitudes of people and forces have been excluded from written history. Individuals have always exerted political influence and pressure without seeking political offices, voting, or even thinking of themselves as political actors. Women and minorities in this country who have been denied the right to vote have not lacked options in making their wishes heard by those in power. They have used pressure tactics—argumentation, persuasion, resistance, and disobedience—as effective tools to make their voices heard. But more than that, ordinary people throughout history often influence political processes simply by doing whatever it is that they do and by the decisions and actions of their day-to-day lives. For example, no legislative body would have debated the idea of passing laws for the apprehension and return of runaway slaves unless significant numbers of women and men decided to risk their lives and the lives of their families and friends by defying their owners' "right" to keep slaves. Many scholars use the term "agency," referring to anybody and everybody as potential political actors simply because they are active agents in their own lives.

Defying a spouse or a slaveholder might not seem as significant to some students of history as colonists defying an overseas empire, yet those acts just as certainly have consequences and the potential to affect a group, a society, a nation, or even the world. Illegal border crossings, hunger strikes, suicide bombings and attacks, signatures on petitions, or participation in a protest march inarguably have a political impact at some level, whether or not that is the intent of those who undertake such actions. Do the ordinary people who do such things exert as much influence on political institutions or upon history as presidents or monarchs? Perhaps not. But would Mahatma Gandhi, Dr. Martin Luther King Jr., or Nelson Mandela have had political power without their respective multitudes of followers whose names seldom appear in history books? It is my aim in this volume to write an inclusive and realistic political history of the decade preceding secession and war. I do not intend to gratuitously elevate or to ignore one kind of political actor or another and in fact strive to show that the elites and the ordinary folk usually had a keen understanding of the interplay between them.

My other surprise really upset my fine, patient, and dedicated friend at Scholarly Resources, Matthew Hershey. While my mission was to update and revise David Potter's book from 1976, I found more often than I could have imagined that my best sources for understanding the minutiae of events from this era, and especially for uncovering enlightening and memorable quotations, came from an older source, an eight-volume work written by Allan Nevins on the era of the Civil War referred to collectively as *The Ordeal of the Union*, published between 1947 and 1971. Mr. Hershey rightly insisted that I make note of this, and I hereby gladly comply.

I am very grateful for the careful and critical readings of this work by John Moretta, Courtney Q. Shah, Kelley Ray, Augie McLamb, and to my friend and colleague Linda Reed and her graduate students at the University of Houston. Matthew Hershey and Steven Woodworth have been a pleasure to work with at every step of this project, and their constructive feedback on various drafts of the manuscript has always provided me with tremendous help. I am also grateful for the assistance of Linda Pote Musumeci at Scholarly Resources and to copy editor Jennifer L. Morgan. I have benefited from the support of friends and family in all aspects of my life and am particularly thankful for encouragement on this effort from the Thursday Dinner group. The labors of all these people have greatly improved this book; any errors of fact or interpretation are my own.

PROLOGUE
After the Compromise

HENRY CLAY, THE venerable senator from Kentucky who had engineered political compromises over Missouri in 1820 and tariffs in 1833, tried early in 1850 to solve all outstanding political problems between the North and the South. His cumbersome Omnibus Bill proposed to create a free state of California; organize the rest of the southwestern territories without, somehow, addressing slavery at all; exchange a vast portion of northwestern Texas in return for a federal bailout of that state's debt; stop the slave trade in Washington, DC; and enact a tough new Fugitive Slave Law. Clay's bill had something for everyone to like—and to hate—depending on his ideas about slavery.

John C. Calhoun, for a generation the unequaled giant of Southern politics, had warned the North that the so-called Compromise did not solve the issues at hand but instead threatened to strike at the heart of white Southern society. On March 4, 1850, he threatened Northern senators that if they would not settle these problems "on the broad principle of justice and duty, say so; and let the States we both represent agree to separate and part in peace, tell us so; and we shall know what to do, when you reduce the question to submission or resistance."[1] Calhoun died on March 31.

William Henry Seward, the powerful young senator from New York, had opposed the same measures as Calhoun did but based his objections on what he termed a "higher law" than the Constitution—God's law—which compelled men of conscience to stop the sin of slavery. Seward emerged as a leader of antislavery Whigs and, eventually, of a new, more powerful antislavery party.

Beyond the halls of Congress more radical voices already had chimed in on the slavery conflict. From New York, Gerrit Smith had announced, "I never yet saw a slaveholder, who drank in the idea of human equality. No slaveholder can drink it in & remain a slaveholder."[2] Robert Barnwell Rhett, already a two-decade veteran secessionist from South Carolina, had warned his fellow Southerners that their acceptance of Clay's "Compromise" would lead Northerners to believe "that we value a union with them more than we value the institution of slavery."[3]

While Seward and Smith, Calhoun and Rhett fanned the flames of extremism, Daniel Webster, the great orator and esteemed senator from Massachusetts, denounced radicals in both the North and the South with a fervent appeal to patriotism. On March 7 he proclaimed, "I wish to speak today, not as a Massachusetts man, not as a northern man, but as an American. . . . I speak today for the preservation of the Union."[4] His moderation won him few accolades from his own constituents, so steeped had they become in antislavery sentiment. In fact, many New Englanders burned effigies of Webster and pronounced him another Benedict Arnold.

Across the South informal groups gathered into "Southern Rights Associations" to press for resistance to any act of Congress antithetical to slavery. Particularly strong in the Deep South, they pressured their elected leaders to act forcefully and immediately. The leaders did. In June 1850, for the first time in American history, an assembly of only slave-state representatives gathered together. They met in Nashville, Tennessee, to discuss their opposition to the North and to Clay's proposal. They even debated whether or not to secede. Moderates won the day at the Nashville Convention. Delegates decided not to act precipitously—not to act at all—since Clay's bill had not yet passed Congress. They would wait and see what transpired and vote to assemble again before year's end. Meanwhile, the governors of Mississippi and South Carolina took steps to prepare their states for armed resistance to federal authority and to assist other slave states that might rally to their side. Sectional tension had never been so extreme, not even when Andrew Jackson prepared a military force to enter Charleston, South Carolina, in 1833 at the culmination of the Nullification Crisis, an overt attempt by a single state to defy the national government.

Amid the turmoil and peril of 1850 a crafty and pragmatic young senator from Illinois, Stephen A. Douglas, seized the spotlight. A Democrat who professed not to care about slavery one way or another, Douglas favored Clay's bill as a means to restore calm to the nation. But Douglas realized that the greatest obstacle for this bill was its complexity. Douglas also hoped that by seizing the moment from Clay, he would gain the nation's gratitude and thereby pave his way to the White House. Douglas used every trick in the politician's arsenal—persuasion, deal making, flattery, and innuendo—to broker a deal. He divided the bill into its basic component parts and forged short-lived voting blocs in order to ram one bill after another through Congress. The result was called the

Compromise of 1850. It gave neither the North nor the South everything they had hoped for, but each side felt compelled to grab whatever advantage they could get from it.

No one much liked the Compromise. Radical Southerners who favored secession, the "fire-eaters," were incredulous that their section submitted to any measure that attacked and weakened slavery in the slightest. In the North, abolitionists also wrung their hands, wondering how so many could ignore the moral imperative to stop slavery for the sake of a short-term political deal. Although neither extreme would give up their opposing crusades, each had been rebuffed for the moment. And most Americans, upset and alarmed by the crisis they had just put to rest, tried desperately to turn away from the politics of threats, of sectionalism, of pro- and antislavery.

Their hope was in vain. Overtly abolitionist or secessionist officeholders were few, especially after the Compromise of 1850. But in religion, education, literature, popular songs, international trade and diplomacy, science and technology, and certainly in politics, issues involving slavery had long since become ingrained into the fabric of American life. That these forces emerged with greater rapidity, vigor, and consequence throughout the 1850s is less surprising than the fact that they had receded even for a while.

Clear social distinctions had already emerged that generally characterized both the North and the South. To state the obvious, the social ideal for most white Southerners had long been the acquisition of land and slaves. True, the vast majority of whites never owned any slaves, and only a tiny minority of slaveholders counted as planters. The cost of a prime fieldhand—a young adult, healthy and already trained for his work—could reach over $2,000 in Louisiana or Texas, at a time when the annual salary for a U.S. senator was $5,000. Southerners who owned twenty or more slaves—no more than 0.5 percent of the white population of the section in the 1850s—ranked as owners of plantations, rather than farms. And yet the possibility was real enough that an ordinary white person might be able to purchase a single slave some day, or at least be bequeathed one as an heir. For many, in fact, this was a real aspiration.

The yeomanry of the South, whether or not they owned one or more slaves, tended to be just as proud of their social standing as planters and quite jealous of their independence. They saw themselves as the embodiment of Thomas Jefferson's ideal American, independent of government at any level and wholly self-sufficient.

With the continuing modernization of the nation's economy, some small farmers dabbled in the market economy by growing crops for sale—most often cotton—rather than literally isolate themselves from a larger world. As this happened, however, these farmers automatically got drawn into a transatlantic economy: the price of cotton in Liverpool affected their profits or losses, whether or not they understood that in the Carolina or Georgia backcountry. Some yeomen admired the planter class; others resented this elite group, who tended to dominate political office as well as the regional economy. Virtually all whites, however, banded together in support of slavery because of ubiquitous racism, and the yeomanry definitely knew that, armed with their votes and their numbers, they could wield real power over the master class.

Independence meant everything to Southern whites across the social spectrum. To be anything less than fully independent, or simply to have others consider one less than independent, unequal, servile, or submissive, to a vast number of white Southerners sounded like qualities that they projected upon their African American slaves. Few could tolerate that. Especially among elite white men, the juxtaposition of liberty and slavery matched that of honor and dishonor. To whites, slaves could not strike back, could not defend their good names (and often had no control over their names at all), could not defend their families; in short, they had no honor. Despite ample evidence that in fact African Americans both had their own codes of honor and did all they could under horrendous oppression to protect their own, in the depth of their racism, whites often feared the perception of "slave-like behavior" among themselves or in the eyes of other whites. Without a bold, forceful response, one risked admitting to shame, dishonor, inequality, and degradation. Therefore, while duels tapered off quickly in the North in the nineteenth century, in the South, while they were never commonplace, "affairs of honor" became a hallmark among elite white men. To kill one's adversary was most decidedly not the main function of duels, but rather, the choice to place one's own life at risk rather than accept a public insult or personal slander stood paramount. Simply to meet a foe on the field of honor often satisfied a particular community to the fact that both parties had honor; both chose to risk giving up life rather than survive insulted, degraded, or submissive.

Some social ideas and ideals managed to cross the Mason-Dixon Line, but very different social norms characterized the antebellum

North. For instance, while the Southern ideal was to attain wealth through acquiring land and slaves, in the North, a section that had chosen to do away with slavery, the ideal means toward financial success obviously came through a determination to work hard for oneself. But a powerful value emerged out of this obvious and elementary situation. To oversimplify, in the South, whites may have respected the toiling yeomanry but ideally would have others—black slaves—do hard labor so whites could enjoy leisure and lavishly entertain guests. Physical labor, to many Southern whites, ranked as a quality best ascribed to black slaves, along with dishonor and subjugation.

On the contrary, Northern whites considered labor virtuous and financial gain through honest hard work a just reward. Self-reliance, thrift, ingenuity, and toil were inherently ennobling, not degrading. The ideal of free labor grew and spread across the North, both among the farming majority of their population and the emerging industrial sector of the region. In fact, the material and industrial advances of the North relative to the South convinced many a Yankee that free labor received God's favor and that slave labor left Dixie behind the march of progress and freedom.

A key to the free labor ideal lay in the belief that all people—men, mostly—must have an opportunity to compete fairly for work in the marketplace, whether on the farm or in the factory. Government had an obligation to ensure a level playing field at the start, thereby allowing those who were best suited to advance economically and receive the fruits of their labor. Northerners who championed these ideals in the territories called themselves Free-Soilers, people who wanted public lands reserved for free labor. In the North, reality collided with ideals just as it did in the South. Few industrialists had any qualms about exploiting the cheap labor of women, children, or foreigners, and many great capitalists demanded and received protective tariffs from the federal government that interfered with free trade in Americans' favor. But despite all that, the ideal and value of free labor remained, as it does in our times.

During the 1850s conflicting sectional values and perceptions of labor smashed into one another predictably and inevitably with each successive political battle over the nation's western territories. Northerners worried about how they could compete economically with slaveholders, men who owned their laborers rather than paid them. Northerners knew full well that a slave-based economy was a choice, not a necessity, and that it could not exist without active support from both local and national governments. How could anyone believe it was fair, right, and American for governments to tip the playing field in favor of slaveholders, of men who eschewed honest labor? White Southerners worried about getting locked out of the unrelenting westward march of the nation just because they owned slaves. Such a possibility could only stem from Northerners' belief that there was something wrong with slavery and therefore something wrong with the slaveholder: that he was unequal to them, less than or not as good as Northerners. This, of course, stood as an affront to sectional honor, and one could not walk away from such a gross insult.

Few in the North or the South could imagine a halt to the march westward. The South enjoyed incredible physical and economic expansion during the 1850s. The cotton empire continued to grow, especially in the Deep South and toward the West. Tobacco started to experience renewed vigor in the Upper South with new methods of cultivation, crop rotation, and fertilization, and the small but highly capitalized and very profitable rice- and sugar-producing regions also did well. As white Southerners continued to stream westward, they often brought slaves with them or bought them as soon as circumstances permitted in their new environs. The slave trade itself made up a major part of the area's economy. During the nineteenth century approximately one million slaves were moved from the less profitable East Coast to the new cotton kingdom of the Southwest.[5] Fully one-quarter of these slaves moved during the 1850s, swelling the slave populations by 1860, especially in Louisiana (36 percent), Mississippi (41 percent), Florida (57 percent), Arkansas (136 percent), and Texas (314 percent). Profits soared. In 1850, Georgia, Alabama, Mississippi, and Arkansas combined had just under 4.7 million acres of cotton under cultivation; they increased that to over 7.1 million acres ten years later. Those same states combined for a yield of 594 pounds of cotton lint per acre in 1850 and 770 pounds per acre in 1860. Despite the potentially inflationary effects of the increases in both slave populations and agricultural production, during the 1850s prices increased for cotton, sugar, land, and slaves.

The South enjoyed tremendous agricultural expansion during this decade, and industry made great strides in the region as well. During the 1850s the value of manufactured goods in the South increased a solid 79 percent. The South had long boasted great industrial accomplishments, from the first steam-locomotive line in the United States to the Tredegar Iron Works in Richmond, Virginia, one of the largest in the country and one in which hundreds of enslaved and free workers toiled side by side. In fact, there was no aspect of industry or manufacturing in the North that the South lacked entirely. And yet, by the end of the 1850s the annual per capita value of manufactured goods in the region stood at only $17.09, while in New England it was $147.47. Agriculture in general, and cotton in particular, remained key.[6]

As 250,000 African American slaves moved westward within the South, over ten times that number of immigrants—just under 2,600,000—arrived in the United States during the 1850s. The vast majority came from Ireland and Germany, but tens of thousands arrived from China, mainly finding work in the West, on or near the Pacific Coast. Some combination of famine, warfare, and religious persecution in Europe compelled most of those immigrants to pour into the North. They overwhelmingly headed to the North because slave labor would have reduced their earning power as wage workers, who could seldom compete with unpaid slaves. In addition, most large farmers in the South preferred owning black labor to hiring whites.

This influx of cheap labor had many profound and often horrible results. Terrible conditions existed in factories and tenements in Northern industrial cities, where labor and life itself seemed cheap for all but the most enlightened capitalists. Disease and crime spread rapidly; seasonal layoffs led to periods of great poverty and suffering. The shifting ethnic profile of these immigrants (less often British and Protestant, more often Irish or central or eastern European and Catholic) and their sheer numbers resulted in a tremendous backlash of bigotry by citizens whose ancestors had immigrated to the United States in more distant times. Combined with the emergence of the nineteenth-century industrial city, many in the North concluded that crime, disease, and poverty were caused by immigrants, rather than being inflicted upon them through employers' greed and callousness.

Northern cities swelled in number and in size. By 1855, 52 percent of all New Yorkers were of foreign birth. More and more native-born Northerners spoke of "them" taking "our" jobs, of "they" who do not act like "us." As if to foreshadow baseball player John Rocker in 2000, in the mid-1800s one New Yorker recorded his disgust after sharing a hot railroad-car ride with "stale, sickly odors from sweaty Irishmen in their shirtsleeves, . . . German Jew shop-boys in white coats, pink faces, and waistcoats that looked like virulent prickly heat; fat old women, with dirty-nosed babies."[7]

Among the multiethnic Northern populace existed a small but conspicuous population of free African Americans. Only a few hundred thousand in number, most were descended from enslaved parents or grandparents from the North before that section's states outlawed slavery at the end of the 1700s. A few scattered hundreds more had escaped Southern slavery by fleeing northward, and many of these continued on toward Canada. But these and other blacks faced a horrible paradox in the North. The growing tide of antislavery and abolition in the region did little to combat racism. In other words, a preponderance of Northerners believed it wrong to enslave anyone, but nevertheless held distinct prejudices against people of color. While in the slave South a modicum of racial integration had to exist—masters did not abandon their slaves but almost always lived among them—it was in the North that states first passed laws to segregate black from white. Across the region stood isolated and often squalid black communities such as "New Guinea" and "Nigger Hill" in Boston and "Little Africa" in Cincinnati.[8]

During the 1850s the United States presented a great specter of diversity, from one section to another and within each portion of the country. Ideas, occupations, systems of labor, national origins, and religious practices as likely divided Americans as brought them together. Tremendous sentimental and patriotic values pervaded the populations of both North and South. Each took great pride in their national identity, character, and history, even though the respective sectional manifestations of them had resulted in the regions drifting apart for quite some time. Many Americans of this era spoke and wrote of "mystic bonds" or "mystic chords" of memory, of history, and of culture that had forged an American identity, but the ties that bound together North and South faced incredible strain with each passing year of the decade, with a tension that would snap those bonds one by one.

NOTES

1. Richard Current, T. Harry Williams, and Frank Freidel, *American History: A Survey*, 5th ed. (New York: Knopf, 1979), 353. For a concise study of the Compromise of 1850, see John C. Waugh, *On the Brink of Civil War: The Compromise of 1850 and How It Changed the Course of American History* (Wilmington, DE: Scholarly Resources, 2003).

2. Michael A. Morrison, *Slavery and the American West: The Eclipse of Manifest Destiny and the Coming of the Civil War* (Chapel Hill: University of North Carolina Press, 1997), 57.

3. Eric H. Walther, *The Fire-Eaters* (Baton Rouge: Louisiana State University Press, 1992), 138–39.

4. Quoted in Robert V. Remini, *Daniel Webster: The Man and His Time* (New York: W. W. Norton, 1997), 669.

5. Walter Johnson, *Soul by Soul: Life inside the Antebellum Slave Market* (Cambridge, MA: Harvard University Press, 1999), 5–6.

6. See William J. Cooper Jr. and Thomas E. Terrill, *The American South: A History*, 2 vols., 3d ed. (New York: McGraw-Hill, 2002), 1:304–15.

7. Mary Beth Norton et al., *A People and a Nation: A History of the United States*, 2 vols., 4th ed. (Boston: Houghton Mifflin Co., 1986), 1:280, 271–72 (quote).

8. Bruce C. Levine, *Half Slave and Half Free: The Roots of Civil War* (New York: Hill and Wang, Noonday Press, 1992), 61.

Chapter One

1852

"The Vile Wretch in Petticoats"

THE COMPROMISE OF 1850 supposedly put an end to contentious sectional issues. Most ordinary Americans hoped so, and many political leaders did as well. Even before the ink had dried on the series of bills that President Millard Fillmore signed into law late that year, contenders across the country began their preparations for the presidential contest of 1852, hopeful of a return to less trying times.

The Whig Party had captured the White House in 1840 and in 1848 but in neither case by huge numbers of votes. In both victories their nominees—William Henry Harrison and Zachary Taylor—lacked substantial prior political experience and instead ran on their records as military heroes. In both cases other Whigs, such as Henry Clay and Daniel Webster, expected to exert real power behind these figureheads. And in both cases the victorious Whig presidents died in office: Harrison after only one month, Taylor after only sixteen months.

Taylor's successor, Millard Fillmore, proved ineffectual and colorless as a leader. Although he desired a nomination in his own right in 1852, Fillmore faced the formidable opposition of his fellow New York Whig, William Henry Seward. In 1850, Senator Seward had pronounced that a "higher law" than the Constitution compelled men of morals to act against slavery. Fillmore, on the other hand, signed into law and enforced the Fugitive Slave Law of 1850, gaining him the enmity of most of New England and Seward's powerful faction in New York, thereby assuring his defeat within his own party. The three Whig presidents, Fillmore, Taylor, and Harrison, were never great party or political leaders; men like Seward and Clay and Webster were.

In 1852, as Henry Clay lay slowly dying in his hotel room in Washington, DC, the aged Daniel Webster decided to mount an effort to win his party's nomination. Serving out his final months as secretary of state in Fillmore's cabinet, Webster corresponded with men across the country who eagerly pledged their support. Webster actually believed that his candidacy made sense. He had stood as the great voice of unionism during the debates over South Carolina's right to nullify federal law in the 1820s and again during the critical debates of 1850, and since compromise and national cohesion had emerged triumphant, why should not he as well? Webster spoke at Faneuil Hall in Boston in May, announcing that he had no platform other than his character and life's accomplishments and needed no more than his dedication to the Union to run for president. One true friend of Webster's noted, however, that "a set of

unworthy parasites and flatterers" had swarmed around the septuagenarian, hoping for favor and appointed office from the great Webster.[1]

The infighting and intrigue among Whig contenders all but guaranteed the nomination of another war hero, this time General Winfield Scott. Born in Virginia in 1786, a year before the writing of the Constitution, Scott had forty years' experience in the army. He had commanded troops in the War of 1812 and led the invasion of Mexico in 1846 and had managed to avoid politics and therefore sectional issues. Desperate for victory, most Northern Whigs rallied to Scott's standard. Even Seward endorsed him enthusiastically, if only to snuff out the candidacy of Webster, who had supported the fateful Compromise that Seward had labored hard to destroy.

Daniel Webster
Library of Congress

Some of Scott's supporters lashed out so bitterly at Fillmore that it astonished even Seward, who remarked that one attack reminded him of a series of sermons he once heard: "Hell—more Hell—still more Hell."[2] Scott needed all the help he could get, if only because of one remark he had made on slavery in 1843 that now made its way to the public. Slaveholders, he said, must "employ all means, not incompatible with the safety of both colors, to ameliorate slavery, even to extermination." Although Scott had also correctly declared that Congress could not touch slavery within states, his remarks helped bolster his candidacy among some Northern voters but did nothing positive for him in the South. Besides, Southern Whigs feared the influence that the Free-Soiler Seward might exert in a Scott presidency.[3]

Democratic presidential hopefuls smelled victory. True, they had lost two of the last three contests, but Taylor had won by only a narrow margin, and President Martin Van Buren's efforts for re-election in 1840 were doomed by his inaction during a miserable economic depression, the Panic of 1837. As the party of Andrew Jackson prepared to retake the White House, leading the charge were some of their most influential old warhorses.

Old and battle tested indeed, five of them had seen combat in the War of 1812. Senator Lewis Cass of Michigan had won his party's nomination in 1848 but had lost the election to Taylor by the slender margin of 1,360,101 to 1,220,544 votes in the popular contest and 163 to 124 votes in the electoral poll. In 1847, Cass had introduced the idea of popular sovereignty as a solution to the territo-

Lewis Cass
Library of Congress

rial issue. Even if Congress had the power to regulate slavery in the territories, he had equivocally stated, the best solution lay in letting the people of each territory decide for themselves. Pennsylvania's James Buchanan had built strong party credentials as a congressman, senator, minister to Russia, and secretary of state, despite persistent rumors about the perpetual bachelor and his intimate friendship with his longtime boarding house companion, William R. King of Alabama, whom Washington insiders called Miss Nancy. William L. Marcy had served as both a governor and a U.S. senator from New York and had acted as President James Polk's secretary of war during the Mexican invasion. William O. Butler of Kentucky was Cass's running mate in 1848, just after rising to the rank of major general in the Mexican War. And Sam Houston, a protégé of Andrew Jackson, had a checkered and glorious career in both politics and war, leaving Tennessee under a cloud of alcoholism and marital strife, then rising to military and political might in Texas.

Against these five "old fogies," every one of them born in the 1700s, stood a "Young American." Stephen A. Douglas, born in 1813, had soared to national prominence by delivering the Compromise of 1850 and led a movement that members called Young America. These pugnacious, ambitious, and dauntless men hoped to wrench their party away from arguments over slavery and instead revitalize its Jacksonian spirit of aggressive expansion and national power. They drew support from merchants in the North and cotton planters in the South, from German and Irish immigrants to railroad interests and land speculators. Under Douglas's leadership these young guns did exert a mighty influence on their party, although not always with the results they had hoped for.

To a great extent, many of the problems for Douglas and Young America stemmed from Douglas himself. His short-fused temper, his ability to consume whiskey in amounts extraordinary even for his times, and his bellicose nature, combined with his remarkable rise to prominence, alienated established politicians. Overseeing a campaign headquarters that churned out appellations such as "ten cent Jimmy Buchanan" and "Cass whose reputation was beyond the C." did not win him friends among party regulars.[4]

As these six slugged it out for their party's nomination, a dark-horse candidate quietly emerged from New Hampshire. Friends of Franklin Pierce had begun to organize a movement to support him back in 1851, and that effort slowly but steadily continued heading into the Democratic convention in June 1852. A young man (still among the youngest ever elected president, at the age of forty-eight), a congressman and senator, Pierce had won some fame as a brigadier general under the command of Winfield Scott during the Mexican War. He emerged as a perfect compromise candidate. Everyone who met him seemed to like him and vice versa. Young enough to satisfy most Young Americans, Pierce also had the distinct advantage of not being Stephen Douglas and therefore not antagonizing the old fogies of the party. Plus, this New Englander was an old-fashioned strict-constructionist and stood firmly upon the Compromise of 1850, even defending absolutely the Fugitive Slave Law, thus making him an enticing possibility for the Southern branch of the party.

The Democratic convention assembled at Baltimore on June 1. Pierce's backers worked quietly and diligently behind the scenes, trying to convince supporters of other candidates to switch to Pierce as a compromise if early balloting proved inconclusive. The balloting dragged on and on, as so often was the case for the Democratic Party. On the first ballot, Cass led with 116 votes, Buchanan came in second with ninety-three, Douglas had but twenty, and the rest combined for three; but the rules called for a two-thirds majority, or 192 votes. Thirty-two ballots later, Cass only increased his total to 133, with the others roughly where they had started as well. Buchanan's forces, determined to stop Cass if they could not win the nomination for their candidate, then decided to seek alternatives. By the forty-seventh ballot more and more delegates had turned to Pierce. The next ballot ended things with a landslide, Pierce winning 282 to Cass's two, Douglas's two, and Houston's one. To balance the ticket geographically, the convention selected Alabama's William R. King to run with the man from New Hampshire.

Whigs entered their party's convention less deeply divided than Democrats but with greater apprehension. Sensing that Scott offered the best chance for their party's victory, antislavery Whig Horace Greeley grumbled to a confidant, "I suppose we must run Scott for President, and I hate it."[5] The Whigs also assembled at Baltimore. On June 16 they began their meeting by voting on a platform, something they had consciously chosen not to do in most previous campaigns. That platform centered on maintaining the Compromise of 1850 as the final settlement of all sectional disputes. Next, they turned to selecting a candidate. Unlike the Democrats, the Whigs settled on a simple majority—149 out of 296 delegates— for nomination. On the first ballot, President Fillmore led Scott by 133 to 131, with Webster receiving but twenty-nine votes. For the next fifty ballots, little changed. As party stalwarts, Webster and Fillmore could have logically struck a deal to have one drop out and support the other, but neither would cooperate with his opponent. On the fifty-third ballot, Pennsylvania delegates broke ranks and led the victorious movement toward Scott.

Henry Wilson, a radical antislavery Whig, was overjoyed by the outcome, if only because it marked the end of Webster's chances. "We have dirked him! We have dirked him!" Wilson shouted, thrilled to dispatch the Northern man who dared not defy the forces of slavery.[6] Others were not so happy. While Democrats easily rallied around Pierce, Whigs expressed grave concern over their candidate.

Southerners worried considerably over what influence William H. Seward might wield in a Scott administration. One, Thomas Clingman of North Carolina, grumbled, "If we support him we must expect to constitute a tail to the army of abolitionists in front."[7] Some Northern Whigs anxiously pondered Scott's lack of political service and experience, his nativist streak, and his vanity—Scott's nickname was Old Fuss 'n' Feathers. Scott himself even remarked that he "respected the presidency more than he desired it."[8]

Webster could not hide his disappointment. After forty years of serving the people, he had garnered a hair more than two dozen votes. "How will this look in history?" he wondered. On June 29 he received another blow, the news that Henry Clay had died. Calhoun had passed away in 1850, and now Clay; only Webster remained of the "Great Triumvirate" that had dominated national politics since the 1810s. Finally, Webster joined them, dying quietly at his home in Marshfield, Massachusetts, on October 24.

The Whig rank and file did not even wait for Webster's political death in July. Immediately, following the custom of the day, each party began to churn out official campaign biographies, pamphlets that served as the chief means of appealing to the masses. A *New York Tribune* staff writer cranked one out for Scott in a week, and his party distributed hundreds of thousands of copies. Other authors wrote additional biographies, some appealing to ethnic Irish and German voters, others to factory workers. In all, over one million Scott pamphlets flooded the nation.

Democratic Party manager B. B. French wrote Pierce's official campaign biography, but a man with far better writing skills joyfully created another one. A friend of Pierce from their days together at Bowdoin College in Maine, novelist Nathaniel Hawthorne, pressed for time, kidded his buddy, "I am taking your life as fast as I can—murdering and mangling you."[9]

It was fitting that Hawthorne, a man of letters, entered politics in 1852 because at the same time literature, whether creative or polemic, stormed into politics. Among those Northerners most upset by the Compromise of 1850 were the Beechers of New England. Lyman Beecher had raised his children with a reforming zeal unsurpassed by contemporaries, even though they lived in an age of enthusiasm and reform. He was a temperance advocate and abolitionist, and the Rev. Mr. Beecher's adult children would make names for themselves that rivaled or surpassed their father's. Like so many Northerners, all of the Beechers were astounded by the portion of the recent Compromise of 1850 that compelled Northerners to assist Southerners in apprehending slaves who attempted to escape. Under the new law, if a Northerner refused to aid slave catchers, that Northerner risked a term in jail, a loss of his own freedom. As Edward Beecher preached the evils of this to his congregation in Boston and Henry Ward Beecher did the same to his in Brooklyn, Edward's wife wrote to her sister-in-law, Harriet, "Hattie, if I could use a pen as you can, I would write something that will make this whole nation feel what an accursed thing slavery is."[10]

Harriet Beecher Stowe had published essays in magazines for years, including pieces in the antislavery publication *National Era*. She decided to write a few stories, perhaps four, for that periodical. She vowed that "the time is come when even a woman or a child who can speak a word for freedom and humanity is bound to speak." Stowe pledged to present to the American public through fiction a portrait of slavery "in the most lifelike and graphic manner possible." She miscalculated only one thing: four chapters became forty-four, serialized in the *National Era* from mid-1851 to the spring of 1852.[11]

The story of *Uncle Tom's Cabin; Or, Life Among the Lowly* struck to the marrow of its readers. Melodramatic, exciting, suggestive, Stowe's serialized story had a power and appeal that convinced Stowe's sister Catherine to find a publisher for a bound edition. On March 15, 1852, the deal was struck for what would prove the most influential book of the era. It sold over 1.2 million copies in its first year in print. Eventually, it sold over three million copies in the United States, and another 3.5 million overseas, ranking it as the best-selling American book ever, to that point.

Despite record sales, professional reviews were mixed. For one, the *North American Review* concluded that despite its "genius," *Uncle Tom's Cabin* had several critical "defects" and was "often tame and inadequate in description," but granted that its "high moral and religious sentiment, and dramatic power shine in every page." How could the *North American Review* account for record sales of a book with such mixed literary qualities? "Its foundation in truth" answered that.[12]

A novel—a work of fiction—spoke "truth" to over one million readers in the North. However, few booksellers in the South dealt with so scurrilous a thing as Stowe's work. "It is a fiction, not for the sake of more effectually communicating truth; but for the sake of more effectually communicating a slander," groused the *Southern*

Literary Messenger from Richmond, Virginia, striving to destroy the reputation "of the vile wretch in petticoats who could write such a volume." Deeper South, in Charleston, South Carolina, the *Southern Quarterly Review* concluded that Stowe had conceived her novel with "malignant bitterness" and produced a work "whose touch contaminates with its filth."[13]

As if to respond to Stowe, several defenders of slavery produced a compilation of four extensive essays in 1852, titled simply enough *The Pro-Slavery Argument*. In fact, plans for this book had been in the works since 1849. An early secessionist and law professor at the College of William and Mary, Nathaniel Beverley Tucker, urged his friend and intellectual protégé, James Henry Hammond of South Carolina, to compile a volume of these works. "Such things" included one of the earlier defenses of slavery published by Tucker's colleague at William and Mary, Professor Thomas R. Dew, in 1833. Tucker died in 1851, but the next year Hammond posthumously honored the wishes of his mentor by producing *The Pro-Slavery Argument*, which included works by South Carolina judge (chancellor) William Harper and Hammond's friend William Gilmore Simms, the most prolific novelist of the Old South.

Most Southern whites had long since abandoned any defensiveness toward the peculiar institution. Earlier generations, especially during America's fight for independence and freedom, had admitted that slavery seemed at odds with American principles of liberty and natural rights, but generally fell back on excuses to rationalize their exploitation of African peoples. The English had forced the institution upon them during colonial days—or New England shippers had, many used to say. Slavery might well be a blight upon the country, but virtually everyone accepted as fact racial inequality and black inferiority, so with the institution a reality, what could one do? Set free the slaves, but consign them to a life of landlessness, poverty, and helplessness? Or grudgingly continue to own them and thereby act as their racial stewards and protectors? Of course, no one ever forced a prospective master to purchase a human being, and a number of white Southerners never had qualms about enslaving people of African origin. But as antislavery and abolitionism grew during the nineteenth century and political conflicts over slavery became more frequent, defensiveness gave way to a peculiar new idea: slavery in fact benefited the slave as well as the master. Enslavement of African Americans was a positive good, rather than a necessary evil.

Stowe and these four Southerners who put together *The Pro-Slavery Argument* all had the same goals in mind for their polar-opposite books. None really thought that they could persuade their antagonists to simply give up, either on slavery or on calling for abolition. Rather, each book aimed at drawing into a phalanx Northern or Southern readers to fortify their resolves respectively to defend or to attack the institution of slavery to the bitter end. And both, of course, did help bolster the growing sectional rift that would result in America's bloodiest war.

No piece of Southern proslavery writing would ever rival the impact of *Uncle Tom's Cabin*. For that matter, neither would anything else produced from the North. But there was another thing about Harriet Beecher Stowe and her effort that struck at the heart of Southern society: this Northern woman dared step out of her culture's proscribed role for her gender and plunge into the public, masculine arena of politics. Before the 1850s, and to some degree during that decade, the spirit of social reform that pervaded the North had made deep inroads in the South as well. But with the revitalized sectional conflict, ever more white Southerners saw something sick about a Northern society that seemed to link reforms in education, prisons, and temperance with radical issues that offered to turn upside down their carefully constructed social hierarchy. These radical issues were women's rights and antislavery. Even though these reformers often squabbled with one another, to the revulsion of many white Southerners, elements of abolitionism and women's rights movements did often fuse reformers from both groups, so that men and women, black and white, sometimes did work together conspicuously to change Northern society—and to threaten the status quo in the South.

Ironically, one of the most notable Southerners to fire back in this war of words and ideas was a woman. Louisa McCord, born in Columbia, South Carolina, in 1810, actually grew up in Philadelphia, where her father, Langdon Cheves, served as president of the Bank of the United States. Cheves was a prominent and wealthy man whose entrance into national politics in 1813 occurred right on the heels of that of his more famous congressional colleague, John C. Calhoun. Despite the fact that Philadelphia was the earliest American home of antislavery, Louisa grew up fully aware of, and consciously benefiting from, the Southern social order. In 1840 she married a respectable Carolina lawyer and politician, David James McCord, and settled down to family life on his Congaree

River plantation, Langsyne, to raise three children. But she also began writing.

In 1852 the *Southern Quarterly Review* published her essay, "Enfranchisement of Women." She opposed the idea. McCord defended the pedestal reserved for white, elite Southern women like herself. While some Northern women clamored for more active public and political roles, and some even followed the lead of Emilia Bloomer, who advocated that women discard traditional dresses in favor of pants-like "bloomers," McCord denied that she "must discard decency and my petticoats." She further explained, "We are no undervaluer of woman. . . . Her mission is, to our seeming, nobler than man's, and she is, in the true fulfillment of that mission, certainly the higher being. . . . Each [woman] can labor, each can strive, lovingly and earnestly, in her own sphere. . . . Woman, we grant, may have a great, a longing, a hungering intellect, equal to man's," but McCord concluded that more than enough challenges existed in the home to occupy these abilities. McCord bashed "petticoated despisers of their [own] sex,—the would-be men . . . Moral Monsters . . . In ceasing to be women, they yet failed to make themselves men."[14]

The printed debate about social constructions for men and women, for black and white, for slave and free was not isolated to white men and women. One of the earliest and most powerful black

Martin R. Delany
Courtesy of the Ohio Historical Society

voices to participate in these publication wars belonged to Martin Delany. Born in 1812 in Charles Town, Virginia (now West Virginia), Delany was the son of a slave father and free black mother. In Virginia, as in all slave states, the legal condition of a child followed that of his or her mother, so Delany was born free. Only two generations separated Delany from his African homeland. One grandfather was a chief in a Golah village. Another was a Mandingo prince. Both were enslaved and shipped across the Atlantic. Proud of his family and of his people, Delany named his first son Toussaint Louverture after the leader of the Haitian revolution against the French in the 1790s. At the age of nineteen, Delany went to Pittsburgh, where he studied medicine and rose to prominence in the city's black community.

In 1843, Delany established the first black newspaper west of the Allegheny Mountains, the *Pittsburgh Mystery*. When that endeavor failed in 1847, Delany became copublisher of the *North Star* that same year in Rochester, New York. His partner was an abolitionist with special credentials: Frederick Douglass had been born and raised a slave in Maryland before he escaped North, following that North Star to freedom. Delany left the *North Star* in 1848 and enrolled at Harvard Medical School in 1850, but he left during the winter session because white students protested his attendance. At the time no licensing requirements existed for physicians, so he returned to Pittsburgh and opened a medical practice.

In 1852, Delany published a book called *The Condition, Elevation, Emancipation and Destiny of the Colored People of the U.S., Politically Considered*. In it he drew upon his personal experiences in Boston, the center of abolitionism, to condemn white abolitionists for their refusal to work for racial integration as well as for freedom. Convinced that racial justice and equality would never occur in the United States, Delany proposed the establishment of a black "promised land" somewhere in Central or South America. His proposal for colonization attracted the attention and support of many African Americans. It also drew the ire of most white abolitionists and a conspicuously silent reaction from his recent associate, Frederick Douglass.

Although Douglass never commented publicly on Delany's treatise, he issued his own powerful broadside on July 5, 1852, in a speech titled "What to the American Slave Is Your Fourth of July?" He answered his own question: "The Fourth of July is a sham . . . to cover up crimes which would disgrace a nation of savages. There is not a nation of the earth guilty of practices more shocking and bloody than are the people of the United States at this very hour."[15]

Matters of racial equality and social, legal, and economic justice continued to divide and distract black and white abolitionists to the very end of slavery in 1865. A microcosm of this discord came when a group of blacks and whites assembled in Ohio for a Convention of Colored Freemen in the fall of 1852. Organizers invited three leading white abolitionists to address the gathering: Cassius M. Clay, Horace Mann, and Benjamin Wade. Clay of Kentucky, a relative of the famed Henry Clay, stood out conspicuously as one of a handful of white Southern abolitionists and made more of a name for himself through his proficiency at slicing up antagonists with his bowie knife. Mann had established his name as a great education reformer, championing free public education in Massachusetts. When John Quincy Adams died in 1845, Mann reluctantly accepted the nomination to replace him in Congress, where he proved a solid Free-Soiler. Wade won election to the Senate in Ohio due to his opposition to the Compromise of 1850, especially the Fugitive Slave Act. All three of these great foes of slavery suggested that the best African Americans could hope for, even in the free states, was to separate themselves from whites and to focus on acquiring some wealth rather than toiling for political rights.[16]

As a few stepped up efforts to change the political landscape through words spoken or written, most Americans simply went about their daily lives, unaware that the deep divisions between North and South could transform even mundane matters into volatile ones. One of the most common activities of the 1850s was simply an extension of a phenomenon as old as European settlement on the Eastern seaboard—the steady march westward across North America. As white Southerners continued their part in this saga, they tested the cohesion of the Union. After all, slaveholders had the right to roam about the country like any other free people. Just because California—or, for that matter, Massachusetts or any other state or territory—prohibited slavery, did that mean a law-abiding resident of a slave state could not take his or her servant along when traveling across the country?

Take the case of Jonathan Lemmon, a slaveholder in Virginia who, in 1852, decided to move to Texas. The fastest way to make the trip meant going first to New York City, then gaining passage on a steamship directly to Texas. So Lemmon took his wife and their eight slaves to New York, where they lodged for several days, waiting for their ship. Lemmon was hardly alone in this; until the 1840s, New York and Pennsylvania, for example, allowed sojourners to remain in those states with their slaves for nine and six months, respectively. But by the 1850s, Northerners felt they could or should no longer make these concessions. Officials in New York in 1852 obtained a writ of habeas corpus to bring before a superior court judge "the bodies of eight colored persons . . . confined and restrained of their liberty . . . under the pretense that they were slaves." Lemmon sued to recover his property. The case went to one court after another and was headed for the United States Supreme Court when the Civil War interrupted the national appellate process.[17]

No federal Supreme Court ruling before the war would directly touch the question of whether or not masters could take their slaves to free states and territories without forfeiting ownership and thereby automatically, if unwillingly, setting them free. During the 1850s a case that involved these questions slowly worked its way to the nation's highest court, where an infamous decision would be rendered in 1857. That decision would center around issues of citizenship and politics and help drive the North and the South even farther apart.

Meanwhile, masters continued to take their slaves with them wherever they went, as they had done ceaselessly since the 1620s. James Gadsden of South Carolina sent a petition of over 1,200 names to the California assembly in 1852, asking that body to allow the petitioners, residents of South Carolina, to emigrate to the Golden State and bring with them their slaves. The Carolinians asserted that only with the "peculiar institution" would California's rich soil prove truly productive. Naturally enough, the free state legislature denied Gadsden's constituents their bold request. Nevertheless, many whites from South Carolina and elsewhere continued to bring their slaves with them to the free state of California; about 600 slaves were there by year's end. And while resisting efforts like Gadsden's, the California assembly in 1852 passed a peculiar bill. For all those masters who brought slaves to California before that state created its own constitution in 1849, the assembly granted one year's notice for them to remove their slaves. And they passed another year's extension in 1853. And another in 1854.

As enslaved African Americans worked the gold mines in California—a free state—free African Americans there faced the same general legal and social repression that Martin Delany and all other African Americans did across the North. In 1852 a California law passed that flatly stated: "Black and mulatto persons are rendered incompetent as witnesses to give evidence against white persons." In other words, just like their enslaved brethren in the South, free blacks could not give testimony against whites in court. Three leaders of the black community of San Francisco, Mifflin W. Gibbs, William Newby, and Jonas Townsend, petitioned the state assembly on March 10, pointing out: "That this provision . . . in effect denies to all such colored persons, the protection of law in the enjoyment of the rights of property and personal security; and the vicious and unprincipled take advantage of this disparity and prey upon those rights with impunity." The petitioners pled for an end to this particularly dangerous form of discrimination, and did so "in the name of republicanism and humanity." Similar movements occurred in other California cities, including the capital, Sacramento, but all of these efforts were in vain.[18]

Although matters of race and slavery remained active around the country in 1852, for a while they stood conspicuously silent in the halls of Congress. Both major parties had just adopted platforms vowing to defend the Compromise of 1850 as a final adjustment of sectional issues. One mark of the effectiveness of the settlement came from Robert Barnwell Rhett, the man who replaced the late John C. Calhoun as senator from South Carolina. Rhett had established his secessionist credentials as far back as 1828 and confirmed them time and again thereafter. As the Southern disunion movement fizzled in 1851–52, Rhett could not fathom that his own people, Carolinians, would capitulate to the North yet again. Rhett concluded that his constituents were no longer worthy of his presence in Washington as their representative. "I am a secessionist—I am a disunionist," Rhett proclaimed on the floor of the Senate. "I will secede, if I can, from this Union. I will test, for myself and for my children, whether South Carolina is a State or a humbled and degraded province, existing only at the mercy of an unscrupulous and fanatical tyranny." Then Rhett resigned.[19]

Rhett realized that the most extreme fanaticism had vaporized with the passage of the Compromise of 1850, but clearly the American public remained quite edgy about the issues involved in that pact, especially the Fugitive Slave Law. Antislavery forces in the North had expected to have a new and powerful fighter on their side with the election to the Senate in 1851 of Charles Sumner, a Free-Soiler from Massachusetts. Sumner looked and acted every bit the part of a senior statesman despite his relative youth, having just turned forty. Tall and solidly built, at 6 feet 2 inches and 185 pounds, Sumner cultivated his outward appearance through his wardrobe and formality, projecting the qualities of a man who always means business. In fact, he was often stuffy and condescending. "Did you ever see a joke in one of my speeches?" he once asked a friend. "No sir, I think I never did," came the answer. Sumner continued, "Of course you never did. You might as well look for a joke in the Book of Revelations."[20]

Even more worrisome to his coalition of supporters than his brusque manner were the signs he gave, once in office, that he was moving both away from antislavery and toward the Democratic Party. Only three Free-Soilers had been elected to the Thirty-first Congress: Sumner, Salmon P. Chase of Ohio, and John P. Hale of New Hampshire. Personally and professionally these three spent a lot of time together, but Sumner, trying to avoid social or political isolation from his fellow senators, made it a point to befriend others, even likely adversaries. Very quickly he became friends with Pierre Soulé of Louisiana and Andrew P. Butler of South Carolina. Both of these Southerners staunchly defended slavery in Congress, and Butler had even helped write the Fugitive Slave Law of 1850, which was so abhorrent to Sumner's constituents. If that did not distress his supporters, many of them registered grave disappointment that Sumner did little to challenge the South, since he had given every indication he would. Sumner spoke out often enough but on relatively commonplace matters, such as the elimination of the navy's ration of distilled spirits, international postage rates, and public lands in Iowa.

A test came for Sumner's fealty to antislavery in the spring of 1852, when abolitionists led by William Lloyd Garrison and Wendell Phillips petitioned him to work for the release of two federal prisoners, Daniel Drayton and Edward Sayres. In 1848 the two served as captain and mate of the schooner *The Pearl*, which they used in an attempt to aid the escape of no fewer than seventy-six slaves from Virginia. Federal authorities apprehended them all, returning the slaves to captivity and the abolitionists to jail and a trial. Slaveholders in Virginia and Maryland hailed their conviction and eight-year sentence to prison. Sumner had campaigned in part on the infamy of the Fugitive Slave Law, condemning James M. Mason of Virginia for writing it and President Millard Fillmore for signing it into law.

When the petition arrived from Garrison and Phillips, Sumner chose not to introduce it to the Senate. Phillips warned Sumner that a backlash against him was welling up in Boston. Garrison, perplexed, published an "Inquiry After a 'Back-Bone' " in his newspaper, *The Liberator*, complaining that Sumner had yet to act against slavery in his first several months in Washington. What critics did not know was that Sumner had opted to work for a presidential pardon for the abolitionists and believed that public agitation would prove counterproductive. (Drayton agreed, saying, "I thought . . .

that I had been made enough of a martyr already.")[21] On August 11, Fillmore finally issued a pardon. With due concern for the safety of Drayton and Sayres, Sumner personally went to their cell and arranged for their immediate trip North, supplying a carriage and an armed friend. Sumner had done his job.

Or had he? Proslavery Southerners railed about the "escape" of two convicted slave stealers. And while moderate Northerners approved of Sumner's course, the Garrisonian *Boston Commonwealth* complained that for seven months now Sumner had sat in the Senate without uttering one word against the Fugitive Slave Act, "though men, women and children are hunted daily, ruthlessly shot down or dragged back to bondage."[22] Discretion and caution had won the release of these prisoners, but once again they only stoked the fires of fanaticism in both the North and the South. The most extreme fanatics of both sections could not stomach the nominations of the two major political parties, so each nominated their own men. In August the Free-Soil Party held its convention in Pittsburgh. This party emerged from several sources. Back in 1840 a relative handful of abolitionists had created the Liberty Party and nominated for president the rarest of things, an abolitionist from Alabama, James G. Birney. He received about 7,000 votes nationwide. The Liberty Party nominated Birney again in 1844, this time garnering 65,000 votes, 2.5 percent of all those cast. By 1848 they turned to John P. Hale of New Hampshire. But shortly after Hale's nomination, a new antislavery coalition materialized.

Composed of Democrats who favored restrictions on the expansion of slavery, the so-called conscience Whigs of the North, who could not support their party's slaveholding nominee, and assorted other disgruntled groups, the Free-Soil Party was not as extreme as the outright abolitionist Liberty Party, but it had clout. Its members included former president Martin Van Buren and Charles Francis Adams, son of recently deceased president-turned-abolitionist John Quincy Adams. Even Liberty Party members saw the superior strength and appeal of the Free-Soilers and so disbanded themselves and canceled Hale's nomination, choosing instead to join forces with the newcomers and their ticket of Van Buren and Adams. Their efforts fetched 291,000 votes, about 10 percent of all votes cast. Van Buren even beat out Democrat Lewis Cass in popular voting in New York, Massachusetts, and Vermont.

John P. Hale and George W. Julian won the Free-Soilers' nomination in 1852. Hale graduated from Bowdoin College in Maine in

1827, attending that school at the same time that Pierce and Hawthorne did and graduating with John Brown Russworm, the first African American to graduate from Bowdoin and the third to graduate from any American college. Initially a Democrat, Hale ranked among the first Americans to break with his party over slavery. Julian, from Indiana, came to Congress in 1848 as an established Free-Soiler, although he had entered politics as a Whig. Their party platform, in stark contrast to those of both major parties, denounced the Compromise of 1850, demanded an end to the addition of any more slave states or territories, and called for popular election for all public officials, for free homesteads, and for cheap postage. In the industrial town of Lowell, Massachusetts, coalitions

of workers' organizations had already elected state assemblymen who promised to restrict both the spread of slavery and the number of hours per day that men had to work. With party leaders such as Sumner, Seward, and Henry Wilson, many Free-Soilers looked hopefully to the November elections.

Like the Free-Soilers, some Southern extremists could not abide by either of the two major political parties. William Lowndes Yancey of Alabama stood among the leading secessionists, or "fire-eaters," of the

John P. Hale
Library of Congress

South during the debates over the Compromise of 1850. Like his fellow disunionists, Yancey was mortified that Southern resistance had evaporated so quickly after so many politicians in the region had threatened to take drastic steps to defend their rights and interests. Already weary of national political parties, considering them entities that quashed principle in favor of winning office and power, Yancey and fellow Southern extremists sought an alternative to Pierce or Scott in 1852. The fact that many of Yancey's radical colleagues now drifted back to the Democratic Party and Pierce, who ran on a platform vowing enforcement of the Compromise, only heightened Yancey's concerns about parties and principles.

Ironically, after surveying the political landscape, Yancey himself strived to convince fellow radicals that their best option in 1852 was in fact Pierce. As in so many of Yancey's early political battles, he failed to convince many others to follow his course. An Alabama Southern Rights Convention gathered in Yancey's hometown, Montgomery, in September in an effort to launch or support an independent ticket. That small convention nominated its own presidential ticket. They selected George M. Troup of Georgia, at age seventy-two a longtime champion of strict construction and Southern rights. In fact, in 1827, Governor Troup had threatened to use the state militia to defy President John Quincy Adams's efforts to protect Indians in Georgia. Troup prevailed over Adams. The Southern Rights Convention picked as Troup's running mate John A. Quitman, secessionist leader of Mississippi and a major general during the Mexican War. Both men accepted. Delegates in Alabama also selected a slate of state electors.

Although not a traditional sort of American political convention, another small gathering assembled in Syracuse, New York, on September 8. The National Woman's Rights Convention continued to insist that adult women receive the right to vote, to legally possess their own property, and to gain all other constitutional rights that men had. One resolution stated simply and clearly: "That the demand of Woman is not for privileges, nor favor, nor employments, nor honor, but for RIGHTS."[23]

This assembly, like so many before and after, had multiple links to abolitionism. Many of the earliest women's rights activists, such as Lucretia Mott and Susan B. Anthony, first entered the public sphere through their labors as abolitionists. Conversely, many leading male abolitionists joined the crusade for women's rights in their efforts to bring freedom to millions of Americans deprived of basic civil rights. The renowned abolitionist Gerrit Smith attended this meeting to support women's rights. Several women at Syracuse denounced the Pierce ticket for its proslavery stance. Elizabeth Oakes Smith of New York fused together the two crusades through her resolution "that as the imbruted slave who is content with his lot and would not be free if he could, if any such there be, only gives evidence of the depth of his degradation, so the woman who is satisfied with her inferior condition, averring that she has all the rights she wants, does but exhibit the enervating effects of the wrongs to which she is subject."[24]

Women's rights advocates, abolitionists, Free-Soilers, and secessionists demonstrated how many waves of discontent with the political status quo swept across the American landscape. But in 1852 their combined efforts proved futile. On election day, Pierce won easily. He received 1,601,474 popular votes to Scott's 1,386,580. Scott's respectable showing among American voters nationally belied his weakness and the approaching demise of his Whig Party. In the entire country, Whigs carried only 434 counties to their rival's 1,100. Pierce's electoral vote total surpassed Scott's by 254 to 42. The Free-Soilers took 291,000 votes, about 10 percent of the popular total. The Southern Rights ticket barely registered. It carried two counties in Alabama and captured just over 2,000 votes statewide, with only 126 votes in Georgia and 3,500 in all.

Southern radical resistance seemed dead. About half of the Free-Soil rank and file drifted back to the two major parties or abstained from voting at all. The Whigs had failed to excite enough Americans with issue-oriented platforms or competent presidential candidates. Although scores of individual officeholders would continue to identify themselves as Whigs, as a national political party the Whigs were mortally wounded. Pierce and the Democrats had prevailed, were united, and stood together on their pledge to honor the Compromise of 1850 and thereby eliminate sectionalism once and for all.

NOTES

1. Robert C. Winthrop, quoted in Allan Nevins, *Ordeal of the Union*, 2 vols. (New York: Charles Scribner's Sons, 1947), 2:23.
2. Nevins, *Ordeal of the Union*, 2:27.
3. Ibid., 2:27.
4. Ibid., 2:11.
5. Ibid., 2:26.
6. Ibid., 2:29.
7. William J. Cooper Jr., *The South and the Politics of Slavery, 1828–1856* (Baton Rouge: Louisiana State University Press, 1978), 330.
8. Nevins, *Ordeal of the Union*, 2:29.
9. Ibid., 2:32.
10. Jeanne Boydston, Mary Kelley, and Anne Margolis, eds., *The Limits of Sisterhood: The Beecher Sisters on Women's Rights and Woman's Sphere* (Chapel Hill: University of North Carolina Press, 1988), 156.
11. Ibid., 156–57.
12. Ibid., 158.

13. "Vile Wretch . . ." in John McCardell, *The Idea of a Southern Nation: Southern Nationalists and Southern Nationalism, 1830–1860* (New York: Norton, 1979), 212; all others in Boydston, Kelley, and Margolis, *Limits of Sisterhood*, 156–58.

14. Michael O'Brien, ed., *All Clever Men, Who Make Their Way: Critical Discourse in the Old South* (Fayetteville: University of Arkansas Press, 1982), 339–56.

15. Charles M. Christian, *Black Saga: The African American Experience; A Chronology* (Washington, DC: Civitas/Counterpoint, 1999), 154.

16. Leon Litwack, *North of Slavery: The Negro in the Free States, 1790–1860* (Chicago: University of Chicago Press, 1961), 173–74.

17. Paul Finkelman, *An Imperfect Union: Slavery, Federalism, and Comity* (Chapel Hill: University of North Carolina Press, 1981), 4–5.

18. Christian, *Black Saga*, 153.

19. Eric H. Walther, *The Fire-Eaters* (Baton Rouge: Louisiana State University Press, 1992), 145.

20. David Herbert Donald, *Charles Sumner and the Coming of the Civil War*, 1st ed. (New York: Knopf, 1960), 218.

21. Ibid., 221; Edward L. Pierce, ed., *Memoir and Letters of Charles Sumner*, 4 vols. (Boston: Roberts Brothers, 1877–1893), 3:277n.

22. Donald, *Charles Sumner and the Civil War*, 222.

23. Virginia Bernhard and Elizabeth Fox-Genovese, eds., *American Feminism: The Seneca Falls Woman's Convention of 1848* (St. James, NY: Brandywine Press, 1995), 183.

24. Ibid., 185.

CHAPTER TWO

1853

"Frank, I Pity You"

WITH THE NEW YEAR came a brief respite in the political battles between North and South. Most Americans awaited the inauguration of President Pierce and hoped for fewer confrontational days
and more ordinary times. Many began to enjoy consumer items that
would become hallmarks of everyday life in America. While its
popularity lay in the century to come, the potato chip made its debut in 1853. In the West, especially in the mining regions, some
Americans began to purchase new, well-constructed blue jeans
manufactured by Levi Strauss. Back East, well-to-do consumers
with a penchant for music in their homes could now buy pianos
made by an American manufacturer named Henry Steinway.

One of the most popular American composers of his day hesi-
tated to have his name published with his music. Stephen Foster, a
Pennsylvanian, began his career writing music for a minstrel
group—white performers who painted their faces black. Foster
gained some knowledge of African American dialect and music and
produced nostalgic tunes such as "O, Susanna," "Camptown
Races," and "The Old Folks at Home" (better known as "Swanee
River"). Although these gained great public favor, Foster sensed a
great deal of public prejudice against "Ethiopian songs," so in 1853
he published anonymously another tune destined to be an American classic, "My Old Kentucky Home."

> The sun shines bright in the old Kentucky home,
> 'Tis summer, the darkies are gay.
> The corn top's ripe and the meadow's in the bloom,
> While the birds make music all the day.
> The young folks roll on the little cabin floor,
> All merry, all happy and bright;
> By'n by Hard Times come a knocking at the door,
> Then my old Kentucky home, good night![1]

This songwriter's imagery of happy times for contented, carefree slaves contrasted absolutely with a new book that appeared early in 1853. The title said it all, as so many long-winded nineteenth-century book titles did, *Twelve Years a Slave: Narrative of Solomon Northup, a Citizen of New-York, Kidnapped in Washington City in 1841, and Rescued in 1853, from a Cotton Plantation Near the Red River, in Louisiana.* A free black man hired to run an errand in Washington, DC, and careful to procure papers from New York to prove his status as a free man before crossing below the Mason-Dixon Line, Northup was nevertheless abducted and sold into slavery. Held in slave pens and shipped off first to Virginia, then to New Orleans, Northup's experiences ran the gamut of the institution. Northup was stripped of his name and called Platt or just "boy," even though he was an adult. Northup had both a relatively kind master and an overtly cruel and violent one. He saw a baby wrenched from her mother's arms at a slave sale. He worked as a skilled laborer and in cotton and sugarcane fields. One master forced him to whip others or face the whip himself. Northup learned how to sabotage this by cracking the lash just above the skin of the intended victim, who would cry out as though in agony to satisfy the master. Finally able and willing to trust a few white men to carry a letter back to New York that explained his predicament and location, Northup made it home in January 1853.

Almost immediately Northup set to work with a local lawyer and writer to publish his story. It appeared in print by July, but a few newspaper stories preceded it. William Lloyd Garrison's *The Liberator* quoted Frederick Douglass as saying, "It is a strange history . . . its truth is stranger than fiction." An antislavery newspaper captioned an article about Northup "Uncle Tom's Cabin—No. 2." Harriet Beecher Stowe, working early that year on publishing a volume of hard, authentic information to prove that her fiction had been based upon facts, noticed "the singular coincidence that this man was carried to a plantation in . . . that same region where the scene of Tom's captivity was laid."[2]

Northup's account sold out its first printing of 8,000 copies in one month, an impressive figure, though it paled in comparison to Stowe's novel. To make certain that no one could miss the coincidences, both authors made direct reference to each other. In Stowe's *Key to Uncle Tom's Cabin*, she included Northup's letter from Louisiana that finally led to his rescue. Northup in turn dedicated subsequent editions of his book to Harriet Beecher Stowe, "Whose

Name, Throughout the World, is Identified with the Great Reform: This Narrative, Affording another Key to Uncle Tom's Cabin."[3]

More Americans continued to show their fascination with Stowe's melodramatic condemnation of slavery. In 1853 the first in a long series of stage versions of *Uncle Tom's Cabin* premiered in New York City's Purdy Theater on March 15. In a telling example of the schism between so many white Northerners' antislavery sympathies and their simultaneous racial bigotry, the manager of the theater cordoned off separate seating for blacks and whites.

In Boston, Sarah Redmond, an African American born into a family of antislavery activists, tried to enter a theater in the city known for its leadership in antislavery and abolition. Because she was black, policemen forcibly ejected her from the white-only facility, shoving her down a flight of stairs at that. Redmond sued for damages as well as to force the owners of that theater to admit blacks. She won. In 1856, Redmond joined leading white members of the American Anti-Slavery Society, including Wendell Phillips and sentimental songwriter Stephen Foster, in a series of public lectures. During the Civil War she moved to London, and she later studied medicine in Italy. Redmond practiced medicine there until her death in 1894.

Another African American who had a long association with white abolitionists published the first novel ever by a black American. William Wells Brown had received training as a printer by Elijah Lovejoy. An abolitionist who died trying to defend his printing press from a proslavery mob in Alton, Illinois, in 1837, Lovejoy's martyrdom made many Americans, including a very young Abraham Lincoln, see that the violence of slavery spread even to free states. Years later William Wells Brown wrote a piece of fiction called *Clotelle, or The President's Daughter*, about the trials of a mulatto child born at Monticello, the home of Thomas Jefferson. Brown had trouble finding an American publisher who would print the novel. A British firm finally did in 1853. Brown would later publish the first play by an African American (*The Black Man*), and after witnessing the role of African Americans during the Civil War, he produced a book entitled *The Negro in the American Rebellion* in 1867.

The same free state of Illinois that had witnessed a proslavery mob murder of Elijah Lovejoy in 1837 passed a law in 1853 that dramatized how powerfully racism continued to flourish there. In January a bill designed to prevent free blacks from taking up residence in the Prairie State came to the floor of the state assembly.

Little debate followed, and the "Black Law" received the governor's signature on February 12 (which happened to be the birthday of Illinois lawyer Abraham Lincoln). Anyone who tried to help an African American settle in the state could receive a fine of up to $500 and one year in the county jail. African Americans who stayed in Illinois over ten days and intended to remain were fined $50 by the state. But if that person could not afford to pay—and many black Northerners could not—he or she faced a horrible prospect. A sheriff would advertise for ten days, then sell the labor of the inmate for a set amount of time to anyone who would pay the $50 fine and court and jail costs. During this period of forced servitude, the African American, with few exceptions, had to do the bidding of the person who paid his or her fine . . . in this free state.

Northern laws and social behavior such as the example in Illinois infuriated abolitionist William Lloyd Garrison. Like most radical abolitionists, Garrison attacked Northerners who supported slavery or denied any responsibility for it almost as ferociously as he assailed slaveholders in the South. All Americans, Garrison said, shared blame for this national sin; all bore responsibility to end it. In an address to a gathering of women's rights advocates in 1853, Garrison condemned sin in any form, as he frequently did. Abolition and women's rights were of a piece to him. Garrison reminded this audience that in no slave state could slaves legally marry, that their "marriages" were legal fictions and allowed only by their masters. Garrison correctly noted, "The marriage relation is abolished among three and a half millions of [enslaved] people." Because Southern churches supported slavery, Garrison judged, "If this does not involve them in all that is impure, and licentious, and demoralizing, I know not what can do so." He continued, "I believe in sin, therefore in a sinner; in theft, therefore in a thief; in slavery, therefore in a slaveholder; in wrong, therefore in a wrongdoer; and unless the men of this nation are made by women to see that they have been guilty of usurpation, and cruel usurpation, I believe very little progress will be made."[4]

While tempers continued to be hot over slavery around the country, political agitation in Congress receded. Even at that, things did not bode well for the Pierce administration before he arrived in Washington for his inauguration. Prior to his party's convention he had published a letter stating that the thought of running for president was "utterly repugnant" to him.[5] His young son, 11-year-old Benjamin, wrote to his mother, Jane, "I hope he won't be elected for I should not like to be at Washington and I know you would not either."[6] Benjamin and Jane Pierce shared great apprehension at the prospect of living life under the microscope that has always scrutinized first families. Jane Pierce especially worried about renewed inquiries about her husband's drinking, a personal habit that had contributed to his resignation from the Senate in 1842. Pierce's novelist-friend Nathaniel Hawthorne, upon learning of Pierce's election, had written, "Frank, I pity you—Indeed I do, from the bottom of my heart!"[7] Playfully, Hawthorne echoed Pierce's family's concerns about the incessant pressure and criticism ready to face any occupant of the White House.

Franklin Pierce
Library of Congress

Hawthorne provided one of the last humorous moments for the Pierce family for quite a while. As they made their way back to New Hampshire after spending Christmas in Massachusetts, a horrible accident occurred on January 6, 1853. The front axle of their railroad car broke. The engine continued to pull for a while, snapping the coupling to their car and sending it off the tracks and diving down a 12-foot embankment. Instinctively, Pierce grabbed his wife as their car began to tumble. Then he reached for his son. As their car settled, the Pierces momentarily believed that they had eluded disaster, but when the president-elect removed his son's cap, he found that some sharp object had sliced off the top of Benjamin's head. Jane Pierce never really recovered from the traumatic death of her son and refused to move to Washington until the end of 1853, and even then she declined attending any formal dinners at the White House. For much of her husband's presidency, Jane Pierce dressed in black and penned letters to her departed child.

On March 4, Pierce took the oath of office as America's fourteenth president. Tens of thousands of visitors poured into the capital to witness the event. Many admired the new statue of Andrew

Jackson in Lafayette Park across the street from the White House. New construction sprang up everywhere. Handsome homes appeared in the northern part of town. Gas lamps were installed at the entrances to the White House, a new hall was opened at the Library of Congress, and plans were laid to erect a huge, new dome over the Capitol building. And yet, dilapidation was everywhere. The still unfinished Washington Monument stood 120 feet high with planks covering its top, doing little to prevent rain seepage. The Tiber Canal that ran through the city was not much more than an open sewer, and the Mall remained slovenly, save for the grounds immediately in front of the Smithsonian building.

Despite all this, optimism and the sound of drums and brass bands rose from all quadrants of the city during the morning of the inauguration. A northeast wind whipped a snow that melted as it hit the ground. At noon, as President Millard Fillmore, President-elect Pierce, and other dignitaries marched from the Willard Hotel toward the Capitol, the sun struggled to break through the clouds. As many as 80,000 people watched Pierce deliver his address without any notes, and his powerful, clear voice actually made his remarks audible to about 15,000.

Nevertheless, his and his wife's grief over their son's death weighed heavily upon them both. And as if Pierce needed anything to get his administration off to a worse start, he had a vice president who did not like him and who never made it to his post. William King had expressed great revulsion at his coupling with Pierce at the Democratic Convention in 1852. Whether from his devotion to his close friend Buchanan or from disgust at compromise winning out over qualifications, or both, he simply did not relish his new job. He need not have worried about it. As 1853 began, King was in Cuba. He had resigned from the Senate late in 1852 not so much to prepare for his new duties as to take his doctor's advice and winter in the warm tropical climate to ease his tuberculosis. A special act of Congress allowed him to take the oath of office overseas rather than in Washington. He died in Cuba on April 18, 1853. Pierce simply served without a vice president.

Nineteenth-century presidents seldom consulted with their vice presidents over national policy. Cabinet secretaries, therefore, carried tremendous importance. In the formation of his cabinet, Pierce decided to try to please all factions of his party, and in the process he inadvertently selected men who would dominate him and tilt the sectional balance of power toward the South. To help him make his decisions, Pierce initially met with William Marcy of New York, a staunch unionist who was dead set against slavery's extension into the territories. But Pierce also called in a friend from his days in the Mexican War, Jefferson Davis of Mississippi. Davis had come home from war threatening secession if the Compromise of 1850 passed into law.

Davis clearly had greater influence than Marcy. Certainly, Pierce appointed prominent Northerners to key positions, but most tended to be quite like Pierce himself, strict constructionists and very acceptable to the South. Caleb Cushing of Massachusetts received the

post of attorney general and soon thereafter wrote that the spirit of antislavery had to be destroyed. Marcy received the post of secretary of state, but Davis more than offset his authority in the cabinet as Pierce's new secretary of war. The new secretary of the navy, James C. Dobbin of North Carolina, was an ardent proslavery expansionist. Pierce's diplomatic appointments even more clearly toed the line for the South. He sent Pierre Soulé of Louisiana to Spain, where the proslavery senator set his eyes on the ac-

William L. Marcy
Library of Congress

quisition of slaveholding Cuba. South Carolina's James Gadsden received Pierce's appointment as commissioner to Mexico. This was the same Gadsden who the previous year had labored to send slaves to the free state of California. Other proslavery agents went to the Netherlands and to Portugal.

Sectional politics had become so intertwined within the fabric of American society that they even influenced Pierce's appointment of a new director of the Census Bureau. The previous director had not yet published results of the 1850 survey and fell victim to a patronage battle: Pierce fired him. In his place, Pierce selected James D. B. De Bow of New Orleans, another presidential payoff to the South. De Bow had already established a name for himself as a statistician through his commercial journal, *De Bow's Review*, and his work on gathering statistics for the state of Louisiana.

In all likelihood, Pierce knew little more than this about his new census director. De Bow, originally from South Carolina, emerged as a leading secessionist during the debates over the Compromise of 1850. Merging two of his great causes, De Bow had already proclaimed that statistical information made up part of the arsenal in sectional political struggles and that his South was losing that race. Northerners, he wrote, had used statistics "as powerful instruments of aggression, and the South, having nothing to show in return, has been compelled to see her cause greatly prejudiced."[8] De Bow worried less about total population and its direct impact on congressional representation and more about measures of social progress such as crime, poverty, education, wealth, manufacturing, and anything else that, should secession ever come, would help show fellow Southerners "our resources of resistance."[9] Most Americans acclaimed De Bow's final product the best census report to date, not to mention De Bow's three-volume compendium, *Industrial Resources, Etc., of the Southern and Western States.* No doubt exists, however, that he fudged some numbers to make the South look better on issues such as wealth and education, and the North worse, especially on crime and pauperism. When reprinting excerpts of the compendium in his own *Review*, De Bow even commented that his work ought to "entirely exhaust the subject" of slavery and race relations—in favor of the South.[10]

In Pierce's appointments of De Bow and most others, the president not only relied heavily on his Southern friends such as Jeff Davis but also never even consulted party stalwarts such as Lewis Cass. And in appointing Pennsylvania's James Buchanan minister to Great Britain, Pierce clearly schemed to keep his recent rival out of the public eye. Of greater consequence for Pierce and for the nation was that in doling out appointments to extremists in the South or the North, he bypassed the very unionists who had driven through Congress the great Compromise that Pierce had vowed to enforce. These strategic problems betrayed a greater problem still. From the start of his administration, Pierce clearly enjoyed the privileges of office and radiated a charming, affable personality that set guests at ease during official visits. But he lacked real resolve or conviction. He was pliable and easily swayed. He tried too much to make every faction in his party happy, even while events unfolded that proved much more was on the line than Democratic infighting.

These matters, however, lay ahead. On inaugural day, Pierce's address resonated with optimism. He promised to observe strict construction of the Constitution and to stand by the Compromise of 1850, and he gave special assurances to the South in this regard. To all Americans he promised a vigorous return on Manifest Destiny, the territorial expansion that Pierce considered "essential for the preservation of the rights of commerce and the peace of the world."[11]

A great campaign had already been launched in the country's efforts at commercial expansion. In January 1852, President Millard Fillmore had authorized an ambitious naval expedition led by Commodore Matthew C. Perry to establish diplomatic and commercial relations with the mysterious empire of Japan. That nation had pretty well avoided allowing Western powers to land on her shores since the 1600s, and wayward Western sailors often faced tortuous death there by crucifixion. American concerns for its seamen and for expanding bases of operation across the Pacific, as well as the economic possibilities of being the first Western nation to tap the Japanese market, combined with national bravado and cockiness to make Japan the next great American crusade.

Matthew Perry was just the man to lead that effort. He was the younger brother of one of America's greatest military heroes, Oliver Hazard Perry, who at twenty-eight years of age defeated the mighty British on Lake Erie during the War of 1812 and thrilled his countrymen by reporting, "We have met the enemy and they are ours." (Oliver Perry died in 1819 at age thirty-four.) Matthew Perry had a more varied, if less auspicious, career than his famed sibling. He commanded one of the country's first steam-powered vessels in 1837, patrolled the coast of Africa in 1843 as part of an ongoing American effort to suppress the African slave trade, and helped take Vera Cruz during the recent war against Mexico. On November 24, 1852, Matthew Perry led America's Eastern Squadron from Norfolk, Virginia, to the Orient.

At Yedo Bay (later called Tokyo) on July 8, 1853, Japanese people witnessed an amazing scene. Through the morning fog and haze appeared Perry's squadron of four black-painted ships. As the vessels drew closer, Japanese witnesses were amazed that two of them moved effortlessly at moderate speed without sails; no steamship had yet appeared near the Japanese coastline. Perry and his crew saw a fortified harbor bedecked with colorful flags and protected by what appeared to be a 200-year-old Portuguese cannon. Dignitaries from both sides managed to communicate, despite the fact that an American interpreter spoke Chinese, not Japanese. Perry presented to the Shogun of Japan a letter from President Fillmore requesting trade and better treatment of American sailors confined in Japan (many castaways from whaling expeditions were held in irons). Perry would return in 1854 with a larger fleet and sign the Treaty of Kanagawa, beginning the formal opening of trade and diplomatic relations between the two countries.

As the Empire of the Rising Sun opened itself to Young America, an old adversary emerged on the southern border of the United States: General Antonio López de Santa Anna climbed once more to power in Mexico. The general's new regime lacked revenue, though, and that was just fine for the expansionist American commissioner in Mexico City, James Gadsden, whom Jefferson Davis had strongly supported for the post. The Carolinian negotiated a deal for the acquisition of over 45,000 square miles of land below the Gila River, a parcel of land the size of Pennsylvania, for $15 million. Gadsden had hoped for a better deal, especially desiring a port on the Gulf of California.

Northerners in the U.S. Senate hoped to nix the deal. Some called the desert land worthless. Others condemned it as an effort by slaveholders to use federal money to expand their region. Rumors abounded that Gadsden was really after more: Tamaulipas, Nuevo León, Coahuila, Chihuahua, Sonora, and Baja California. Whether or not Gadsden truly desired this, other Southerners at that time and later assuredly looked to Mexico as a means of expanding slavery through one Mexican state after another. With some reservations the Senate ratified the Gadsden Purchase, but for only $10 million.

Some Americans simply could not wait for the federal government to further national expansion. "Filibusters," or men who took it upon themselves to enlarge America's territory, made their mark during the 1850s. A great number of these men spoke the language of Manifest Destiny with a distinct Southern accent; to them and many of their supporters the solution to sectional conflict with the North came through the promise of acquiring lands suited to the expansion of slavery.

No filibuster gained more fame or infamy than did William Walker. Born in Tennessee in 1824 and afforded an exceptional education at the medical school of the University of Pennsylvania as well as through various studies in Europe, Walker grew dissatisfied with the medical practice he had established back home in Nashville. Always restless, Walker moved to the more exciting international port city of New Orleans, where he studied law, set up a practice, and quit that profession all in rapid succession. He shifted to journalism, helping to edit the *New Orleans Crescent*. He also fell in love with a woman named Ellen Martin, who was both deaf and mute. Always ready to adapt and a quick study, Walker learned sign language to communicate with her. When cholera took Martin's life in 1849, the brokenhearted Walker fled New Orleans for California during the excitement of the gold rush.

In California, Walker resumed law and newspaper work and became involved in politics. This thin man of average height, at 5 feet 6 inches, who was personally quite shy (if he spoke at all, he usually kept both hands in his pockets), incongruously developed a colorful public life. In the Wild West this man of the South became involved in several duels and briefly went to jail for contempt of court when he defended freedom of the press. By 1853, Walker again gazed over distant horizons, this time applying to the Mexican government to establish a small colony in Sonora (much as Moses Austin and his son Stephen F. Austin had done in the Mexican province of Texas a generation before). Mexican officials turned him down. Walker decided to go anyway.

Recruiting forty-five men from the Barbary Coast of San Francisco and dodging American officials, Walker departed for Baja California in autumn. Landing at La Paz under a Mexican flag that he flew from his ship to keep port officials off guard, Walker and his force abducted the local governor and easily took over the town. By year's end, Walker declared himself president of the independent Republic of Lower California and cast his gaze across the Gulf of California toward the huge province of Sonora. Conquest of that would have to wait.

Far more Americans set their sights on Cuba, the great sugar-producing island held by Spain since the days of Christopher Columbus. Some Cubans who chafed at colonial rule had already tapped into American desires to annex Cuba and heightened them with appeals to American republican ideals; the Spanish monarchy ruled despotically over this tropical paradise. Between 1849 and 1851, Narciso López, a Cuban expatriate, secured the support of American filibusters, particularly from the Southern states. After failing to win the support and involvement of Robert E. Lee or Jefferson Davis, López found an ally in John A. Quitman, governor of Mississippi. Quitman, a veteran of the Mexican War and one of the few Americans who had entered Texas in 1836 in an effort to help that republic win its independence from Mexico, offered López money, military advice, and help in recruiting troops. López did manage to land an invasion force of 600 in Cuba in 1850 but was repulsed. Upon his return to New Orleans federal officials arrested him for violating American neutrality acts. They also indicted Governor Quitman. After three hung juries the government dropped all charges. Vindicated in his mind, López then gathered 400 men for another invasion in 1851. One of his colonels, William Crittenden of Kentucky, was a nephew of the attorney general of the United States. This time, López and many of his men were killed. Crittenden was executed for his involvement in the action, but American willingness to risk life and fortune for Cuba did not wane.

By 1853, British efforts directed toward Cuba riveted the attention of white Southerners in the United States. Having long since assumed the mantle of leadership in transatlantic antislavery movements, the British were particularly appalled by the smuggling of slaves directly from Africa to Cuba. That year alone at least 12,500 Africans were stolen from their homelands and forced into servitude by the Spanish. The British aimed to stop this and to press toward emancipation on the island itself. As one Southerner put it, should the British try to impose emancipation in Cuba, America must declare war. "There will be no dissenting voice in this part of the country," he predicted, and forecast as well that such a war would elevate into public office enough Southern war heroes to "perhaps ultimately change the character of the government itself."[12]

Pierre Soulé, Pierce's commissioner to Madrid, was the perfect man to pour fuel on the expansionist fire. A native of France who came to the United States in 1825, after escaping prison for his efforts to help topple the Bourbon dynasty—which also ruled Spain —Soulé made himself well known in Spain before he arrived for his enthusiastic public support of the López expeditions. In fact, as he departed New York for Spain in August, he delivered a speech designed to rally Cuban exiles in America and to put Spain on notice. A banner at the dock read:

> The Antilles flower, the true key of the Gulf,
> Must be plucked from the crown of the old Spanish wolf.

The tact and reserve characteristic of most successful diplomats clearly did not inhabit Pierre Soulé.[13]

It did not take long for Soulé to exacerbate matters even further. At a grand ball for all diplomats in Madrid in 1853, Soulé confronted his French counterpart, M. de Turgot, a man who knew of Soulé's active resistance to the French crown. A Spanish dignitary, the Duke of Alba, joined de Turgot's wife in ridiculing Mrs. Soulé for her ostentatious dress and corpulent figure. An enraged Soulé grabbed the duke by his elbow and glowered at the offender. One thing led to another, and finally a hesitant Alba accepted Soulé's challenge to a duel with swords. Neither party was hurt, but then Soulé went after de Turgot, challenged him to a duel with pistols, and felled the Frenchman with a bullet to the leg. Soulé ended his usefulness as a diplomat before it had begun, but he had also confirmed for himself that the only way to deal with Bourbons was by force.

For most Americans neither Walker's bizarre invasion nor Commodore Perry's exotic expedition nor even possible designs on Cuba held as much interest and fascination as the idea to link the Mississippi Valley and the West Coast with a railroad. From the beginning of time until the early nineteenth century, the fastest human beings could travel was only as fast as the swiftest animal could carry or pull them or as a strong wind could fill a sail. That changed with the invention of the steam-powered locomotive. Now human beings could lay down tracks and propel themselves at unheard-of speeds in any direction on land, as fast as 24 miles per hour by 1829 and over 40 miles per hour by the 1850s.

Still mostly a novelty well into the 1840s, railroad building exploded by the 1850s, and travel by train became almost commonplace in America by the end of the decade. About 6,000 miles of track existed in the United States in 1848. In 1852 mileage stood at 10,800. By 1859 the country would have over 30,000 miles of track in use, by far the most of any nation on earth. Railroad fever gripped the nation as all who lived along train routes saw the economic boom that accompanied the new lines. Railroad building, however, often proved enormously expensive. It cost over $20,000 a mile on level ground and up to $45,000 in hilly, rocky New England. Still, as investment and expertise grew, cost savings made it possible for travelers to ride sometimes for as little as a penny a mile. Although it took several transfers between different companies' trains, by the middle of the decade, passengers could travel the 886 miles from Baltimore to St. Louis in just under forty-eight hours and pay under $26. And even at that, huge profits accumulated for a new generation of American business tycoons, such as Cornelius Vanderbilt of New York.

The continued exploitation of gold and other natural resources on the Pacific Coast, combined with the growing ease, speed, and familiarity of travel by rail, led to an obvious conclusion for many. Rather than spend months traveling by foot or draft animal over land, or weeks sailing from the Atlantic Coast around South America or to a land crossing in Central America and back aboard a ship, why not connect the American continent by rail?

Many challenges stood in the way. The longest continuous rail line in the world in 1852 was the Erie Railroad, at 537 miles. That railroad cost $23,580,000; the entire federal budget in 1853 stood at just over $60,000,000. The Erie line had required the toil of 5,000 men and 1,250 horses for several years to link Baltimore with Wheeling (in present-day West Virginia) on the Ohio River. At the time only 10,417 men served in the U.S. Army. Who, or what corporation, could afford to link the East and the West? Who would hire all the men and assemble all the necessary materials? What was the best route? How would the federal government get involved?

Back in 1844 a merchant from New York had hoped to lead this unprecedented effort. Asa Whitney had asked Congress to sell him a 60-mile-wide stretch of federal land between Milwaukee and the Columbia River on the West Coast. He had hoped to buy it cheap, sell it at a profit, and thereby finance what would have been the longest railroad on earth. Whitney proposed as well that once he finished the railroad—fifteen to twenty-five years in the future— he would then turn it over to the federal government.

Most Americans in Congress and beyond strongly disliked the idea of federal aid and even more so the concept of federal ownership of a railroad, especially if one man was to be in charge. Beyond that, everywhere south of Milwaukee, politicians and local merchants did not like the thought of losing the eastern terminus of a line that would bring money and construction jobs now and wealth from the West later and, in turn, West Coast ports' growing trade with Asia. Even so, most critics agreed that the costs and scale of a transcontinental railroad required federal involvement, some way, somehow.

In 1845 a young, Democratic freshman congressman from Illinois, Stephen A. Douglas, proposed a plan of his own. It paralleled Whitney's in many ways, but like Douglas himself it was more

ambitious and audacious. Chicago, not Milwaukee, would serve
as the eastern terminus (Douglas happened to have investments
there), and Douglas wanted the railroad to head directly to San
Francisco—a sleepy port town in California, then part of Mexico.
Brimming with Young America confidence, Douglas simply reasoned that as the railroad progressed and settlers followed it west,
the United States would surely annex that region in time to complete the railroad. A bill to that effect failed in Congress in 1845,
but war secured California three years later.

For the next several years, Congress considered new bills for a
transcontinental railroad. Eventually, New Orleans, St. Louis, and
Chicago stood as the most likely spots for the eastern end. The
California gold rush of 1849 and the admission of California as a
state in 1850 reinvigorated the clamor from businessmen and from
the general public to better unite the East and the West. But greed
crushed one design after another. In 1852 congressmen from Missouri, Illinois, and Iowa tried to achieve federal organization of the
vast territory west of Iowa, the huge northern remnant of the Louisiana Purchase, from the Indian Territory (Oklahoma) to Canada.
They proposed calling it Nebraska and suggested the destruction
of Indian land titles there to facilitate the removal of tribes from
the route of the railroad. Horrified Texans, who dreamed of running a route from New Orleans across the Lone Star State's 880
longitudinal miles, desperately tried to stop this. In an act of sheer
hypocrisy, Texas congressmen, who had never had much concern
or compassion for Indians within their state, objected arduously to
the terrible unfairness of this bill for Native Americans on the Great
Plains.

Stephen Douglas took up the challenge again early in 1853. He
now chaired the important Senate territorial committee and ranked
among the most celebrated and dominant national political leaders since the deaths of John C. Calhoun in 1850 and Henry Clay
and Daniel Webster in 1852. Douglas threw his considerable support to the Nebraska bill in March. Another supporter of this measure, Senator David Atchison of Missouri, warned Douglas not to
anticipate support from slave states because Nebraska lay north of
the Missouri Compromise's 36°30' line, closing it to the expansion
of slavery. Slave-state senators proved Atchison right; every one of
them but Missouri's voted to table the bill.

By December 1853, Douglas had good reason to suspect that
Southerners might prevail. He already knew that President Pierce

owed his election largely to Southern support and that Secretary of War Jefferson Davis had enormous authority with the president. Since the start of the year, James Gadsden helped acquire northern portions of Mexico, bolstering the odds of a line linking New Orleans and San Diego. Senator Atchison told Douglas that he could no longer support the Nebraska Bill and joined the phalanx of other slave-state congressmen, stating that he would rather see the territory "sink in hell" than surrender it to Free-Soil settlers.[14] Douglas's bid had failed even with Atchison's backing. Without strong support from the South, Douglas knew he could not succeed. The ambitious and pragmatic Little Giant, as people called him, knew that he had to enlist the support of the South for his railroad idea to fly, and as the year drew to a close he prepared to do just that.

Blackwood's Magazine in Edinburgh, Scotland, spoke of "that control in and over the Government of the United States which is exercised by a comparatively small number of persons," yet is "more absolute than that of any European aristocracy—almost as uncontrolled by public sentiment as an Asiatic potentate."[15] This article echoed a swelling chorus that had begun rising from the American North since the 1830s, spreading chants of a "Slave Power" conspiracy to dominate the United States. How else, many wondered aloud, could the South have elected so many slaveholders to the White House? Seven of the nation's eleven elected presidents prior to 1852 had owned slaves, and one of the few exceptions, Martin Van Buren, had the patronage of slaveholder Andrew Jackson and the powerful backing of the Southern states. And now Pierce, from New Hampshire, not only had substantial electoral support from the South but also created a cabinet that leaned distinctly toward Southern interests. How could this be, many pondered, when the free states had had the majority of the population and the majority of seats in the House of Representatives and in the Electoral College since 1800? The Supreme Court, too, in the 1850s had a strong Southern or pro-Southern majority. To a growing number it seemed that disreputable and treacherous men in the North plotted with the Slave Power in return for personal gain, public office, and patronage. In the days ahead, Stephen A. Douglas of Illinois would absolutely confirm this suspicion for a multitude.

NOTES

1. http://ingeb.org/songs/othesuns.html, accessed July 29, 2003.

2. Sue Eakin and Joseph Logsdon, eds., *Twelve Years a Slave* (Baton Rouge: Louisiana State University Press, 1968), ix, xii.

3. Ibid., frontispiece.

4. Virginia Bernhard and Elizabeth Fox-Genovese, eds., *American Feminism: The Seneca Falls Woman's Convention of 1848* (St. James, NY: Brandywine Press, 1995), 190–92.

5. Allan Nevins, *Ordeal of the Union*, 2 vols. (New York: Charles Scribner's Sons, 1947), 2:16.

6. Michael A. Morrison, *Slavery and the American West: The Eclipse of Manifest Destiny and the Coming of the Civil War* (Chapel Hill: University of North Carolina Press, 1997), 126.

7. Nevins, *Ordeal of the Union*, 2:41.

8. Eric H. Walther, *The Fire-Eaters* (Baton Rouge: Louisiana State University Press, 1992), 206.

9. Ibid., 207.

10. Ibid., 214.

11. Nevins, *Ordeal of the Union*, 2:45.

12. Cave Johnson, quoted in Nevins, *Ordeal of the Union*, 2:67.

13. Ibid., 2:68.

14. David M. Potter, *The Impending Crisis, 1848–1861* (New York: Harper & Row, 1976), 155.

15. David Brion Davis, *The Slave Power Conspiracy and the Paranoid Style* (Baton Rouge: Louisiana State University Press, 1969), 19–20.

CHAPTER THREE

1854

"It Will Raise a Hell of a Storm"

SHORTLY AFTER CONGRESS reconvened following a Christmas and New Year recess, Senator Stephen Douglas again took up the question of Nebraska. On January 4 he reported a bill that called for organization of a Nebraska Territory. That bill left the question of slavery for the people of Nebraska to decide locally upon their admission to the Union as a state, precisely as Douglas's Compromise of 1850 had done for New Mexico and Utah. A report accompanying his bill mentioned the Missouri Compromise restriction from 1820 that prohibited slavery precisely where Douglas hoped to organize a territory. Douglas personally believed that this restriction would remain in place unless overturned by the Supreme Court, but as long as that legal barrier persisted, it doomed Douglas's bill, since slave-state congressmen had nothing to gain and therefore would not support it.

The next day the *Washington Sentinel* printed a new version of Douglas's bill, now running to twenty-one sections. The new part specifically called upon the people of Nebraska to decide for themselves whether or not to have slavery; that had only been implied in the first version. Douglas, in an effort to woo representatives from the South, now clearly intended his bill to overturn the Missouri Compromise restriction on slavery. It worked. Southern delegates began to deliberate. Most still thought Douglas offered too vague a promise, although Southerners quickly started to sense an opportunity to burst from their geographic confinement and capture a vast new domain for their section and for slavery.

On January 16, Senator Archibald Dixon of Kentucky, successor to the late Henry Clay, offered an amendment to the Nebraska Bill calling for an explicit repeal of the 36°30′ line created by Clay in 1820. Douglas did not like that. Leaving things vague or implied worked better for him; this had always let him finesse matters to suit his ends. But Douglas wanted Nebraska and wanted a transcontinental railroad. According to Dixon's wife, as she, her husband, and Douglas talked during a carriage ride, Douglas concluded, "By God, sir, you are right, and I will incorporate it in my bill, though I know it will raise a hell of a storm."[1]

Stephen A. Douglas
Library of Congress

A few more technical problems delayed things. Settlers and congressmen with various interests and motivations preferred to divide the territory in two—Kansas and Nebraska. Douglas agreed. Committees prepared their reports for the following week, but Douglas considered it imperative to make sure that President Pierce would sign the measure. Several powerful Southern senators had already met with Pierce and pressed him hard on the Kansas-Nebraska Bill. One newspaper had reported the occurrence of a heated cabinet debate over the bill, with Jefferson Davis and Navy Secretary James C. Dobbin arguing vociferously for the measure and others as adamantly urging Pierce not to support it. Douglas wanted to know where Pierce stood and, with the aid of Jeff Davis, convinced the president to break his own tradition of refraining from conducting business on the Sabbath. On Sunday, January 22, Douglas and Davis met with Pierce and got the assurances they wanted.

The next day, January 23, Kansas-Nebraska came to the floor of the Senate for a vote. It caused a hell of a storm. Many senators—like most Americans—had considered the Missouri Compromise a permanent settlement, almost a sacred compact. Now it stood a good chance of dying. Under Douglas's bill the people of each territory would decide for themselves whether or not to have slavery. But how? When? How often? Who constituted "the people"? Settlers? Squatters? The bill contained no specific instructions about when or how elections should take place. At some time during the settling process? When 30,000 people had taken up residence in a territory (a population figure required for territorial governments)? Or when a territory applied for statehood? And in the meantime, who would decide if slavery was allowed? White Southerners believed that slavery must be allowed in each territory unless and until its people decided to apply for statehood; only then could they reject it. Northerners asserted that a handful of settlers in the remote Western plains could not be allowed to decide such a volatile question for millions of Americans across the country. Douglas, defending Cass's great democratic principle of popular sovereignty, said that settlers on the scene ought to be able to decide early and to have the ability to vote upon it repeatedly if they chose to.

Robert Winthrop, a congressman from Massachusetts, summarized the thoughts and feelings of many Northerners. In a letter to a friend he wrote, "We are guardians of the infant commonwealths which lie cradled in these new Territories. We must do to them, as we would be done by. If I thank God that Massachusetts is not a slave State, how then can I turn round and let Nebraska and Kansas become one by refusing to interpose for their protection?"[2]

Others reacted with greater outrage. Before the bill had even hit the floor of Congress, on January 19, Senators Charles Sumner and Salmon P. Chase, along with Representatives Joshua R. Giddings, Gerrit Smith, and two others, drafted "An Appeal of the Independent Democrats." Less an appeal than a manifesto, these self-styled independents warned that Kansas-Nebraska threatened free institutions and even the permanency of the Union:

> We arraign this bill as a gross violation of a sacred pledge; as a criminal betrayal of precious rights; as part and parcel of an atrocious plot to exclude from a vast unoccupied region immigrants from the Old World and free laborers from our own States, and convert it into a dreary region of despotism inhabited by masters and slaves. . . . Even if overcome in the impending struggle, we shall not submit. We shall go home to our constituents, erect anew the standard of freedom, and call on the people to come to the rescue of the country from the domination of slavery. We will not despair; for the cause of human freedom is the cause of God.[3]

Douglas did his best to immediately cut off the challenge of these Independent Democrats. "Why should we gratify the abolition party in their effort to get up another political tornado of fanaticism and put the country again in peril for the purpose of electing a few agitators to the Congress of the United States?" he asked. Then he exploded with rage, arraigning Chase and Sumner as "the pure, unadulterated representatives of Abolitionism, Free Soilism, [and] Niggerism in the Congress of the United States."[4]

Douglas's efforts to dismiss the moral underpinning of these radicals only helped draw all his opponents closer together. Chase answered Douglas for the tiny group: "Now, sir, who is responsible for this renewal of strife and controversy? Not we, for we have introduced no question of territorial slavery into Congress—not we who are denounced as agitators and factionists." Others joined Chase. William Henry Seward of New York declared, "The slavery agitation which you deprecate so much is an eternal struggle between conservatism and progress, between truth and error, between right and wrong." Sumner encouraged all congressmen, regardless of section, to unite "according to the sentiments of the [founding] Fathers and the true spirit of the Constitution, in declaring Freedom, not Slavery NATIONAL." Democratic Senator Hannibal Hamlin of Maine defied pressure from Pierce and Attorney General Caleb Cushing and scolded, "Douglas, your bill is a gross moral

Hannibal Hamlin
Library of Congress

wrong. . . . It is vicious in principle, and if enacted, will produce infinite mischief. I shall oppose it."[5]

The indignation of countless Northerners matched that of these representatives and swept across the region. While Congress debated Kansas-Nebraska, on February 23 the periodical *Independent* published a letter by Harriet Beecher Stowe. "The Providence of God has brought our nation to a crisis of most solemn interest," she began. The issue before Congress would affect "the temporal and eternal interests" of people around the world and for generations to come. "Through our nation, it is to affect the interests of liberty and Christianity throughout the whole world," she wrote. After starting her letter in the manner of a politician, Stowe shifted immediately to a gendered vantage point. "I do not think there is a mother among us all, who clasps her child to her breast, who could ever be made to feel it right that that child should be a slave." And if there could be no mother who could think that right, Stowe asserted, no woman could think it right "to inflict on her neighbor's child what she would think worse than death were it inflicted on her own." Continuing to avoid and therefore to transcend race by writing in universal terms, Stowe continued, "I do not think there is a wife who would think it right *her* husband should be sold to a trader, and worked all his life without rights and without wages." With a not-so-subtle depiction of rape, she added that she did not believe "there is a brother who would think it right to have his sister owned as property, with no legal defense for her personal honor, by any living man." Would Northerners allow Kansas-Nebraska to extend these horrors across "a region of fair, free, unoccupied territory, nearly equal, in extent, to the whole of the free States?"

Stowe then outlined a yet greater fear, one that emerged in part from a recent Supreme Court decision and in part from the paranoia of those who believed in a Slave Power conspiracy. She referred to the Lemmon case of 1852 that declared it legal for slaveholders to maintain their human property while remaining for a time in free states. Like a growing multitude in the North, Stowe saw an ominous and ghastly future if the Lemmon decision stood and Kansas-Nebraska became law. "Should this come to pass, it is no more improbable that there may be, four years hence, slave depots in New York city, than it was four years ago, that the South would propose a repeal of the 'Missouri Compromise.' "[6]

In stark contrast to Northerners' outrage, initial reactions from the South were generally quiet or perplexed. Certainly most white men there felt that this act simply redressed a wrong embodied in law since 1820 and believed that vindication, not victory, came in the form of Kansas-Nebraska. Why, then, did Northerners seem so upset? Writing to his fellow Alabama senator, J. L. M. Curry stated, "It is difficult for us to comprehend or credit the excitement that is said to prevail in the North on account of the Nebraska question."[7] Back home in Alabama, Curry explained, few spoke of it at all, publicly or privately. Some in Dixie still did not quite trust Douglas or other Northerners who supported him. The most skeptical and radical of these actually complained about depending on Northern allies and grumbled, "We are at the mercy of the plundering unscrupulous North and are not freemen."[8]

Others, though, tackled head-on an issue that few in the North ever understood. Senator Andrew P. Butler of South Carolina publicly acknowledged that slavery would likely never gain a foothold in the relatively dry, cold Great Plains. Nevertheless, he continued, the South must have Douglas's bill. Butler explained, "I am willing to take this bill as it is. I am willing to take it, even upon the assumption that no slaves will go into Nebraska or Kansas. I am willing to take it upon the ground that, if you adopt it, it will take a festering thorn from the side of the South. I am willing to take it upon the ground that by it sentiments of honor are regarded."[9]

Curiously, most white Southerners drooled at the prospect of Douglas's bill while simultaneously denying that popular sovereignty could exclude slavery from territories. They continued to insist that it could only happen when a territory applied to Congress for statehood. They lined up solidly behind Douglas for an opportunity to expand slavery, not for the specifics of the bill itself.

On March 4 the Senate approved the Kansas-Nebraska Act by 37 to 14. Only two Southerners voted against it, Democrat Sam Houston from Texas and John Bell, a Whig from Tennessee. Only four Northern Democrats voted against it. House Democrats from the North worried; they now had to either vote their party's line and thereby upset their constituents or stand by their section and alienate their Southern allies. So they stalled as long as they could,

Alexander Stephens
Library of Congress

allowing Whigs who opposed the measure to speak at length —for days—against it. But one Whig, Georgia representative Alexander H. Stephens, diminutive in stature but towering in intellect and ambition, led the effort to pass the bill. On May 22 the House approved Kansas-Nebraska by the slender margin of 113 to 110. Pierce signed it into law on May 30.

In Congress only forty-two Northerners had supported the Kansas-Nebraska Act and eighty-nine opposed it; seventy-one Southerners supported it and just eleven voted against it. Among Northern Democrats only thirty-nine opposed the bill; every single Northern Whig and Free-Soiler voted it down. Of the few Southerners to vote nay, most were

Whigs and from the Upper South. The votes on Kansas-Nebraska reflected a great shift in national politics. Democrats reigned supreme, led by the South but aided by Northerners such as Douglas and Pierce. These votes provided the nails for the Whig Party coffin. Southern Whigs could not offer their electorate better protection for slavery than Democrats could. Whigs in the North proved simply impotent and irrelevant. But out of the Whigs' ashes in the North arose something quite new.

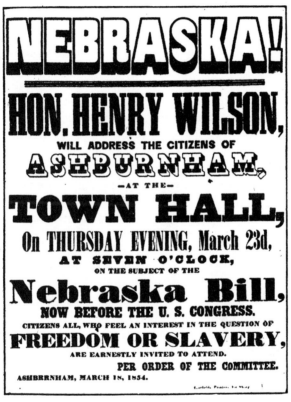

Notice of meeting in Massachusetts against Douglas's bill. From Allan Nevins, *Ordeal of the Union*, 2 vols. (New York: Charles Scribners's Sons, 1947), 2:125.

Even before final passage of the bill, dissenting politicians in the North began to desert their party organizations. Although more likely Whigs than Democrats, these defections spread across the entire section and both major parties. Astute politicians such as Whig Party boss Thurlow Weed of New York and conscientious

Free-Soilers like John P. Hale of New Hampshire saw opportunity through the tumult, a chance to build something new. In some places these men called themselves "Republicans"; in others, the "People's Party" or "Fusion" or just Anti-Nebraska. The movement varied as tremendously from state to state as did its names. One group of Republicans in Illinois leaned strongly toward abolitionism, so much so that the Free-Soil Whig they sought to help build their organization, Abraham Lincoln, initially refused to join. In February a gathering of Anti-Nebraska men at Ripon, Wisconsin, adopted the label Republican. Thirty congressmen had endorsed the party name by May, as did a subsequent state convention in Michigan. Whatever their names and whatever other political goals they pursued (and there were many), members of these groups all stood foursquare behind opposition to the expansion of slavery to the territories.

Two prominent senators who would soon lead the Republican Party now taunted the "Slave Power." William H. Seward of New York announced, "Since there is no escaping your challenge, I accept it in behalf of the cause of freedom. We will engage in competition for the virgin soil of Kansas, and God give the victory to the side which is stronger in numbers as it is in right."[10] Charles Sumner pronounced Kansas-Nebraska the worst and best bill ever produced by Congress—the worst for giving slavery a temporary victory, and the best by annulling all previous compromises with slavery and making impossible any compromises in the future. Like Seward, Sumner concluded, "Thus it puts Freedom and Slavery face to face, and bids them grapple."[11] The citizens of Boston punctuated Sumner's sentiments the very next day.

On May 26 a crowd gathered at Faneuil Hall to protest the arrest and return south of Anthony Burns, a fugitive slave. Burns had escaped from his master in Virginia and obtained work as a tailor in Boston. A local vigilance committee had promised to protect him "by every and any means necessary."[12] They could not stop the arrest of Burns; local authorities had deputized several local citizens—including gamblers and pimps—as a show of force. But on May 26 three leading citizens of Boston launched an effort to block the return of Burns to his master. Thomas Wentworth Higginson led the attempt, and Wendell Phillips and Theodore Parker egged on the crowd, which swarmed from Faneuil Hall to the courthouse that held Burns.

Higginson came from an old and distinguished New England family. He entered Harvard Divinity School at age thirteen and later was ordained as a Unitarian minister. An early advocate of women's suffrage, trade unions, free public education, and temperance, Higginson's most important reform effort quickly became radical abolitionism. In fact, Higginson swore in 1847 "to promote the Dissolution of the Union" if politicians could not achieve the end of slavery in the South. In May 1854, as Henry David Thoreau put it, Higginson became "the only Harvard Phi Beta Kappa, Unitarian Minister, and master of seven languages who has led a storming party against a federal bastion with a battering ram in his hands."[13]

A grandson of the commander of rebel troops at the Battle of Lexington in 1775, Theodore Parker, like Higginson, graduated from Harvard and became a minister. Known for his egotism and dogmatism, Parker himself announced that he valued "truth over friendship, candor over decorum," and "war over any peace that compromises liberty," earning him a reputation that matched Higginson's radicalism.[14] Several of the men deputized to guard Burns threatened Parker's life in return for his promise to intercede. Parker responded brazenly, choosing to sit between some of those very deputies during Burns's hearing, close enough so that their clothing made contact with each other. He later recorded boastfully, "The malaria of their rum and tobacco was an offense in my face. I saw their weapons and laughed as I looked at these drunken rowdies in their coward eye."[15]

Wendell Phillips, yet another Harvard-educated reformer, earned himself a reputation as an orator that rivaled the great Daniel Webster's. He had urged rejection of Texas annexation in 1845 and opposed war against Mexico in 1846 in his determination to stop the spread of slavery and, like Higginson, periodically called for dissolution of the Union. Referring to sexual exploitation of slaves by masters, Phillips publicly charged white Southerners with transforming their section into "one great brothel."[16] In 1850 he had condemned the Fugitive Slave Law, insisting that it "is to be denounced, resisted, disobeyed."[17] Later that year, Parker harbored a fugitive slave in his home, protecting her and himself with a loaded gun.

Now these three led a mob. Gathering first at Faneuil Hall, a site famous since the American Revolution as a gathering spot for rallies of resistance to oppression and calls for liberty, each unleashed a flood of words. A sign posted outside the hall read: "Shall he [Burns] be plunged into the hell of Virginia slavery by a Massa-chusetts judge . . . ?" Phillips asserted, "There is no law in Massa-chusetts, and when law ceases the people may act in their own sovereignty." Another speaker, Samuel Gridley Howe, announced, "No man's freedom is safe until all men are free." Finally, the in-censed crowd poured out of Faneuil Hall and swarmed toward the courthouse a few blocks away. There the Rev. Mr. Higginson and his men, using as a battering ram the banister from the steps of a local museum, led the throng and pounded open the door of the courthouse. A volley of shots greeted them, scattering many. Higginson shouted, "You cowards, will you desert us now?"[18] In they went. More gunshots rang out. One deputy cut open Higginson's chin with a saber. Other deputies beat back the intrud-ers with clubs. The would-be rescuers had to retreat. A fugitive slave from Kentucky, Lewis Hayden, who had established his house as a station on the Underground Railroad, waited outside with his gun. Hayden fired at the deputies as they pursued Higginson and his men, covering their escape. The mob failed to force their way in, but not before they killed one of the guards.

President Pierce responded immediately and forcefully, send-ing 2,000 federal troops to Boston to escort Burns to the harbor, where a ship waited to return him to slavery. A marine band pur-posely played "Carry Me Back to Old Virginny" to mock both Burns and the crowd, estimated by some at 50,000, about one-third of the entire population of the city. The people of Boston lined up in grim procession with black crepe, and many displayed portraits of Pierce—turned upside down—from windows. The cost of the troops, the ship, and the cleanup after the procession totaled some $100,000, leaving Higginson to remark that Burns thus became "the most expensive slave in the history of mankind."[19] One year later, Bostonians gathered enough money to purchase Burns from his master and set him free.

While a growing number of Northerners saw a Slave Power conspiring to take over the country, when the people of an entire city like Boston contrived to violate the Fugitive Slave Act, many in the South could only conclude that abolitionists wantonly and publicly designed to destroy slavery. Many in the South blamed Sumner directly for the attempt to stop the rendition of Burns, ig-noring the fact that his remarks in Congress had not yet reached Boston at the time of Higginson's effort. The *Washington Star* warned

Sumner to watch his "walk, talk, and acts." Burns's seizure and threats on Sumner's life galvanized New Englanders' support for the senator. A future governor of Connecticut, Joseph Hawley, told Sumner, "I have revolvers and can use them," and offered to come to Washington for Sumner's protection. More existentially, another fan wrote, "Should you fall, you will . . . kindle a fire of freedom that will blaze and burn the length and breadth of the land the light of which will irradiate the fartherest corners of the earth."[20]

Emboldened by his supporters and revolted by the rendition of Anthony Burns, Sumner planned a formal oration calling for the repeal of the Fugitive Slave Law. Before he could act, though, his fellow Massachusetts senator, Julius Rockwell, presented the Senate with a petition of 2,900 citizens calling for the withdrawal of the odious law. Some Southerners knew that many of the signers had participated in the effort to rescue Burns and denounced them as traitors and murderers. They insisted that a repeal of the Fugitive Slave Law would result in disunion. Sumner responded plainly, "If the Union be in any way dependent on an act . . . so revolting in every regard, then it ought not to exist."[21]

One day, as Sumner continued his antislavery agitation, the aged Andrew P. Butler, senator from South Carolina, entered the chamber. Butler had been among the few to befriend Sumner when the Northern senator first came to Washington, but now Butler's anger took over. He seized the floor and condemned Sumner's remarks as unsuited for the dignity of the Senate floor. Then Butler asked Sumner how in the world white Southerners could expect the return of their runaway slaves without the Fugitive Slave Law to enable it. Sumner replied, "Does the honorable Senator ask me if I would personally join in sending a fellow-man into bondage? 'Is thy servant a dog, that he should do this thing?' " he asked, copying abolitionist Wendell Phillips's poignant use of Scripture. An irate Butler shouted back, denouncing Sumner for implying that it was a dog's duty to enforce federal law. Virginian James M. Mason added his lung power, chastising Sumner for his "vapid, vulgar declamation" and fanaticism that proved Sumner's "reason is dethroned."

Others piled on. John Pettit of Indiana declared that Sumner had sunk "to a depth of humiliation and degradation which it would not be enviable for the lowest of God's creatures to occupy." Two days later, on June 28, still more senators joined the verbal assault.

Clement C. Clay of Alabama castigated Sumner as a leper, a serpent, and a "filthy reptile." Clay added that Sumner ought to be relegated to the "nadir of social degradation which he merits."[22]

Sumner replied, How could Southern senators attack him for his aversion to returning fugitive slaves? After all, many Southerners, even those dedicated to slavery, were uncomfortable with slave trading, and most were revolted by stealing slaves—free people—from Africa. Dramatically, Sumner challenged his Southern comrades by asking how many of them would personally wish to hunt down a runaway slave, to "stoop to any such service." He offered, "Until some one rises and openly professes his willingness to become a Slave-Hunter, I will not believe there can be one," and waited for a show of hands. He got none. Then Sumner turned specifically upon Mason and Butler, rebuking them for their "plantation manners" and concluding that the two must have thought themselves still on "a plantation well stocked with slaves, over which the overseer had full sway." As the debate ended, Sumner had solidified his reputation as the leading Senate spokesman against slavery, to the delight of antislavery Northerners and the disgust of honor-conscious white Southerners.[23]

While Sumner and others turned up the summer heat with their inflamed rhetoric in Congress, Stephen Douglas embarked on a speaking tour across the North in an effort to cool passions and win support for the Kansas-Nebraska Act. In Trenton, New Jersey, remonstrances by wage workers and labor leaders overwhelmed what had been a carefully orchestrated rally for Douglas, sending the senator off with hoots of derision as his train left town. In Cleveland he saw an effigy of himself hanging from a tree. Newspapers along his route called him Benedict Arnold and Judas, for selling out the North. Years later, Douglas recalled that he could have traveled clear across the North by the fiery light of his own burning effigy.

His ill-famed tour ended in his home state, in Chicago, on Saturday, September 1. A crowd of about 8,000 people awaited Douglas late in the evening. Leading Democrats tried to orchestrate a sympathetic reception, carefully selecting a meeting hall in a neighborhood with likely supporters and actually hiring men to cheer Douglas and to restrain hecklers. It did not work. As Douglas spoke, more and more people interrupted, shouted, and hissed at the Little Giant, who stubbornly proceeded with his long defense of Kansas-Nebraska. After midnight, with the meeting degenerating further,

Douglas finally ended it by shouting, "Abolitionists of Chicago, it is now Sunday morning. I'll go to church, and you may go to hell."[24]

By early October, Douglas faced less hostile crowds and even seemed to start to win back some support. In Springfield he spoke at the statehouse. The next day, at the same place, Abraham Lincoln responded with a three-hour oration. With minor variations he repeated it a few days later in Peoria. "No man is good enough to govern another man, *without that other's consent*," Lincoln proclaimed. Invoking the Declaration of Independence, Lincoln charged, "The spirit of Seventy-six and the spirit of Nebraska are utter antagonisms. . . . Near eighty years ago we began by declaring that all men are created equal; but now from that beginning we have run down the other direction, that for some men to enslave others is a 'sacred right of self-government.' These principles cannot stand together," he concluded.[25] Clearly, Lincoln condemned American slavery.

Even so, this Free-Soil Whig had enormously mixed feelings about political and legal realities. The Constitution granted states control over domestic institutions, and slavery was one of these. As a lawyer, Lincoln knew that neither the Northern people nor Congress could do anything about slavery in the Southern states. He even argued that all Americans should respect the Fugitive Slave Act. However, Lincoln denounced slavery. With great candor he admitted, "If all earthly power were given to me, I should not know what to do, about the existing institution. My first impulse would be to free all the slaves, and send them to Liberia," an African nation created by the United States specifically for this purpose. And yet, he knew that there was neither money nor shipping enough to carry off over 3.5 million slaves, and he also knew that many would perish in transit or upon arrival. "What then? Free them all, and keep them among us as underlings?" He considered that not much different than slavery. Free them and make them socially and politically equal to whites? Lincoln responded to this with the racism typical of Northern masses: "My own feelings will not admit of this; and if mine would, we well know that those of the great mass of white people will not."[26] The solution? At least keep the institution confined; do not let it grow; do not allow it into Kansas or Nebraska. Lincoln was well on his way toward becoming a Republican.

As proslavery Southerners looked toward the Great Plains for territorial expansion, "President" William Walker issued a decree from La Paz, Mexico, on January 18, annexing the province of Sonora to his would-be Republic of Lower California. Walker's regime won no respect from the local population. In fact, his men had free rein to plunder and pillage, and they even looted a Catholic mission. Although other filibusters and adventurers had swelled Walker's American forces to about 150, the Mexican people and their government had had about enough. Simultaneously, President Pierce issued his own proclamation: a decree against filibustering. American expansion was all well and good as long as the American government did the invading, not private citizens. In fact, so many filibustering expeditions had been planned or executed that Congress had already passed several neutrality laws rendering the practice illegal. Under direction from Secretary of War Jefferson Davis, federal authorities in San Francisco arrested several of Walker's supporters there and stopped supplies and more men from sailing for La Paz.

Walker moved on again. Rather than sailing across the narrow Gulf of California, he marched his men all the way north to and across the mouth of the Colorado River, finally reaching Sonora. Worn out and lacking food and supplies, his men turned upon one another and deserted; Walker hastily retreated back to the United States rather than face a Mexican military force sent to stop him. Federal authorities in California arrested him and his men for violating neutrality laws. Walker's trial in San Francisco turned into a showcase for American expansionism and racism. The judge clearly sympathized with Walker, and the jury took all of eight minutes to find Walker not guilty and to declare their gratitude for any American who tried to "civilize the Greasers." Vindicated, Walker took the rest of the year to plan another, grander conquest overseas, one that would gain him much more glory than he could have achieved in Mexico.[27]

Elsewhere in Latin America, on February 28 Spanish authorities in Havana, Cuba, seized an American merchant vessel, the *Black Warrior*, citing an error in the ship's manifest. The seizure and subsequent refusal to compensate the United States for the loss of property prompted many expansionists, including members of Congress, to call for war against Spain, focusing on American absorption of Cuba. Secretary of State William L. Marcy considered both a military strike to take Cuba and an effort to purchase the island. Even though Spanish authorities released the ship on March 16, after the payment of a $6,000 fine, on April 8 the American minister to Madrid, Pierre Soulé, the man who had dueled with French and Spanish gentlemen the year before, presented the Spanish government with a claim for damages. With no response from that government, Soulé issued an ultimatum demanding immediate satisfaction, using much the same language as supposed gentlemen in affairs of honor, or duels.

Secretary Marcy, though, tried to temper the situation. On August 16, Marcy ordered Soulé to join the American commissioner to England, James Buchanan of Pennsylvania, and to France, John Y. Mason of Virginia, in Ostend, Belgium, to mold a policy for the American acquisition of Cuba. The meeting occurred on October 9 with the full support of President Pierce. Soulé led the affair from the start, and the result bore his aggressive, expansionist mark. The "Ostend Manifesto" declared that Cuba was indispensable for the security of slavery in the United States and that America should make every effort to purchase it. If Spain refused to sell the island, the American diplomats continued, "then by every law human and divine, we shall be justified in wresting it from Spain, if we have the power."[28]

Northerners reacted to the document with horror and indignation. The *New York Evening Post* called it "atrocious." The *New York Tribune* labeled it the "Manifesto of Brigands" and a "buccaneering document" that threatened "to grasp, to rob, to murder, to grow rich on the spoils of the provinces and toils of slaves." Secretary Marcy distanced himself by disavowing any part in the formation of the policy, and even Soulé faced so much pressure that he felt compelled to resign his post by December 17. Between the Ostend Manifesto and Kansas-Nebraska, it seemed obvious to more and more Northerners that a grasping Slave Power would stop at nothing to expand its realm.

Few whites in the South could comprehend this hostile Northern reaction to the Ostend Manifesto. In their minds, slavery was part and parcel of the United States, a source of pride as well as profit, and a benefit to blacks as well as whites. In fact, the first two books published in the United States to use the term "sociology" in their titles both appeared in 1854, were produced by Southern authors, and vehemently defended slavery.

Henry Hughes wrote *Treatise on Sociology: Theoretical and Practical*. Raised in Port Gibson, Mississippi, he graduated in 1847 at age eighteen from nearby Oakland College and then studied law in New Orleans and a wide variety of subjects in France. Whatever temptations cosmopolitan Paris offered Hughes, they could not overcome his desire to return to his little town on the Mississippi River, where he established a law practice. But Hughes also began to speak out on public issues and to write.

In his *Treatise*, Hughes made some efforts to attain scientific objectivity. He tried to avoid discussing slavery per se, preferring instead to describe systems of "warranteeism." Hughes explained, "Warranteeism does not violate the personal liberty of the warrantee. It allows economically all rights consistent with the economic order; politically, all rights consistent with the political order." Hughes effectively described the warrantor as a paternalist, one who had a duty to take care of the "economic, political, and hygienic" needs of his charges. "It is their duty to administer by all just means, the public industry of their warranty; prescribing the hours, quantity, quality or other accidents of labor."[29]

Of course, African American slavery in the South, not principles of sociological inquiry, informed—actually dictated—Hughes's perspective. Doubtless, Hughes genuinely believed the proslavery argument that he shared with so many contemporary white Southerners. Shamelessly he described the supposed truth of slave life in the South, or rather, the lives of warrantees under kind warrantors: "They are not slaves; they are not persons who have no rights. Their slavery is nominal only; and the name, a wrong to the warrantee States."[30]

Some of these same ideas appeared in George Fitzhugh's book *Sociology for the South*, although Fitzhugh never pretended to cloak his argument in science, nor did he shy away from calling masters "masters" and slaves "slaves." Fitzhugh, a Virginian born to a planter family with declining fortune, left the land as an adult to pursue a career in law. He liked to argue but had little taste for listening to the sad stories of prospective clients and therefore acquired few. Shunning law, Fitzhugh turned to writing, mostly pamphlets and articles, and later books, the majority of which dealt with slavery and race. In one piece that gained him some renown in 1851, titled "What Shall Be Done with Free Negroes?" Fitzhugh argued for the adoption of some sort of peonage system so that whites could better control this anomalous class, or have the state hire out those who did not support themselves, or ship free blacks to Africa.

Fitzhugh offered a series of articles that he combined in book form as *Sociology for the South: Or the Failure of Free Society*. He began by apologizing for using this new term, "sociology." Fitzhugh brazenly declared, "The fact that, before the institution of Free Society, there was no such term, and that it is not now in use in slave countries" proved that slave societies have always been so happy and harmonious that they required "no doctors . . . to treat of its complaints, or to propose remedies for their cure." Fitzhugh asserted, "The ancients took it for granted that slavery was right, and never attempted to justify it. The moderns assume that it is wrong. . . . The South can lose nothing, and may gain, by the discussion. She has, up to this time, been condemned without a hearing."[31]

Fitzhugh painted quite a contrast between Northern and Southern labor systems. In the North, he explained, where "liberty and free competition" divide capital and labor, the result injured the working classes. Free workers had to find a home, find a job, and take care of themselves besides. In contrast, "slavery relieves our slaves of these cares altogether, and slavery is a form, and the very best form, of socialism." Slaves in the South need not worry about starving to death, receiving support in infirmity or old age, reduction of wages or loss of jobs—all possibilities that existed in free, competitive society but not in the slave South. There, "the master increases in provision for the family as the family increases in number and helplessness. It is a beautiful example of communism, where each one receives not according to his labor, but according to his wants." Adding a theological dimension as strained as his socioeconomic ones, Fitzhugh commented, "It is remarkable . . . that sin began by the desire for liberty and the attempt to attain it in the person of Satan and his fallen angels. The world wants good government and plenty of it—not liberty."[32]

Substituting supposed medical science for supposed social science, Dr. Josiah Nott of Mobile, Alabama, added yet another layer to the proslavery argument in 1854 with his book *Types of Mankind*, a collection of his previous lectures on ethnology, a presumed science of ethnic types. Unlike most proslavery advocates, who claimed that the origins of African peoples came from God's curse upon Cain and his descendants, Dr. Nott argued that careful study of white and black races actually proved they were of different species, different types of mankind. "The Almighty in his wisdom has peopled our vast planet from many distant centres, instead of one, and with races or species originally and radically different," he explained. Nott asserted that blacks' "highest contribution is attained in the state of slavery," that they could never rise "above the grade of mediocrity in the whites." Nott concluded that whites, on the other hand, had a destiny "to conquer and hold every foot of the globe" they could and to control all other "inferior races."[33]

Although not a direct response to Hughes, Fitzhugh, or Nott, a young Free-Soiler in Illinois scratched out some of his own thoughts on proslavery argumentation. As though taking aim at Southern "scientists," Abraham Lincoln wrote, "The most dumb and stupid slave that ever toiled for a master, does constantly *know* that he is wronged." Lincoln also noted that "although volume upon volume is written to prove slavery a very good thing, we never hear of the man who wishes to take the good of it, *by being a slave himself*."[34] At about the same time, Lincoln tried to settle in his own lawyer's mind what logic lay at the root of slavery, providing a poignant rebuttal to the likes of Josiah Nott:

> If A. can prove, however conclusively, that he may, of right, enslave B.—why may not B. snatch the same argument, and prove equally, that he may enslave A?—
> You say A. is white, and B. is black. It is *color*, then; the lighter, having the right to enslave the darker? Take care. By this rule, you are to be slave to the first man you meet, with fairer skin than your own.
> You do not mean *color* exactly?—You mean the whites are *intellectually* the superiors of the blacks, and, therefore have the right to enslave them? Take care again. By this rule, you are to be slave to the first man you meet, with an intellect superior to your own.
> But, you say, it is a question of *interest*; and, if you can make it your *interest*, you have a right to enslave another. Very well. And if he can make it his interest, he has the right to enslave you.[35]

While the implications of Kansas-Nebraska motivated Lincoln to work out his thoughts on slavery and racism, the act caused one hell of a storm in the congressional elections during the fall of 1854. It mostly devastated Northern Democrats, with voters expressing tremendous anger toward Douglas and his supporters, including President Pierce. Southern Democrats weathered the storm fairly well, losing only four of their sixty-seven seats, but their Northern counterparts got hammered: sixty-six of ninety-one Democrats from the North got voted out of office. In Ohio every man who won a seat in Congress ran as an Anti-Nebraska candidate, as did all but two in Indiana. In Iowa, James W. Grimes led Anti-Nebraska forces to a stunning victory, capturing the state house and the governorship for himself. Grimes vowed *"war and war continually* against the abandonment to slavery of a single foot of soil now consecrated to freedom."[36]

Southern Democrats now controlled the national party, unlike any time before, but that party was severely weakened. A Democrat in Charleston observed the tumultuous political landscape and concluded "that the Nebraska excitement will soon die out—that it will not harm the country, that it will very properly turn out of office the majority of Northern Democrats, who hoped to profit by it." Nevertheless, he worried, "Can we of the South maintain brotherly relations with men whose power is based upon sectional agitation, *against our section*?"[37]

Other forces also unleashed their powers during this election year. Nativism, a prejudicial reaction by those already in America to new immigrants, had been gathering into a legitimate political force since the 1830s. Mostly building in the North, the section that absorbed the lion's share of these newcomers, nativist organizations began to make an impact in politics by the 1840s. The rise of these groups paralleled the incredible flood of European immigration at the time. From 1845 to 1854 some 2,939,000 immigrants arrived, fully 1,200,000 of them Irish, fleeing the famine that ravaged their homeland. Like the Irish, many of the others were Catholic, and Protestant Americans generally had no love for "papists," or those who followed the Pope. In politics, local and state issues that tended to divide people between Catholic and Protestant played right into the hands of nativist organizations, especially questions about temperance, Sabbath-breaking, and various other evangelical—and mostly Protestant—reforms.

Most notable among these nativist political groups were the Order of United Americans, created in 1844, and the Order of the Star-Spangled Banner, founded in 1849, both in New York City. Like those of many other such groups, their founders created these orders as secret societies. Members were not supposed to divulge to nonmembers anything about meetings or activities; if asked anything, they were to reply, "I know nothing." Outsiders quickly decided to follow suit and derisively called nativists Know-Nothings. But Know-Nothings, who later called themselves the American Party, seemed to have the last laugh. Especially after the introduction of Kansas-Nebraska shook the foundations of national politics, Know-Nothings picked up many new members, or at least potential partners in coalitions. As Free-Soilers gathered to form the Republican Party, Know-Nothings were already way ahead of them in organization and in numbers.

The growth of the Know-Nothings was no less than meteoric. Two years before, an official count of Know-Nothing membership stood at a paltry forty-three; by the end of 1854 they counted over one million. Many joined because of nativist issues per se, but many more did so because of their antislavery convictions. Anson Burlingame, a Know-Nothing congressman from Massachusetts, spoke for these by arguing, "Slavery and Priestcraft . . . have a common purpose: they seek [to annex] Cuba and Hayti and the Mexican States together, because they will be Catholic and slave. I say they are in alliance by the necessity of their nature,—for one denies the right of a man to his body, and the other the right of a man to his soul."[38] But also, since neither Whigs, Democrats, nor even Free-Soilers offered a potent party mechanism to rally these forces, many antislavery men in the North used the Know-Nothings, as Joshua Giddings said, "as a screen—a dark wall—behind which members of old political organizations could escape unseen from party shackles, and take a position, according to the dictates of judgment and conscience."[39] Most of these quickly deserted the American Party for the emergent Republican Party.

By 1854 Northern voters had a spectacular array of political choices. They could vote for Republicans, Democrats, Whigs, Free-Soilers, the People's Party, the Fusion Party, Anti-Nebraska, Know-Nothings, Know-Somethings (antislavery nativists), Maine Lawites (who called for temperance laws), or Rum Democrats (who opposed temperance), not to mention curiosities like Hard Shell Democrats, Soft Shell Democrats, Half Shells, Adopted Citizens, and Hindoos.

Reacting to all this party commotion plus continued waves of women's rights and abolitionist meetings in the North, a newspaper in Alabama boasted of the South's moral superiority over Northern culture: "You will rarely see mobs assembling to burn churches or to violate the constitution [in the South]. . . . There, no Angel Gabriel sounds his horn, disturbing the quiet Sabbath and calling together bands of rowdies. There, no Salem witchcraft, nor Blue Laws, nor Bloomerism, nor Woman's Rights, nor Mormonism, nor Millerism, nor Anti-Popery, nor Spirit-Rapping, nor Socialism, nor other monstrous productions have sprung up to choke the healthy growth of freedom." And when free blacks in New York spoke out for suffrage for themselves as well as for all women and then endorsed Whig gubernatorial candidate Myron H. Clark—an advocate of Maine laws, Anti-Nebraska, and antislavery—this newspaper lashed out, "Now that the Niggers and the disaffected Know-Nothings have declared for Myron, it only remains for the 'strong-minded' women . . . to pitch in, to make his election sure. He would then be the Whig-Nigger-Know-Nothing-Woman's-Rights candidate for the great Empire State."[40]

Sectional antagonisms rose to levels not seen in a generation, greater than the worst days of the crisis of 1850, when secession had become a distinct possibility, and rivaled only when South Carolina had defied President Andrew Jackson during the Nullification Crisis of 1832–33. In both of those previous conflicts, radical Southerners had taken preparations to defy the nation by force of arms. By the end of 1854, though, violent resistance in the North to federal law had become established and efforts in both sections to win Kansas for their respective sides rapidly turned into an arms race.

Before Kansas-Nebraska even passed into law, wealthy businessman and abolitionist Eli Thayer of Worcester, Massachusetts, with financial support from Amos Lawrence, organized the Massachusetts Immigrant Aid Society. Granted a charter by the Massachusetts assembly and allowed to raise capital stock up to $5 million, Thayer's organization hoped to send whole groups of Free-Soilers to Kansas. Their support aided more farmers from the Midwest in their migration to the embattled territory than it did people from the Bay State, and by the end of the year the society had helped to relocate only about 650 Northerners. Charles Francis Adams, son of John Quincy Adams, gave $25,000. Theodore Parker and Samuel Gridley Howe, two of the men who had tried to stop the rendition of Anthony Burns, added their assistance. Grateful Free-Soilers honored their main sponsor by naming their chief settlement Lawrence, Kansas, a town that remained the bastion of free-soilism in that territory. Early in 1855 the organization reincorporated as the New England Emigrant Aid Society.

Not to be outdone, proslavery zealots rose to the challenge. Many feared not only losing Kansas and Nebraska to a cordon of free territories and states but also the weakening of slavery on the western border. Virginia senator Robert M. T. Hunter believed, "The game must be played boldly. . . . If we win we carry slavery to the Pacific Ocean, if we fail we lose Missouri Arkansas Texas and all the territories." As David Atchison of Missouri said, "We are playing for a mighty stake." Recalling an episode fifteen years before, when people in Missouri violently and ruthlessly forced from their soil members of the Mormon faith, Atchison wrote to Jefferson Davis, "We are organizing. We will be compelled to shoot, burn & hang, but the thing will soon be over. We intend to 'Mormonize' the Abolitionists."[41]

Both North and South got their first chance to prevail in November. Pierce's appointee as territorial governor for Kansas, Andrew Reeder, a Democrat from Pennsylvania who had never before held a public office, called for elections. The poll represented the first real test of popular sovereignty in action. Men such as Atchison refused to let it be a fair test. With others of like mind, Atchison gathered men to charge across the border into Kansas and guarantee a proslavery victory. Called border ruffians or even Pukes by their Free-Soil victims, many in fact were coarse and vicious, with less direct interest in slavery than hatred for Yankees, whom they considered "sanctimonious" and dedicated to "sickly sycophantic love for the nigger."[42] Their presence and their intimidation of Free-Soilers won the first round. Later, a congressional committee rejected over 1,700 of their votes as fraudulent. But this scenario was just the beginning; Kansas had merely begun to bleed.

NOTES*

1. Allan Nevins, *Ordeal of the Union*, 2 vols. (New York: Charles Scribner's Sons, 1947), 2:96.
2. Ibid., 101.
3. Hans Trefousse, *The Radical Republicans: Lincoln's Vanguard for Racial Justice* (New York: Knopf, 1969), 69–70.
4. Nevins, *Ordeal of the Union*, 2:114.
5. Trefousse, *Radical Republicans*, 71–73.
6. Jeanne Boydston, Mary Kelley, and Ann Margolis, eds., *The Limits of Sisterhood: The Beecher Sisters on Women's Rights and Woman's Sphere* (Chapel Hill: University of North Carolina Press, 1988), 180–82.
7. J. Mills Thornton III, *Politics and Power in a Slave Society: Alabama, 1800–1860* (Baton Rouge: Louisiana State University Press, 1978), 351.
8. John McQueen of South Carolina, quoted in Eric H. Walther, *The Fire-Eaters* (Baton Rouge: Louisiana State University Press, 1992), 147.
9. Lacy K. Ford Jr., *Origins of Southern Radicalism: The South Carolina Upcountry, 1800–1860* (New York: Oxford University Press, 1988), 343.
10. James M. McPherson, *Battle Cry of Freedom: The Civil War Era* (New York: Oxford University Press, 1988), 145.
11. David Herbert Donald, *Charles Sumner and the Coming of the Civil War*, 1st ed. (New York: Knopf, 1960), 260–61.

*Emphasis in all quotations is that of the original authors.

12. Edward J. Renehan Jr., *The Secret Six: The True Tale of the Men Who Conspired with John Brown* (Columbia: University of South Carolina Press, 1996), 65.

13. Ibid., 54, 64–65.

14. Ibid., 39.

15. Ibid., 65.

16. David M. Potter, *The Impending Crisis, 1848–1861* (New York: Harper & Row, 1976), 252.

17. McPherson, *Battle Cry of Freedom*, 82.

18. Renehan, *Secret Six*, 66 (Phillips, Parker, and Howe), 68 (Higginson).

19. Ibid., 70.

20. Donald, *Charles Sumner and Civil War*, 262–63.

21. Ibid., 263.

22. Ibid., 262–64.

23. Ibid., 264–65.

24. Bruce C. Levine, *Half Slave and Half Free: The Roots of Civil War* (New York: Hill and Wang, Noonday Press, 1992), 195.

25. Roy P. Basler et al., eds., *The Collected Works of Abraham Lincoln*, 9 vols. (New Brunswick, NJ: Rutgers University Press, 1953), 2:266, 275.

26. Ibid., 2:253–54.

27. Nevins, *Ordeal of the Union*, 2:369.

28. Potter, *Impending Crisis*, 190.

29. Drew G. Faust, ed., *The Ideology of Slavery: Proslavery Thought in the Antebellum South, 1830–1860* (Baton Rouge: Louisiana State University Press, 1981), 242–44.

30. Ibid., 253.

31. Harvey Wish, ed., *Ante-Bellum Writings of George Fitzhugh and Hinton Rowan Helper on Slavery* (New York: Capricorn Books, 1960), 43–45.

32. Ibid., 58–59, 60.

33. John McCardell, *The Idea of a Southern Nation: Southern Nationalists and Southern Nationalism, 1830–1860* (New York: Norton, 1979), 80–81, 83.

34. Basler, *Collected Works of Abraham Lincoln*, 2:222.

35. Ibid., 2:222–23.

36. Nevins, *Ordeal*, 344.

37. George S. Bryan, quoted in Nevins, *Ordeal of the Union*, 2:345–46.

38. Tyler Anbinder, *Nativism and Slavery: The Northern Know Nothings and the Politics of the 1850s* (New York: Oxford University Press, 1992), 45.

39. Ibid., 50.

40. *Montgomery Advertiser and State Gazette*, September 13, 1854.

41. McPherson, *Battle Cry of Freedom*, 145–46.

42. Ibid., 146.

Chapter Four

1855

"Kansas Has Been Invaded"

AT THE START of the year, Governor Andrew Reeder's office reported a population in Kansas of only 8,601 people, including 242 slaves, clustered mostly along the eastern fringe of the territory's 20,000 square miles. In Reeder's mind this justified calling an election for a legislature, set by the governor for March 30. Careful to ensure a fair vote, the governor appointed three election judges—two Free-Soilers, one proslavery—and several constables to supervise the balloting in each district and mandated that they take an oath to maintain regular procedures and to make sure that voters actually resided in Kansas, owning homes in no other state or territory. There only should have been about 2,900 eligible voters.

Reeder's precautions proved worthless. Rumors spread that the Emigrant Aid Society had sent 20,000 men to steal the election, and proslavery men quickly organized to stop this phantom menace. Calling themselves Sons of the South or Blue Lodge or South Band, some 5,000 vigilantes streamed across from Missouri. One company actually had its own flag and band, besides plenty of weapons, including two artillery pieces. They set up camp near the Free-Soil stronghold of Lawrence the day before the election. In Missouri, David Atchison, up for reelection to the U.S. Senate, personally led about eighty heavily armed men into Kansas and swore to raise enough of a force "to kill every God-damned abolitionist in the Territory." This massive display by proslavery men; their threats, firing gunshots into the air; the intimidation or removal of judges; and the counting of fraudulent votes produced a lopsided proslavery victory: only one of their men failed to win. In all, proslavery candidates took 6,307 votes to a paltry 791 Free-Soil votes out of 2,900 eligible voters. One proslavery man tediously explained to a protesting Free-Soil voter, "Atchison had helped to make the bill [that created Kansas], and had told them they had a right to vote, and he knew a God-damned sight better than I did."[1]

Governor Reeder threw out votes where someone contested their validity, but generally believed that he had no right to intervene unless someone officially challenged the process, and since no one filed an official grievance, he allowed the fraud to stand. Proslavery delegates, claiming victory, rushed to the territorial capital, Shawnee Mission, to demand that Reeder provide certificates of election. They insisted that the governor lacked the authority to set the limits that he had on the election and that newly arrived Southerners had every right to vote. On April 6, Reeder appeared in public to issue his decision. Guarded by personal friends whose fingers remained poised on their guns' triggers, while proslavery men did the same with theirs, Reeder issued certificates to two-thirds of the petitioners and called new elections in the six remaining districts, where Free-Soilers had filed protests.

David R. Atchison
Library of Congress

Five of those six districts elected Free-Soil delegates to the new assembly, with its solid proslavery majority. By mid-April, Reeder finally had enough evidence of the extent of fraud and violence. He scrambled toward Washington, DC, warning the public along the way about the mischief in Kansas and hastening personally to bring the matter to the attention of President Pierce.

Arriving too late to bolster the ineffectual free-soil cause, five brothers decided to move from Ohio to Kansas in the spring of 1855. The Midwest suffered through a prolonged and extreme drought, and promotional literature promised fertile land and endless opportunity to the west. Besides, Owen, Jason, Salmon, Frederick, and John Brown Jr. had a pronounced abolitionist family upbringing, so their decision to move complemented their determination to keep Kansas free of slaves and slaveholders. Owen, Samuel, and Frederick crossed into the territory first, and John Jr. and Jason followed. On their steamboat journey up the Missouri River, Jason

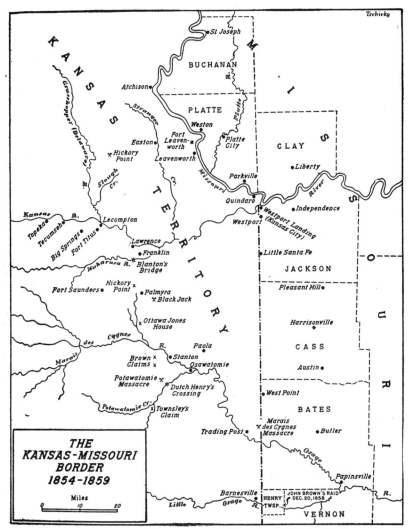

Tschirky

THE
KANSAS-MISSOURI
BORDER
1854-1859

Miles
10   20

From Allan Nevins, *Ordeal of the Union*, 2 vols. (New York: Charles Scribners's Sons, 1947), 2:303.

and John Brown found themselves outnumbered by Southerners, one of whom warned the young men that they were heading for trouble, since proslavery Missourians lay waiting with "Annoyance Associations" to discourage the likes of John Jr. and Jason. Undaunted, John Jr. replied that if anyone tried to stop them they would be ready with the sword, "that final arbiter of all the great questions that have stirred mankind."[2]

Later on their ill-fated voyage, a cholera outbreak took the life of Jason's four-year-old son, Austin. The grieving father and his brother disembarked just long enough to bury the boy when the ship docked for repairs, but when they returned, the ship had left without them. A stagecoach took them to Kansas City, the very core of proslavery western Missouri. They then set off by foot on a trail cut through immense fields of grass and, in April, finally reached Osawatomie, by the Marais des Cygnes River and Pottawatomie Creek, about 30 miles south of Lawrence. There they joined their other three brothers. A few days later the five set out westward about 5 miles, staking out an improvised camp they called Brown's Station.

As the Brown brothers established their settlement, Governor Reeder stopped briefly in his native Pennsylvania to deliver a grave message. "Kansas has been invaded, conquered, subjugated by an armed force from beyond her borders, led on by a fanatical spirit," he exclaimed, and insisted that the nation respond with equal force.[3] Arriving later in Washington, for two weeks in May, Reeder met with Franklin Pierce to discuss the predicament. In no uncertain terms he told his president that proslavery men had wantonly violated the letter of the law and the spirit of democracy. Pierce responded with his typical effort to please everyone while in fact doing nothing. He told Reeder that the chaos in Kansas gave him the greatest suffering he had experienced since the death of his son and that the situation threatened the effectiveness of his entire administration. And yet, he chided Reeder for the governor's inflammatory remarks in Pennsylvania as well as for Reeder's failure to speak out against similar crimes by the Emigrant Aid people (even though Reeder knew of no crimes committed by that group). Reeder would have to return to Kansas and sort things out without presidential help.

It must have shocked Reeder upon his return in June to find that the situation there had actually grown more wild. He called the new assembly to convene at Pawnee City, 100 miles west of the slave border with Missouri, on July 2. The legislature complied but met only to adjourn to proslavery Shawnee Mission, in open rebellion against the hapless governor. There they passed laws that defied the concepts of popular sovereignty, American democracy, fair play, and common sense. Only proslavery men could hold public office. Anyone who denied the legality of slavery in the territory faced prison and hard labor for no less than two years. Anyone who in any way aided a slave's attempt to run away or even merely circulated abolition literature could find themselves sentenced to death. No laws like these had ever existed in any slave state. Every bill received Reeder's veto, and the assembly overrode each one of them.

Most of these laws proved ineffective and were unenforced. But the very lack of the law or its enforcement permeated the region with terror. In April, members of the proslavery Blue Lodge organization stormed into Parkville, Missouri, near Leavenworth, Kansas, in order to silence criticisms from George S. Park and W. J. Patterson, editors of the *Parkville Industrial Luminary*. Armed men barged into the paper's office and seized the press itself with the type, throwing them into the Missouri River. As for Park and Patterson, Blue Lodgers swore "our honor as men to follow and hang them wherever we can take them." Park, who had once fought in Texas under the command of Sam Houston, held his ground and escaped unharmed, but the vigilantes found Patterson and determined to throw him into the river, too. Patterson cried out—truthfully—that he was Canadian and thus won a release, after being warned to drop his abolition propaganda and leave town or face worse from the Blue Lodge.[4]

More grave violence occurred later in April, back across the river in Leavenworth. A public meeting attended by pro- and antislavery men alike degenerated quickly when a Free-Soil lawyer took such offense at receiving a punch by a proslavery politician that the attorney shot him dead. Proslavery forces in Leavenworth responded the next month by holding a meeting that passed resolutions to create a vigilance committee to dispatch any settler who disparaged slavery or interfered with slaves.

National reactions to the violence in Kansas varied tremendously. Abolitionist Horace Greeley's *New York Tribune* reported the Parkville incident to a stunned readership. Other responses were less predictable. The *New Orleans Bulletin* transcended Southern partisanship and denounced the draconian laws passed by the fraudulent territorial assembly. A Democratic senator in California broke with his party and called on Congress to intervene and annul the nefarious laws of Kansas.

On the scene in Kansas, one of the five brothers who had just arrived wrote an account to send to his father, John Brown. The father was raised a strict Calvinist and had a pronounced sense of right and wrong. John Brown saw no greater wrong in the United States than slavery and had already begun to work with other

prominent abolitionists. His sons—these five of Brown's twenty children—had already asked him to accompany them to Kansas in 1854,
but he had declined. Proud that his sons shared his determination
and fanaticism for reform, though, John Brown had written, "If you
or any of my family are disposed to go to Kansas or Nebraska, with a
view to help defeat Satan and his legions in that direction," they had
their father's full support.[5]

Now, in May 1855, John Jr. wrote a letter to his father, who had
just left Rockville, Illinois, for upstate New York. John Jr. told his
father, "If we can succeed in making this a *free* State, a great work
will be accomplished for *mankind*." But John Jr. also got his father's
ire up by warning that proslavery forces had proven that they would
make Kansas a slave state "by means no matter how foul" and that
Annoyance Associations had struck terror into the hearts of Free-
Soilers so thoroughly that most displayed "the most abject and cow-
ardly spirit."[6] Kansas Free-Soilers needed more men, more weapons,
and more nerve. John Brown would try to supply all those needs.

Before making the long trip to Kansas, John Brown had critical
business to attend to in New York. On June 26 radical abolitionists
assembled at Syracuse, home of the wealthy and dedicated abolitionist Gerrit Smith, an old friend of Brown's. Before Brown arrived delegates already had raised $4,600 to support abolitionist
activities. On June 28, Brown had Smith read John Jr.'s letter to the
convention, drawing tears from many in the audience. Then Brown
himself followed with his own remarks, proclaiming assuredly that
"without the shedding of blood there is no remission of sin."[7] Black
abolitionist Frederick Douglass, another acquaintance of Brown's,
rose to support Brown's effort. Only about $60 was collected. But
trifling details like that had never stopped Brown, nor would they
now. He began his preparations for Kansas and arrived on the scene
in October.

In Kansas, matters continued to degenerate. The embattled
Governor Reeder had to contend not only with a defiant and fraudu-
lent assembly but also with a judiciary stacked with proslavery men.
Appointed by Pierce in 1854, Chief Justice Samuel D. Lecompte of
Maryland and Associate Justice Rush Elmore of Alabama out-
weighed the influence of Associate Justice S. W. Johnson of Ohio.
And by summer, Senator Atchison had traveled back to Washing-
ton, DC, to press Pierce for the ouster of the obstinate, fair-minded
Reeder. Using the pretext that Reeder's local land speculation was

illegal, Pierce once again toed the line for the South and removed him, appointing Wilson Shannon as a replacement.

At the time of his appointment, Shannon, a former governor of Ohio, tended his law practice in Cincinnati. He arrived in Kansas in September and announced his support for the Shawnee Mission government, vowing to enforce all its laws. Furthermore, Shannon declared that because Kansas bordered slaveholding Missouri, and because trade along the Missouri River bound the areas further together, he believed that their local institutions ought to be in harmony. The new Northern governor announced himself in favor of slavery, further feeding Northern anxieties about an insidious Slave Power conspiracy.

While John Brown worked his way west toward Kansas to join his boys in their partisan warfare against the proslavery forces supported by the new governor, a London publishing house produced a book by an African American also named John Brown. This ex-slave produced a firsthand account of life in the South, *Slave Life in Georgia: A Narrative of the Life, Sufferings, and Escape of John Brown, A Fugitive Slave, Now Living in England*. Born in Southampton County, Virginia, the slave John Brown subsequently lived in both Georgia and Louisiana. Before making his final escape, Brown faced almost unbelievable punishment for repeatedly trying to run away from one of his masters:

> To prevent my running any more, [master] Stevens fixed bells and horns on my head. . . . A circle of iron, having a hinge behind, with a staple and a padlock before, which hang under the chin, is fastened around the neck. Another circle of iron fits quite close around the crown of the head. The two are held together in this position by three rods of iron, which are fixed in each circle. These rods, or horns, stick out three feet above the head, and have a bell attached to each. The bells and horns do not weigh less than twelve to fourteen pounds. . . . I wore the bells and horns, day and night, for three months . . . their weight made my head and neck ache dreadfully. . . . At night I could not lie down to rest, because the horns prevented my stretching myself, or even curling up.[8]

The fanaticism that compelled the white abolitionist John Brown to violently confront the expansion of slavery had roots in another kind of fanaticism and violence—the virtually unlimited power of white masters over black slaves.

In June 1855, in Missouri, not far from the violence of Kansas, a young female slave named Celia also reached the end of her ability to endure suffering and degradation. Robert Newsom, a widower in his fifties, had purchased the 14-year-old Celia in 1850 with one object in mind—sexual exploitation. On their journey to Newsom's farm immediately after her purchase, Newsom raped Celia for the first of many times. Celia bore two children over the next five years, most likely Newsom's, who followed their mother's legal condition as slaves on their father's small farm. Newsom set up Celia in a substantial brick cabin with a large fireplace complete with hearthstones. The cabin sat in a grove of fruit trees behind the Newsom family home. Ostensibly the farm's cook, Celia was in fact her master's concubine.

Pregnant once more and ill in the spring of 1855, Celia appealed to Newsom's adult daughters to keep their father from assaulting her again. In June, Celia even dared to confront Newsom himself, begging him to let her alone in her condition. He responded by warning her to expect another visit that very night. Celia informed him that she would try to defend herself this time and before returning to her quarters found a large stick and stowed it in a corner of her cabin. On the night of June 23, Newsom made his way to Celia. The two exchanged words, and Newsom advanced toward the 19-year-old woman as she retreated to the corner. Celia grabbed her improvised weapon and struck him hard on the head, dazing him and sending him sinking down onto a stool on the floor. Then she raised the stick with both hands over her head and sent it crashing down onto the skull of her rapist-master, killing him. In a panic, Celia decided to try to destroy the evidence and actually shoved Newsom's body into her fireplace, turning it and reducing as much of it as possible into ashes, fetching out small bones to crush and burying large ones under the cabin's floor.

Contrary to many modern assumptions, "plantation justice" seems to have been the exception rather than the rule in the Old South. At least it was for Celia. Although she had committed the ultimate act of slave rebellion, the surrounding white community immediately set about providing her with their sense of justice, a sense based upon their own notions of propriety, of law, and of the ideal of whites' benevolent care of their slaves—"warranteeism," as Henry Hughes would have said. Rather than receiving instant punishment, Celia was sent into the white legal system. After an initial inquest, a court appointed attorneys to offer Celia a defense, even though no slaves could ever testify against whites. John Jameson, a former congressman and an experienced trial lawyer, headed the team, supported by two less prominent men. If not the most rabid defenders of slavery, none of the three opposed it. They pulled every trick in the book to offer the teenager a vigorous defense, one far more energetic than anyone had reason to expect.

Like so many white Southerners, Jameson and his team believed slavery fundamentally right, moral, and compatible with ideals of American and Christian values. The three acted as men who fully subscribed to the Southern Code of Honor, a code that required men to protect women and children both physically and in their public reputations. Yet within the system they defended, two horrible wrongs had occurred, rape and murder. Because of Celia's torment and her motivation to protect herself, Jameson and the others tried to apply to her case a Missouri law that provided women with the legal right to defend themselves from sexual assault. The law made no reference to color or race. At Celia's trial the judge threw out Jameson's defense. Even after a guilty verdict, Jameson still did not give up. Knowing that the execution date set did not permit adequate time for an appeal, someone—probably Jameson and accomplices—broke Celia out of jail and hid her away to prevent her execution, then returned her to jail after the execution date had passed. They still believed fundamentally in the legal process; they simply tried to buy time for a victimized teenager. Eventually, all of Jameson's efforts came to naught, and Celia was hanged. William Lloyd Garrison's *The Liberator* covered the story, printing it under the title "Catalogue of Southern Crimes and Horrors."[9]

The horrors of slavery, racism, and the sectional conflict all crept into the pages of Walt Whitman's *Leaves of Grass*, first published in 1855. Although far from the focal point of his collection of poems, Whitman's preface referred to "slavery and the tremendous spreading hands to protect it, and the stern opposition to it which shall never cease till the speaking of tongues and the moving of lips cease." Early on he wrote:

I celebrate myself, and sing myself,
And what I assume you shall assume;
For every atom belonging to me, as good belongs to you.

Later Whitman depicted himself as:

A southerner soon as a northerner—a planter nonchalant and
    hospitable, down by the Oconee I live;
. . . At home on the hills of Vermont, or in the woods of
    Maine, or the Texan ranch.[10]

Walt Whitman
Library of Congress

At one point in a poem he
later called "Song of Myself,"
Whitman wrote from the first-
person vantage point of a man
harboring a runaway slave,
and later he wrote as "the
hounded slave," chased by
bloodhounds and angry men.
In "I Sing the Body Electric,"
Whitman depicted a slave at
the auction block who radiated
a proud spirit of resistance:

There swells and jets a heart—
there all passions, desires,
    reachings, aspirations;
. . . In him the start of populous
states and rich republics.[11]

Leaves of Grass also contained a poem called "A Boston Ballad,"
which Whitman had written the year before in response to the rendition of Anthony Burns. Dripping with sarcasm and reproach for
the actions of his government, Whitman wrote:

To get betimes to Boston town, I rose this morning early;
Here's a good place at the corner—I must stand and see
    the show.
Clear the way there, Jonathan!
Way for the President's marshal! Way for the government
    cannon!
Way for the Federal foot and dragoons—and phantoms
    the apparitions copiously trembling.
I love to look on the stars and stripes—I hope the
    fifes will play Yankee Doodle.[12]

When this collection appeared in print, Whitman himself had
begun the process of leaving his old ties to the Democratic Party and
becoming a Republican. Later still, he would become fascinated by
and drawn to that party's leader, its "captain," Abraham Lincoln.

Although Whitman strove to celebrate his country without turning a blind eye to its many deep faults, Frederick Douglass presented readers with a starkly different vision of America in 1855. Douglass published *My Bondage, My Freedom*, an extended and more detailed version of his earlier *Narrative of the Life of Frederick Douglass*, printed in 1845. A distinct difference between his *Narrative* and the new work was the revelation of his growing disenchantment with the Garrisonian abolitionists: they were no longer radical enough for Douglass. "The morality of *free* society can have no application to the *slave* society," Douglass proclaimed. "Slaveholders have made it almost impossible for the slave to commit any crime, known either to the laws of God or to the laws of man. If he steals, he takes his own; if he kills his master, he imitates only the heroes of the revolution. Slaveholders I hold to be individually and collectively responsible for all the evils which grow out of the horrid relation, and I believe they will be so held at the judgment, in the sight of a just God."[13]

Later in the year, in his own *Frederick Douglass' Paper*, Douglass made more explicit his criticisms of the Garrisonian abolitionists. He believed they had good intentions but did not go far enough: "Again, we maintain that no man has a Right to make any concession to Tyranny, which he would refuse to make if *he* were the victim . . . were he, himself the slave." Douglass quoted one Garrisonian as saying, "All the slave asks of us, is to stand out of the way, withdraw our pledge to keep the peace on the plantation; withdraw our pledge to return him. . . . God will vindicate the oppressed, by the laws of justice which he has founded." Douglass reeled at that logic; he considered it an abandonment. Although Douglass himself had literally fought back against a white man and delivered himself to freedom, in general he believed, "The ability of the slave righting himself, presupposes his ability to do so, unaided by Northern interference. O no! the slave *cannot* 'right himself' any more than an infant can grapple with a giant."[14]

As hundreds of African American slaves continued their individual struggles for liberation from bondage in the South, across the North and the territories free African Americans grappled with the giant of racism, with decidedly mixed results in 1855. In Brownhelm Township, Ohioan John Mercer Langston won election as town clerk, becoming the first African American in the United States elected to public office. Much later, in 1889, Langston would win election to the U.S. House of Representatives. In 1855, Brigham Young, leader of the Mormon Church in Utah, announced that even a "single drop" of black blood disqualified men from entering the Mormon priesthood.[15] And from San Francisco, a correspondent for *Frederick Douglass' Paper* displayed his own racism when he reported, "The poor Chinese are, indeed, a wretched looking set. They are filthy, immoral and licentious."[16] The California assembly fixed the same legal restrictions and discrimination against Asians and free African Americans.

White Northerners, though, continued to manifest their perplexing distinction between their acceptance of prejudice against people of color and their revulsion toward slavery. In efforts to circumvent the Fugitive Slave Law of 1850, many Northern states adopted "personal liberty laws," guarantees of due process for all citizens, including fugitive slaves. In February 1855 a committee of the Massachusetts assembly held open hearings to discuss a proposal to do the same. A very odd thing happened. In the audience two diametrically opposed advocates stood to argue their respective sides—John W. Githell, a visiting slaveholder from Alabama, and Lewis Hayden, a former slave from Kentucky. Hayden's mother had received merciless beatings from their master for her refusal of his sexual advances. The master retaliated further by selling off the enslaved family, exchanging Hayden for two horses. By studying the Bible and discarded newspapers, Hayden taught himself to read and write. With his wife and son he escaped in 1844 and fled to Canada. He then returned to the United States in 1845 and became involved with the antislavery movement in Detroit. He moved to Boston the next year. Active in the Underground Railroad, Hayden once greeted would-be slave catchers at his home with two kegs of gunpowder and a torch. Clearly, Hayden was ready to tangle with the likes of slaveholder Githell.

At the hearing, Githell repeated many common proslavery arguments: that masters took good care of their slaves, that slaves were largely content with their lot, and that only the worst of them— the most unruly—even tried to escape. Hayden responded by asking the assembly to consider the intelligence and civic responsibility of men like Frederick Douglass and William Wells Brown, among other famous black abolitionists who had escaped slavery and come to the North, and concluded, "If they are among the worst specimens then you have no fear of letting loose those now in bondage!"[17] Hayden then rhetorically asked Githell if abolitionist William

Lloyd Garrison would gain the same privileges in the South that Githell enjoyed in Boston: the freedom to walk the streets without harassment, to participate in a legislative hearing, and to voice his strenuous opposition to slavery. The Commonwealth of Massachusetts passed its personal liberty law.

For good measure, a few weeks later on April 28, the governor of Massachusetts signed a bill that legally ended both racial and religious segregation in public schools in Massachusetts. Not all African Americans heralded this as a great victory, however. For years several black leaders, including Frederick Douglass and James McCune Smith, had debated the relative merits of school integration and racially exclusive schools. Barbara Ann Stewart, a second-generation black abolitionist born in Canada, became quite active in education issues in her adopted home of New York. A participant in a black national convention in Rochester in 1853 at the age of nineteen and instrumental in organizing the western New York auxiliary of the National Council of Colored People, Stewart was particularly attuned to the twofold prejudice suffered by black women. When she tried to attend a state black convention in 1855, black men refused to enroll her because of her sex. And nothing tested her perseverance—or caused her greater vexation—than the crusade to educate free African Americans.

Stewart voiced her concerns in a letter to *Frederick Douglass' Paper* on June 1, 1855: "Thousands and thousands of intelligent [black] fathers and mothers, whose children are as dear to them as those of their more white neighbors, lay down upon their pillow at night with their minds burdened with care. What shall I do with my children?" Stewart herself believed, ideally, in educating all as extensively as possible, but the realities of life in racist America quickly interceded on her design. She argued that only whites could attain the best jobs in America: "If a porter shop is to be the highest station in life to which my son can aspire; the gentleman's kitchen the only place my daughter can find employment, then what is the use of educating them? The more ignorant they are, the better they will be suited with their condition." Creating trade schools for black youths, she concluded, was the best thing to do under the circumstances; at least that would help them get a job." As to mere knowledge of books, I have no faith in it," a frustrated Stewart concluded. "I have spent all my life in educating my head," yet the best prospect she found for that education came from overseas, from a chance to work as a teacher in Liberia, the African nation created by the

United States for former American slaves.[18] Stewart finally accepted a position at a black public school in Wilkes-Barre, Pennsylvania, but fell ill and died in 1861.

An unusual first in black college education occurred in an unlikely place in 1855: slaveholding Kentucky. Although the state's slave population exceeded 210,000, some white Kentuckians such as Abraham Lincoln and his wife, Mary Todd Lincoln, held pronounced antislavery views. A few others—very few—went further. Foremost among these stood Cassius M. Clay. Together with abolitionist preacher John G. Fee, Clay opened Berea College, the first institution of higher education in the United States based on racial equality. Clay selected a spot in the foothills of the Cumberland Mountains, a part of the state where neither slavery nor proslavery ideology among whites had ever gained much of a hold. Fee called the college Berea, a name taken from the New Testament, after the place where Paul the Apostle had found open-minded people. Originally intended as a church school for black and white men, Berea College soon admitted black and white as well as male and female students. Later in his life, Clay looked back upon this effort and concluded proudly, "We builded better than we knew," and gave all credit to the Rev. Mr. Fee.[19]

Fee could not have succeeded, however, without the powerful backing and raw courage of Cassius Clay. In the summer of 1855 proslavery whites violently drove Fee from other parts of Kentucky, and Clay resolved to face these foes. Although likely an apocryphal account, through the years a story of one confrontation attests to Clay's very real defiance and bravery. Supposedly, he mounted a speaker's platform and produced a Bible, proclaiming, "For those who obey the rules of right, and the sacred truths of the Christian religion, I appeal to this Book." Next, he presented a copy of the Constitution, announcing, "To those who respect the law of this country, this is my authority." For those who recognized "only the law of force," Clay said, as he drew two long-barreled pistols and a bowie knife, "for those—here is my defense!"[20]

No matter how formidable and daring Clay was, he could not appear everywhere at once to defend his cause. In 1859 a group of armed men forced Berea College to close. In 1865 it reopened with about the same number of black and white students. This lasted until 1904—just months after Clay's death at age ninety-three—when the state legislature passed "Jim Crow" laws that prohibited racial mixing. The state then opened a separate black college near

Louisville, and Berea did not register another African American student until 1954, the year of the landmark Supreme Court decision in the case of *Brown v. the Board of Education of Topeka, Kansas*.

The growing civil discord and violence in the United States was matched in 1855 by that in the Central American nation of Nicaragua, which faced mounting internal and external tensions. As thousands of Americans continued to seek the fastest route from the East to the gold fields of the West, many looked toward Central America. Rather than crossing the mountains and deserts of the American West or sailing around South America, many preferred landing in the Caribbean on the isthmus of Nicaragua and traveling over land, river, and lake to the Pacific for the relatively short ocean voyage to San Francisco. The American government had already signed a treaty with Nicaragua in 1849, gaining exclusive rights to build a canal across the narrow isthmus, but that would never materialize. Instead, by 1851 railroad baron Cornelius Vanderbilt gained a monopoly on a cross-country route. From 1851 to 1856, Vanderbilt's Accessory Transit Company shuttled 24,000 Americans per year across Nicaragua. But the French and the English began maneuvering for a piece of the action. International tensions rose in 1854 to the point that an American naval vessel bombarded a British settlement at Greytown (modern Belize) in British Honduras, near Guatemala, in a contest over a viable isthmian route to the West.

Revolution and civil warfare created chaos within Nicaragua by 1854. One group, called variously Democrats or Constitutionalists, invited American assistance and offered large land grants in return. A journalist from San Francisco covering the turbulence in Nicaragua returned to California with an offer from the Constitutionalists to lure to their aid an American who was notorious already for his willingness to invade Latin America. They offered a colonel's commission to William Walker, erstwhile president of the Republic of Lower California. That provided all the legitimacy Walker needed for his next great adventure.

Early in 1855, as Walker set about collecting men and supplies for a military invasion, federal officials in San Francisco had a good idea what Walker was doing but did nothing to impede him. Walker gathered fifty-seven men, described by one historian as "degenerates, villains, and professional adventurers."[21] At least one had murdered a gambler, several had prior experience as soldiers or filibusters, and others, like Walker, simply got bored with ordinary life and swept up in the spirit of Manifest Destiny. Walker dubbed his motley crew "the immortals." He armed each with a rifle, two Colt revolvers, and a bowie knife. They snuck out of San Francisco at midnight on May 4. Twenty days later they landed on the western coast of Nicaragua at Realejo and jumped into the maelstrom of civil war.

The thuggery of Walker's "immortals" and their superior firepower in the form of new revolving pistols made them a formidable and deadly host. Down to fifty-five men, Walker attacked a force of 500 defenders of the government—the Legitimists—and inflicted 200 casualties with no serious losses to his men. By autumn, Walker had captured the capital, Grenada, and scattered opposition forces. He signed a peace treaty with local military leader General Ponciano Corral, establishing Corral as provisional president and Walker as general in chief of the armies. Walker set up a newspaper, *El Nicaraguense*, through which he offered himself, with his distinctive grey eyes, as the embodiment of a local legend about a grey-eyed man who would deliver the Indians from oppression. In early November, Walker, the self-styled "grey-eyed man of destiny," had Corral arrested, tried, and executed for alleged treasonable correspondence. That entire process took all of eighty hours. Walker made himself dictator of Nicaragua.

From the United States, men and supplies streamed in to join Walker and to seek position, place, and power within his regime. One group stole the entire contents of a militia armory in Sacramento, California, on their way south, and others looted what was at hand in San Francisco. The Accessory Transit Company, owing the government of Nicaragua tens of thousands of dollars, ditched the old regime and its debt and supported Walker, providing him with critical financial support. President Pierce issued a proclamation denouncing the invasion of Nicaragua, but in May 1856 he would receive Walker's emissary, virtually recognizing the legitimacy of Walker's regime. Coupled with the Ostend Manifesto, Pierce's actions convinced many antislavery Northerners that the president was "a Northern man with Southern principles" and that the New Hampshire Democrat was involved in some insidious cooperative efforts with the advocates of slave expansion into the Caribbean.

Those suspicions would have been exacerbated had word leaked about Pierce's complicity with another plan to extend slavery. In 1853 the president had met with John Quitman, the renowned filibuster, general, and former governor of Mississippi. Pierre Soulé and Secretary of State William Marcy joined the meeting and encouraged Quitman to lead a filibustering expedition to Cuba. They counted on the Crimean War as a distraction large enough to prevent European intervention and hoped that once Americans toppled the Spanish regime and established a republic, Congress would admit Cuba to the Union as a slave state, the same course that had led to Texas annexation in 1845. By 1854 the leader of the Havana government made clear his desire to phase out slavery from the island and to crack down on the illegal slave trade. Southern Americans who desired Cuban annexation believed they had to make a move.

From the end of 1854 into the new year, Quitman and his compatriots started searching for money, men, and material for an invasion. As William Walker and other filibusters knew, zealous expansionists were not difficult to come by; Quitman received many offers of assistance and much encouragement. One volunteer from New Orleans was John Quitman Moore, who was no relation but rather had been named for General Quitman in recognition of his efforts to annex Texas back in 1836. Another supporter, already in Vera Cruz, Mexico, wrote to his leader that their plan ought to expand to include conquest of Mexico. By capturing Cuba and Mexico both, he explained, the South could free itself from "the mercy of fanatical Northern demagogues" and "the feeble hands of our compromising, vacillating brethren."[22] The complex world of international politics worked to unravel Quitman's plans and this new expedition before it really got started. A new captain-general in Cuba renounced his predecessor's plans to end slavery, then threatened the American consul in Havana that if Quitman attempted to carry out his plan, a military force of armed slaves would be waiting to stop him. He also sent for British warships to resume patrolling Cuban waters. Lack of sufficient finances, weapons, and a sudden abandonment by Pierce ended the scheme. Quitman, however, was not deterred.

In July 1855, Quitman offered himself for election to Congress. With expansionism threatened and a rising tide of Republicans in the capitol, Quitman announced that "the destiny of the South" lay in the results of his campaign.[23] The South had to rely on her own people, not equivocating Northern allies like Pierce, "upon all matters connected with our peculiar institution."[24] Quitman won easily. "My destiny is action, and I will prostrate all opposition or die in harness," he vowed. Ready to face enemies in Washington, especially the "politically corrupt combination, planned by [a]cute Yankee genius" that swore to oppose slavery, Quitman also prepared himself to stand up against wavering Southerners. As he explained to a friend, "There were Tories in '76, there will be Tories in '56. *We* shall have to serve the latter as the patriots of the Revolution treated the former."[25] One of his constituents, who called himself a *"Strict construction State Rights Secession democrat out & out,* in fact a *Red Southern rights man,"* offered thanks to the Almighty that with Representative Quitman the South would have at least "one man in Congress that we can depend on."[26]

Although the latest Cuba and Mexico schemes fell apart, growing fear in the North of the spread of slavery and a Slave Power conspiracy helped feed the swelling power of free-soil and Anti-Nebraska sentiment. Abraham Lincoln shared this belief. Still considering himself a Whig, Lincoln resigned from the Illinois assembly in order to qualify for a bid for the U.S. Senate. Needing fifty-one votes for victory in the assembly, Lincoln took a commanding lead on the first ballot with forty-five to the forty-one garnered by James Shields, the Democratic incumbent. Lyman Trumbull, an Anti-Nebraska man, gained but five votes. By the sixth ballot, Shields remained steady at forty-one, Lincoln dropped to thirty-six, and Trumbull gained three. An early also-ran, Democrat Joel Matteson soared to forty-six votes by the eighth ballot, triggering a desertion of many Lincoln supporters to the more unequivocal Trumbull. On the tenth try, Lincoln's last supporters threw their votes to Trumbull, who carried the election. A disappointed Lincoln realized, "I could not . . . let the whole political result go to ruin, on a point merely personal to myself."[27] The other Illinois senator, Stephen Douglas, suffered a sharper rebuke than Lincoln, as his legislature effectively rejected his doctrine of popular sovereignty in favor of free soil.

Other prominent Republicans and Anti-Nebraska men won election or reelection to Congress in 1855. While making an election speech at Boston's Faneuil Hall, Charles Sumner demanded of his audience, "Are you for Freedom, or are you for Slavery? . . . Are you for God, or are you for the Devil?"[28] His constituents answered by returning Sumner to the Senate. In New York the man who had invoked a "higher law" than the Constitution in the war against slavery, back in 1850, William H. Seward, won reelection as well. After withdrawing awhile from public office, pioneering Free-Soiler John P. Hale again won election from New Hampshire to the House of Representatives. Henry Wilson rode a wave of Know-Nothing support to join Sumner as Massachusetts's other senator. The "Natick Cobbler" drew criticism from many of his Free-Soil colleagues, including Sumner. Theodore Parker wrote to Wilson, "I know you cannot fail to be faithful to this great question of slavery. . . . But your connection with the *Know Nothings* makes me fear for other forms of justice. *The Catholics* are . . . men, the *Foreigners* are men; the North is wide . . . enough for them all."[29]

Henry Wilson
Library of Congress

Wilson would quickly abandon—and long regret—his association with the nativists. Unparalleled election violence in 1855 helped to propel his departure from the group. Nativist mobs rioted and murdered across the country, with major outbreaks in Chicago, Baltimore, New Orleans, and Washington. In Cincinnati, nativists destroyed two ballot boxes while other combatants struggled over a cannon. In Louisville, mobs attacked German and Irish immigrants, burning a brewery and taking the lives of upwards of twenty people in the process. Elsewhere in Louisville, nativists set fire to many homes of immigrants. As a local newspaper reported, "Seeking to escape death from the flames, the wretched inhabitants reached the streets only to meet death in another form. As soon as one appeared at a door he was fired at and generally killed. A number were taken off badly wounded, and others, shot to pieces, returned to their burning houses, preferring rather to be burnt than to meet the infuriated mob."[30]

Election horrors convinced others besides Wilson to disassociate themselves from Know-Nothings and join the Republican Party. Abraham Lincoln explained to a friend, "How can one who abhors the oppression of negroes, be in favor of degrading classes of white men?" Between the determination of slaveholders to expand their institution and the bigotry of nativists, Lincoln considered the nation in an astonishing state of moral decay. The United States had begun in 1776 with a declaration that all were equal. "We now practically read it 'all men are created equal, *except negroes*,' " lamented Lincoln. If nativists took over the government, he prophesied, "it will read 'all men are created equal except negroes, *and foreigners, and catholics*.' When it comes to this," Lincoln concluded, "I should prefer emigrating to some country where they make no pretense of loving liberty—to Russia, for instance, where despotism can be taken pure, and without the base alloy of hypocracy [*sic*]."[31]

Elections in Kansas Territory during the summer and fall of 1855 actually became more fantastic than before. After the overzealous proslavery legislature expelled the handful of Free-Soil assemblymen, many of the Free-Soilers and their supporters correctly concluded that they had no place in the Shawnee Mission government, so they decided to create their own. During the second half of the year, free-staters prepared for a convention in Topeka, and in December they held their elections to ratify their constitution, a step toward electing their men to nothing less than a shadow government. To make matters worse—as seemed inevitable in Kansas— just before the December elections, news spread of the murder of a free-state man by a proslavery settler from Virginia. When fellow free-stater Jacob Branson called a protest meeting, the proslavery sheriff arrested Branson for disturbing the peace, even though he had never sought the arrest of the murderer who started the whole affair. An armed group of Free-Soilers from nearby Lawrence raided the sheriff's posse and liberated Branson. The sheriff told Governor Shannon that "open rebellion against the laws of the Territory" had erupted—again without even passing reference to the murder.[32] Shannon mobilized the proslavery militia, and from across the border in Missouri, Senator Atchison again countered with ruffians to intercede. Rumors swept across the wintry plain that a force of 2,000 to 3,000 proslavery men were massing on the Wakarusa River to attack the town of Lawrence. Before a bullet was fired, locals called the building conflict the Wakarusa War.

The men of Lawrence hastily gathered weapons and threw up earthworks to defend their town. Word spread to nearby Brown's Station, and John, John Jr., Owen, Salmon, and Frederick set out on December 6 to join the resistance. Before entering town they met some Missourians at a bridge that they had to cross. The Browns moved forward deliberately and without wavering, making sure to display their astounding arsenal of knives, broadswords, rifles, and revolvers as they passed without incident. They arrived at Lawrence and met with local militia leaders in the still incomplete Free State Hotel, constructed out of stone and, in fact, less a hotel than a fortress. There John Brown also examined the corpse of Thomas Barber, a free-stater just murdered by the gathering pro-slavery forces on the Wakarusa.

John Brown took command of the "Liberty Guards," one of eleven small companies. Many, including Brown himself, hoped to launch a sneak attack at night and massacre their foes in their sleep. Meanwhile, news arrived to Governor Shannon of the murder of Thomas Barber and the general drunkenness and rowdiness of the proslavery forces. He grew concerned that he could not control these men, whom even he called a pack of hyenas.[33] On December 8, Shannon arrived in person and met with leaders on both sides to draw up and sign a treaty that sent home the Missouri forces and pledged free-staters not to resist local laws. Free-staters considered themselves victorious and disbanded by December 12.

Three days later the Topeka constitution came up for ratification by the settlers of Kansas. Proslavery men generally abstained from participating in what they considered a farce at best and a violation of their own legally established regime at worst. So the results were predictable—a clear victory for the Topeka constitution. Another issue on the free-state ballot also passed overwhelmingly, the "Negro Exclusion clause." Kansas was to remain both free and white. Another round of elections in January would provide a free-state governor and legislature.

In the aftermath of the Wakarusa War, the Thirty-fourth Congress convened in Washington in December. Republicans had their first opportunity to flex some muscle, having overtaken Know-Nothings by 108 to 43 in the House. But the eighty-three Democrats there tried mightily to hold on to power against all comers. They caucused and declared their belief that the recent national elections both rejected nativism and affirmed the Kansas-Nebraska Act. The Democrats rallied behind William A. Richardson of Illinois as their nominee for Speaker of the House. This infuriated Republicans, who coalesced around Nathaniel P. Banks of Massachusetts, a man who had left the Democrats a year before, when Kansas-Nebraska came before Congress, and moved fleetingly through Know-Nothingism to his new party. Know-Nothings first considered Humphrey Marshall, a representative from Louisville, Kentucky, a city that saw one of the worst scenes of violence in a bloody year. Wisely, the party reconsidered and shifted abruptly to a less provocative candidate, Henry M. Fuller.

House rules established that a Speaker must receive a majority vote. Day after day, week after week, balloting took place in vain, with the Republicans holding their plurality but unable to siphon off any other votes. On the sixty-eighth ballot, taken on Christmas Eve, Banks stood at 101, Richardson at seventy-two, and Fuller at thirty-one, with eleven votes scattered among others. The political battle would rage on into January and fail to find resolution until February 1856, when Banks and the Republicans finally emerged victorious. As the sectional crisis escalated, Americans would look back at the speakership conflict of 1855 as short-lived and mild.

NOTES*

1. Allan Nevins, *Ordeal of the Union*, 2 vols. (New York: Charles Scribner's Sons, 1947), 2:384–85.

2. Stephen Oates, *To Purge This Land with Blood: A Biography of John Brown* (New York: Harper & Row, 1970), 86.

3. Nevins, *Ordeal of the Union*, 2:386.

4. Melton A. McLaurin, *Celia, A Slave* (New York: Avon Books, 1991), 67.

5. Oates, *To Purge This Land with Blood*, 85.

6. Ibid., 89.

7. John Stauffer, "Advent among the Indians: The Revolutionary Ethos of Gerrit Smith, James McCune Smith, Frederick Douglass, and John Brown," in *Antislavery Violence: Sectional, Racial, and Cultural Conflict in Antebellum America*, ed. John R. McKivigan and Stanley Harrold (Knoxville: University of Tennessee Press, 1999), 255.

8. Steven Mintz, ed., *African American Voices: The Life Cycle of Slavery* (St. James, NY: Brandywine Press, 1993), 120.

9. McLaurin, *Celia, A Slave*, 82.

10. Walt Whitman, *Leaves of Grass*, http://www.bartleby.com/142/14. html, stanzas 1 and 16, accessed August 8, 2003.

11. Walt Whitman, "I Sing the Body Electric," http://www.bartleby. com/142/19.html, stanza 7, accessed August 8, 2003.

12. Walt Whitman, "A Boston Ballad," http://www.bartleby.com/142/99.html, accessed August 8, 2003.

13. Michael Meyer, ed., *The Narrative and Selected Writings: Frederick Douglass* (New York: Modern Library, 1984), 137–38.

14. *Frederick Douglass' Paper*, November 16, 1855, quoted in Meyer, *Frederick Douglass*, 357.

15. Charles M. Christian, *Black Saga: The African American Experience* (Boston: Houghton Mifflin, 1995), 160.

*Emphasis in all quotations is that of the original authors.

16. Leon Litwack, *North of Slavery: The Negro in the Free States, 1790–1860* (Chicago: University of Chicago Press, 1961), 167.

17. C. Peter Ripley et al., eds., *Black Abolitionist Papers*, 5 vols. (Chapel Hill: University of North Carolina Press, 1985–1992), 4:266–68.

18. Ibid., 4:295–96.

19. H. Edward Richardson, *Cassius Marcellus Clay: Firebrand of Freedom* (Lexington: University Press of Kentucky, 1976), 75.

20. Ibid., 76–77.

21. Robert E. May, *The Southern Dream of a Caribbean Empire, 1854–1861* (Athens: University of Georgia Press, 1989), 94.

22. Eric H. Walther, *The Fire-Eaters* (Baton Rouge: Louisiana State University Press, 1992), 108.

23. Ibid., 109.

24. John McCardell, *The Idea of a Southern Nation: Southern Nationalists and Southern Nationalism, 1830–1860* (New York: Norton, 1979), 260.

25. Ibid., 261.

26. Walther, *Fire-Eaters*, 109.

27. Roy P. Basler et al., eds., *The Collected Works of Abraham Lincoln*, 9 vols. (New Brunswick, NJ: Rutgers University Press, 1953), 2:306–7.

28. David Brion Davis, *The Slave Power Conspiracy and the Paranoid Style* (Baton Rouge: Louisiana State University Press, 1969), 61.

29. Hans Trefousse, *The Radical Republicans: Lincoln's Vanguard for Racial Justice* (New York: Knopf, 1969), 88.

30. Nevins, *Ordeal of the Union*, 2:404.

31. Basler, *Collected Works of Abraham Lincoln*, 2:323.

32. Oates, *To Purge This Land with Blood*, 106.

33. Edward J. Renehan Jr., *The Secret Six: The True Tale of the Men Who Conspired with John Brown* (Columbia: University of South Carolina Press, 1996), 90.

CHAPTER FIVE

1856

"The Rape of a Virgin Territory"

TEMPERATURES AS LOW AS 29 degrees below zero froze the plains of Kansas in the early winter of 1856, but not even nature's might fully cooled the fiery tempers of partisans in that embattled territory. On January 5 a meeting at Osawatomie, presided over by none other than John Brown, nominated candidates for the free-state elections to be held ten days later. On election day the Brown clan, again armed to the teeth, marched to Pottawatomie. They met no opposition this time, however, and elections there went off without a hitch. Charles Robinson won the governor's chair, and John Brown Jr. won election to the assembly in the new Free-Soil government about to form in Topeka.

The peace at Pottawatomie was an aberration. News swept the territory about a buildup of militia forces in Missouri, in outright violation of the accord that had preempted the recent Wakarusa War. During the voting at Leavenworth, free-staters and proslavery men slugged it out at the polls, with one of the latter killed, two more injured, and two free-staters wounded. Days later proslavery men captured Captain R. P. Brown (no relation to John Brown), a local free-state leader, and savagely attacked him with a hatchet and knives. They threw his dying body at the door of his cabin, shouting to his stunned and horrified wife, "Here's Brown."[1]

In support of this butchery a proslavery newspaper cried, "War! War!" It announced, "These higher-law men will not be permitted longer to carry on their illegal and high-handed proceedings." Another paper similarly proclaimed, "Sound the bugle of war over the length and breadth of the land and leave not an Abolitionist in the Territory to relate their treacherous and contaminating schemes. Strike your piercing rifle balls and your glittering steel to their black and poisonous hearts."[2]

On January 24, before news of the latest atrocities in Kansas reached President Pierce, he issued a special message to Congress that blamed all of the violence in Kansas on emigrant aid societies outside of the beleaguered territory. Pierce also condemned the rising Topeka government as "revolutionary" and its actions in opposition to the Shawnee Mission government as "treasonable insurrection."[3]

Winter thawed just enough in February to allow mail routes to reopen and news to reach Kansas from the East. "We hear that Franklin Pierce means to crush the men of Kansas," John Brown explained to his wife back in New York. Almost gleeful about the prospect of such a conflict, Brown wrote, "I do not know how well he may succeed; but I think he may find his hands full before it is over." When federal troops arrived on the scene, ostensibly to remove Americans who trespassed onto Indian lands, Brown was convinced that an invasion had begun. He now believed that free-staters might have to shoot at soldiers of their own federal government, writing to Congressman Joshua Giddings, "I ask in the name of God; I ask in the name of the venerated fore-fathers; I ask in the name of all that good or true men ever hold dear; will Congress suffer us to be driven to such 'dire extremities'? *Will anything be done*?"[4]

Although Pierce blamed only Northern emigrant aid societies for the worsening situation in Kansas, in fact both North and South participated in the escalation of arms and violence. Proslavery expeditions formed across the South to combat their Northern counterparts. One of the greatest proslavery drives into Kansas came from Alabama. In 1855, Colonel Jefferson Buford, a lawyer and state senator from Eufaula in Barbour County, a stronghold of secessionists, decided to stake his life, his son, and $20,000 of his own money on the cause of slavery in Kansas. Part of the money Buford raised came from the sale of some of his own slaves, so determined was he to preserve the future of the institution of slavery in the United States. Buford sought 300 able-bodied men to join him, and in the winter of 1856 he toured Alabama to address the masses; warn them of the crisis; and gather money, men, and munitions. Buford enlisted the skills of one of the South's greatest orators, fellow secessionist William Lowndes Yancey, who spoke for hours at a time to rally support and volunteers. By April, Buford had his 300 men. They gathered in Montgomery, the state capital, paused briefly at a church to receive a minister's blessing, and departed down the Alabama River for Mobile, then moved on to New Orleans and Kansas. Similar efforts occurred in Atlanta and Marietta, Georgia; in

Abbeville and Charleston, South Carolina; and elsewhere. Women sold their jewelry to aid the cause; railroads provided free transportation to the gathering troops.

Similar efforts pervaded the North. Men and weapons poured into Kansas from Vermont, New Hampshire, Ohio, and from the old Northwest. One of the more notable efforts occurred in New Haven, Connecticut, where over 100 men gathered for an expedition to Kansas. This company included several Yale graduates, a minister, and two former state assemblymen. The junior class at Yale presented them with a rifle inscribed *Ultima Ratio Liberarum,* "The Final Reckoning of the Free." New York City mounted a gigantic effort, drawing over 3,000 people to a meeting on April 29 and uniting previously reluctant conservative businessmen and politicians with more radical men like Benjamin F. Butler and newspaper editor Horace Greeley. Congressman Gerrit Smith personally donated $3,000 to the New York State Kansas Committee. At Plymouth Church in New York, the Rev. Henry Ward Beecher, a brother of Harriet Beecher Stowe, led another drive. From his pulpit,

Henry Ward Beecher
Library of Congress

Beecher declared that the cause of freedom in Kansas required rifles more than it needed Bibles. He sent a shipment of Sharps rifles to free-staters, packing them in a box marked "Bibles." Throughout Kansas, combatants on both sides soon referred to these lethal weapons as Beecher's Bibles.

Against this backdrop the free-state Topeka government assembled on March 4, in direct opposition to President Pierce's warning. Charles Robinson assumed the governorship, and the legislature, including Representative John Brown Jr., selected James Henry Lane and former territorial governor Andrew Reeder as their two U.S. senators. The assembly instructed these men to "memorialize" Congress on behalf of their cause, rather than to challenge outright the proslavery government by trying to pass and enforce their own laws. This bitterly disappointed the junior Brown. He now virtually gave up on nonviolent options and vowed that "the war-cry heard upon our plains will reverberate not only through the hemp and tobacco fields of Missouri but the 'Rice Swamps,' the cotton and Sugar plantations of the Sunny South."[5]

Another round of violent conflict erupted shortly after a territorial district court opened at a tavern in Pottawatomie on April 21. Judge Sterling Cato, a secessionist from Alabama, presided, and other proslavery men, such as James P. Doyle, filled the grand jury.

James H. Lane
Library of Congress

Doyle's son Drury served as bailiff. The Browns and other abolitionists could not help but fear that the long arm of the proslavery law had finally come to their community from Shawnee Mission, ready to enforce the odious proslavery statutes. Two days later, proslavery sheriff Samuel Jones narrowly escaped death after an assassin's bullet struck him. Many free-staters condemned the act—at least in public—but proslavery forces exploded with rage. "War to the knife, and the knife to the hilt," threatened the editors of the *Atchison Squatter Sovereign*. They vowed, "Jones' Murder Must Be Revenged!" even though Jones was very much alive. Reason had ceased to prevail.[6]

Retaliation began instantly. Senator David Atchison yet again mobilized his Missourians for a raid, and drunken proslavery men within Kansas killed two free-staters and savagely tarred another (they had no feathers so they substituted cotton, a better symbol of slavery at any rate). By May 2, Buford's expedition of over 300 men arrived, with banners reading "Alabama for Kansas" and "The Supremacy of the White Race" aloft. A group of Georgians came right behind. On May 8, Judge Samuel D. Lecompte ordered a grand jury to indict all the members of the Topeka government for treason. Indictments or subpoenas followed for Robinson, Lane, and Reeder, as well as for the owners of two free-state newspapers and the owner of the fortress-like Free State Hotel in Lawrence. On

May 11 federal marshal J. B. Donelson announced falsely that residents of Lawrence had resisted his authority. This lie served as a catalyst for a gathering of proslavery forces in Lecompton and preparations for all-out combat against the people of Lawrence.

"A proslavery army has concentrated outside of Lawrence, and they have cannon!" a messenger announced on May 21.[7] Most of the town's leaders fled before Marshal Donelson led federal troops into town to serve warrants and make arrests. But the gathering proslavery mob of about 1,000 spoiled for a fight. They found their leader in the avenging figure of Sheriff Jones, now fully recovered from his bullet wound. Jones, his men, and the omnipresent Senator Atchison swarmed into town with no effective force to stop them. They destroyed two printing presses, looted and consumed whiskey and anything else they desired, arrested Governor Robinson and set fire to his home, and then culminated the attack by training their five cannon on the Free State Hotel before burning it to the ground. Atchison had encouraged his followers to attack any armed woman they might encounter. "When a woman takes on herself the garb of a soldier by carrying a Sharpe's [sic] rifle, *then she is no longer a woman*, and, by damned, treat her for what you find her, and trample her underfoot as you would a snake . . . if a man or a woman dare to stand before you, blow them to hell with a chunk of cold lead!"[8] Miraculously, only one man died—a proslavery man crushed to death under a collapsed wall of the hotel—but news spread far and fast of the "sack of Lawrence."

Countless Northerners had long since concluded that various features of Southern life predisposed the master class toward violence and bullying. The sacking of Lawrence and other brutal events of the year 1856 certainly magnified that sense. Timothy Day, a Republican from Ohio, asserted to a friend that white Southerners viewed Northerners as "their natural enemies, and in many instances as their inferiors. The education of a life has taught them to command and to be obeyed."[9] Black abolitionist William Wells Brown, in a speech at New York's capitol building in May, echoed these sentiments. Brown stated that every white boy in slaveholding families, from early in their youth, grew up with the privilege of commanding those around them, even adult black men much older than they. "He has been accustomed to kick and drive the black slave about," Brown explained. So it was only natural that "when he meets white persons, he considers them his inferiors, and his passions break forth on the slightest provocation." Brown characterized the entire Southern delegation to Congress as "the bully, the duelist, the woman-scourger, the gambler, the murderer."[10]

Although clearly carrying generalizations too far and applying them to too many, Northern critiques were borne out by abundant real life examples of this behavior. In this year of 1856, James Henry Hammond, former governor of South Carolina and contributor to the proslavery argument, penned an incredible letter to his adult son, Harry. In it the man who had argued that slavery elevated and protected the enslaved under the paternalistic care of white men referred to his most favored slaves, Sally Johnson and her daughter, Louisa. Hammond had used both mother and daughter simultaneously for his sexual pleasures for many years. A leading member of the master class, a man who expected others—slaves and his children alike—to respond to his bidding, Hammond gently commanded his son:

> In the last will I made I left to you, over and above my other children Sally Johnson the mother of Louisa and all the children of both. Sally says Henderson [a slave] is my child. It is possible, but I do not believe it. Yet act on her's rather than my opinion. Louisa's first child *may* be mine. I think not. Her second is I believe mine. Take care of her and her children who are both of *your* blood if not of mine and of Henderson. . . . I cannot free these people and send them North. It would be cruelty to them. Nor would I like that any but my own blood should own as Slaves my own blood or Louisa. . . . Do not let Louisa or any of my children or possible children be slaves of Strangers. Slavery *in the family* will be their happiest earthly condition.

Hammond signed this letter, "Ever affectionately, J. H. H."[11]

Raised in this kind of environment of exploitation and command and wedded to their Code of Honor, white Southern youths fairly frequently lashed out in public behavior that Northern critics could not help but notice and cringe at. On February 17 and 18, 1856, several students at the College of South Carolina in Columbia (now the University of South Carolina) had a hostile encounter with the town marshal. The youths' hypersensitive spirit of independence led quickly to a frightening escalation of tensions, until 100 armed students squared off against five local militia companies. Only the intervention of a popular faculty member averted violence. A few students left the school of their own accord, a few more at the insistence of their parents, but after a three-week suspension of all campus activities, the remainder returned to their classes with no punishment or adverse consequences at all.

Conversely, many white Southerners worried about the unwholesome impact of Northern societies and values upon their young adult sons, especially those bound for college. Although several fine colleges and universities existed in the South, few disagreed that the best schools in the country were Harvard, Yale, and the College of New Jersey (now Princeton). But all these lay in the North, with Harvard at the very epicenter of abolitionism and other sick "isms" of Northern society, such as campaigns for women's rights and black voting rights. As sectional tensions mounted, more Southern parents became attuned to the argument that Southern sons ought to be educated in Southern schools, taught by Southerners, and made to read Southern books.

Concern for a "pure" Southern education had already played a significant role in the founding of several colleges, including the Virginia Military Institute in Lexington, Virginia (1839), and the South Carolina Military Academy—the Citadel—in Charleston (1842). Both of these provided Southern alternatives for military education so that concerned parents would not have to send their sons to the U.S. Military Academy at West Point, New York. Few intended Southern schools such as these to offer alternatives to Harvard or Yale, but some dreamed of creating a viable alternative. An editorial in the influential New Orleans journal *De Bow's Review* cited the "*political* necessity for the establishment" of a university "around which shall cluster the hopes and pride of the South . . . one pledged to the defence and perpetuation of that form of civilization peculiar to the slaveholding States." This advocate hoped that graduates from such a college would "return home to their native States . . . not a whit the less Kentuckians, or Georgians, or Texans, but more thoroughly Southerners."[12]

An Episcopal bishop emerged as the leader of this movement. Leonidas Polk, himself a graduate of the U.S. Military Academy and later of the Virginia Seminary in Alexandria, was ordained as a priest in 1830 and by 1841 became bishop of Louisiana. By the late 1840s he had established one of the largest plantations in the country, with 400 slaves producing valuable sugar in south Louisiana. Severe weather in 1849–50 damaged his crops and land so badly that he decided to sell out of the farming business and relocate to New Orleans.

That city was the second most populous in the South and the sixth largest in the United States, but neither it nor the state of Louisiana had yet created a respectable university. Polk's concerns about the political and educational plight of the South led to his proposal for a University of the South in 1856 at a convention of Episcopal bishops. "Talk of slavery! Those madcaps at the North don't understand the thing at all. We hold the negroes, and they [Northerners] hold us! They are at the head of the ladder! They furnish the yoke, and we the neck!" Polk exclaimed. "My own is getting sore, and it is the same with those of my neighbors in Church and State."[13]

Polk's fellow clergymen favorably received his motion. The next year, at another meeting of bishops, they established a college administration, set policy for a board of trustees, and began financial planning. Polk wanted a central location within the South, and they finally settled on Sewanee, Tennessee, near Chattanooga. Isolated from even small towns and villages but possessed of abundant land, timber, and coal, the site had the makings for an entire college community and some supply of cash through the sale of coal. Polk and his colleagues targeted an endowment of $500,000, about half that of Harvard at the time. When they had raised $478,000 by 1859 they began preparing for construction. In October 1860 a large crowd gathered for the laying of the cornerstone for the University of the South, but within four months seven Lower South states seceded, and Tennessee would soon join them in a new slaveholders' republic.

To many in the South no amount of education, no sense of reason, seemed capable of stopping a corrupt and degraded free-soil spirit from sweeping the North and threatening the sanctity of the Union. Many believed, for instance, that it made sense for folks from neighboring Missouri to move to Kansas, but, as one Southern newspaper offered, "it was contrary to nature, common sense and common policy, that emigration from Massachusetts should pass through the more fertile Northwest, to settle in that distant Territory."[14] For many, the only explanation for this peculiar behavior had to come from some combination of conspiracy and ignorance.

Theories aplenty arose from the lips and pens of worried Southerners. Senator Asa Biggs of North Carolina proclaimed that Republicans had grown "tired of the Constitution which was formed by our pure and revolutionary ancestors. . . . *Now* every plan is resorted to to evade its sanctions" in a grand design to "crush out an institution which they . . . suppose wrong." Edmund Ruffin, a venerable secessionist from Virginia, concluded that the Republican Party could only gain favor among the "very ignorant . . . or unprincipled or debased and vicious individuals—who also because of their poverty, have but little interest in the . . . welfare of their country."[15]

Others chimed in that much of Northerners' hostility to slavery came from their preference to effectively "enslave" white men, to transform entire poor white families into "hirelings," miserable wage laborers, rather than confining the most grueling work to black slaves. Tennessee senator Andrew Johnson spoke of the North as standing "with her iron-heel upon the necks of seventeen million laborers." James Henry Hammond agreed that working white men in the North fell victim to "the modern *artificial* money power system in which [men] are subject to the domination of capital—a monster without a heart." In stark contrast, wrote South Carolina congressman and secessionist Laurence Keitt, black slavery in the South "rescues the improving and ruling race" from drudgery, giving whites a unique capacity for refinement of manners and minds.[16]

Neither manners nor intellect characterized the debates in Congress in the spring of 1856. Over the winter, illness had limited any action on the floor by Stephen Douglas, and by March the Little Giant still remained somewhat hampered. But that month he erupted with a hearty defense of popular sovereignty and support for President Pierce's territorial government in Kansas. He also lashed out against the new Republican senators whom his own Kansas-Nebraska Act had inadvertently helped propel into power. Douglas exclusively blamed Northern emigrant aid societies for all of the violence in Kansas. He called resistance to the proslavery government treason and rebellion. "We understand that this is a movement for the purpose of producing a collision, with the hope that civil war may result if blood shall be shed in Kansas," Douglas thundered. "Sir, we are ready to meet that issue."[17]

In turn, many Republican senators spoiled for a fight, none more than Charles Sumner. Earlier in the year he had written to a friend, "In protecting this Territory against tyranny we are driven to battle with tyrants, who are the oligarchs of slavery."[18] Sumner vigorously countered Douglas point by point. Had not those Americans who opposed slavery as much right to move to Kansas as those who supported it? Certainly, Northern emigrants loved freedom and hated slavery. "And have they not a right to do so?" he asked. Douglas stuck tenaciously to his cryptic logic that men such as Sumner advocated "foreign interference," while Douglas stood behind "self-government and non-interference," somehow excusing the intervention of Atchison, his Missourians, the Buford expedition, and others for the South.[19] Day after day, week after week, the battle of assertions continued, with Douglas tirelessly taking on all challengers. William Henry Seward joined the fray, arguing that Congress ought to immediately admit Kansas as a free state based upon the

Charles Sumner
Library of Congress

Topeka constitution. Free-staters had not even submitted that document for public discussion in Kansas; Seward's position rested on even flimsier ground than Douglas's.

Presuppositions of men from both sections infected Congress, steadily ratcheting up tensions in the federal capital and radiating from there across the nation over telegraph lines and newspapers. In an open letter to the *Atchison Squatter Sovereign*, South Carolina congressman Preston Brooks wrote: "The admission

of Kansas into the Union as a slave state is now a point of honor with the South. . . . It is my deliberate conviction that the fate of the South is to be decided with the Kansas issue. If Kansas become a hireling State, slave property will decline to half its present value in Missouri as soon as the fact is determined. Then abolitionism will become the prevailing sentiment. So with Arkansas; so with upper Texas."[20]

An uncle of Brooks's, Andrew P. Butler, announced on the Senate floor, "God knows, as I have said, one drop of blood shed in civil strife in this country may not only dissolve this Union, but may do far worse. . . . Really it is broken already; for the spirit which cherished it has been extinguished, and the very altars upon which we ought to worship have been profaned by false fires." Instead of watching the country drift slowly toward disunion, Butler declared, "I would rather that it should be dissolved tomorrow."[21]

When another Southerner nonchalantly spoke of war to the knife and the knife to the hilt, New Englander John P. Hale fired back, "Sir, Puritan blood has not always shrunk even from these encounters; and when war has been proclaimed with the knife, and the knife to the hilt, the steel has sometimes glistened in their hands; and, when the battle was over, they were not always found second best."[22]

Northern concerns about Southerners' violence and Southern apprehensions about Northern rudeness combined horribly and dramatically on the floor of the Capitol. On May 19 and 20, Charles Sumner delivered a speech he called "Crimes against Kansas," one carefully and deliberately crafted to elicit emotional responses from all who heard it. From the start he used metaphors of sexual depravity, calling the drama in Kansas "the rape of a virgin territory, compelling it to the hateful embrace of slavery." Sumner labeled Andrew P. Butler, co-author of the 1850 Fugitive Slave Act, the Don Quixote of slavery, a man who "has chosen a mistress" who was "ugly" and "polluted" in the eyes of the world, but "chaste in his sight . . . the harlot, Slavery." Then he turned on Douglas, castigating him as "the squire of slavery, its very Sancho Panza, ready to do all its humiliating offices," for opening Kansas to slavery.[23] Sumner was just warming up, and an angry, irritable Douglas paced at the back of the chamber grumbling, "That damn fool will get himself killed by some other damn fool."[24]

On the second day of his harangue, Sumner turned his ire again toward Andrew Butler, who at the time was home in South Carolina seeking rest for various infirmities. Sumner referred to the absent Carolinian's slight paralysis of the lip, ridiculing Butler for "incoherent phrases, discharged [with] the loose expectoration of his speech." Sumner dug deeper, declaring that Butler "touches nothing that he does not disfigure," that he could not open his mouth "but out there flies a blunder." Then Sumner turned more generally on South Carolina and "its shameful imbecility from Slavery."[25] Other senators immediately denounced Sumner's caustic speech. Stephen Douglas was beside himself. He fired back at Sumner's "lasciviousness and obscenity." Douglas depicted Sumner as a supreme egotist who practiced his speech "every night before the glass with a Negro boy to hold the candle and watch the gestures" until both words and gestures seemed sufficiently vulgar.[26]

When Sumner regained the floor he fired back at the Little Giant, "No person with the upright form of a man, can be allowed, without violation of all decency, to switch out from his tongue the perpetual stench of offensive personality. . . . The noisome, squat, and nameless animal, to which I now refer, is not the proper model for an American Senator. Will the Senator from Illinois take notice?" Douglas blandly replied, "I will, and therefore will not imitate you, sir." Unwilling to quit the attack, Sumner retorted, "Again the Senator has switched his tongue, and again he fills the Senate with its offensive odor."[27]

The next day, Preston Brooks heard about Sumner's diatribe but had some trouble believing it. Brooks was not only a congressman from South Carolina but also a nephew of Andrew P. Butler and hotheaded even by the most extreme standards of Carolina radicals. Brooks once declared, "*I have been a secessionist from the time I could think.*"[28] He had enthusiastically rushed off to combat in the Mexican War in 1846 and before that had defended his and his family's good name in a duel with another Carolinian, whose bullet struck Brooks in the hip, requiring Brooks to walk with the aid of a cane. Charles Sumner had willfully, publicly, and maliciously slandered Brooks's family, his state, and his section. Well versed in affairs of honor, Brooks knew what he must do and what he must not do. Brooks could not challenge Sumner to a duel. The published pamphlet, *Code of Honor*, clearly stated that duels represented an affair of honor between gentlemen. "Crimes Against Kansas" proved that Sumner was no gentleman, but rather, more like a beast—a dog or a horse that had reared upon its master. In such a case, a man did not challenge the offending animal to a duel but instead had to strike down the villainous creature. The *Code of Honor* even specified how to carry out such chastisement, with a horsewhip or a stick. Brooks did not have his whip with him in the Capitol, but he always carried his sturdy, gold-handled cane.

On May 22, Brooks decided to "disgrace" Sumner. He enlisted the support of fellow South Carolina congressman Laurence Keitt, another passionate secessionist, and Virginia representative Henry Edmundson. The three walked across the Capitol building from their House chamber toward the Senate side. They waited in an anteroom for business to wrap up and for the public galleries to clear of spectators; the three Southern gentlemen preferred not to have ladies present for the "disgrace." Finally, Brooks led the way to Sumner's desk, where the senator sat, unaware even of who Brooks was, let alone of his relationship to Butler. Besides, Sumner's mind was on other matters, and his large frame was wedged into his small desk, which, like others in the old chamber, was bolted to the floor.

Brooks announced, "Mr. Sumner, I have read your speech twice over carefully. It is a libel on South Carolina, and Mr. Butler, who is a relative of mine." A puzzled Sumner looked up from his desktop to see this stranger raising a gold-handled cane high overhead, aimed at Sumner's skull. He tried to stand up immediately but got stuck in his tiny desk as Brooks rained a blow hard upon his head. Reacting more than thinking, Sumner threw up his arms in self-defense, but to Brooks it looked like the senator intended to strike back. So Brooks hit him again . . . and again . . . and again. Later Brooks boasted, "I . . . gave him about thirty first rate stripes. Toward the last he bellowed like a calf." As Sumner gushed blood and slumped helplessly onto the floor, other senators rushed to try to stop the continual beating but could not. Edmundson yelled them off and Keitt, waving menacingly his own ornamental walking stick, warned them all, "Let them alone, God damn you!" The assault stopped only after Brooks's cane shattered, and the gold head rolled away.[29]

Before lapsing into unconsciousness, Sumner murmured, "I could not believe that such a thing was possible."[30] As Douglas and Robert Toombs of Georgia simply watched, other senators helped carry Sumner from the floor and brought him to his lodgings, where a doctor attended to the gory gashes and sedated him. At first, the wounds did not appear too serious. Sumner himself expected to return to the Senate in a few days and was able to testify to a House committee sent to his room. But infection and swelling set in, putting great pressure on Sumner's brain. He could not eat, could barely sleep, and his body was wracked with pain. A full recovery took over three years.

William Cullen Bryant spoke for thousands in the North through his *New York Evening Post*. "Has it come to this? Are we to be chastised as they chastise their slaves? Are we too, slaves, slaves for life, a target for their brutal blows, when we do not comport ourselves to please them?"[31] Sumner's home state paid homage to their martyr by reelecting him in 1857, knowing very well that his service—and critical votes—would remain unavailable for years.

As for Brooks, immediately after the attack his friends Keitt and Edmundson helped him retrieve the gold head of his demolished cane and clean off Sumner's blood, which had splattered onto his skin and clothing, and they accompanied Brooks down

Pennsylvania Avenue to have dinner. Keitt wrote to his fiancée that Brooks "combined in happy proportion freedom of speech and freedom of the cudgel."[32] Gestures of gratitude poured forth for Brooks from across the South. The *Richmond Enquirer* lauded his actions as "good in conception, better in execution, and best of all in consequence. The vulgar Abolitionists in the Senate . . . have been suffered to run too long without collars. They must be lashed into submission." Brooks bragged that fellow congressmen begged for fragments of his cane "as *sacred relics*," and he proudly received tokens of appreciation from many portions of the South in the form of brand new canes, at least one of which was inscribed with the message "Hit Him Again."[33]

On the day after the assault the Senate created a committee of five to investigate matters, acting on a motion by William H. Seward. Virginia's James M. Mason added an amendment requiring election of the committee members, rather than appointment by its chair, ensuring a Democrat majority. Prior to the vote, Senator Butler had returned to the floor to defend his nephew for "acting under the dictates of high honor."[34] The committee decided not to act at all, leaving it to the lower House since it was members of that body who were under investigation.

The House formed a committee of five: three Northerners and two Southerners. The committee investigated, took testimony from Sumner, and finally produced two reports by July. The majority report favored expulsion of Brooks and censure for Keitt and Edmundson. The minority report, using intrepid Southern logic and rigid, strict construction, declared that no specific power existed in the Constitution allowing the House to punish its own for "alleged" assaults and, therefore, refused to offer an opinion. The House adopted the majority report by 121 to 95, not close to the two-thirds margin (144 votes) required for expulsion. Meanwhile, federal court proceedings concluded against Brooks, fining him $300 for assault.

Brooks had had enough. Of course he had assaulted Sumner. He likened it to a husband redressing an insulted wife's honor. For Congress or a court to find his conduct improper represented yet another attack on his honor. Brooks would not have it; he resigned. So did Keitt. That created two vacancies in the House delegation from South Carolina, compelling the governor of that state to call for special elections to fill them. Brooks and Keitt filed for reelection. As Keitt explained clearly, these men would take their fates away from those who had no understanding of true honor and place it "among whom honor is maintained."[35] In elections that fall, both carried the day without a solitary dissenting vote in their entire congressional districts. Clearly, the electorate applauded their actions, vindicated them, and wanted them back in Washington to continue to represent them. Ironically, only months after retaking his seat in the Capitol in August 1856, Preston Brooks died suddenly at the age of thirty-seven. And four months after that, Andrew P. Butler died at his home near Edgefield, South Carolina, before reaching age sixty-one.

"One measure has followed upon another, each bolder than the last, until we have violence ruling in the Federal Capitol, and civil war raging in the Territories," muttered Republicans meeting in New York.[36] As if to punctuate that sentiment, only days after the assault on Sumner, John Brown prepared his own special reprisal for the recent sacking of Lawrence. After wandering alone into a forest to "converse with God," on May 23, Brown gathered together three of his sons and a son-in-law.[37] He told them to fetch special weapons that he had brought from Ohio—broadswords—and to sharpen them. Under cover of night, Brown moved his squad past the proslavery columns that lingered in the region toward a sparse settlement on Pottawatomie Creek. They first stopped at the shabby cabin of James Doyle, one of the members of Sterling Cato's grand jury that helped set into action the events leading to the sacking of Lawrence. Brown approached the place, demanding that Doyle and his two adult sons step out; he commanded Doyle's wife, daughter, and teenage son to remain inside. Upon his orders, Brown's sons slashed open the heads of the Doyle men and sliced off the younger son's arms for good measure. About an hour later, Brown seized proslavery Allen Wilkinson, and his wife and children watched powerlessly as the Browns slaughtered him as well. The same fate came to yet another man farther down Pottawatomie Creek.

Even most free-staters condemned Brown's massacre. The *New York Herald* called Brown and his men "devils in human form," who had surpassed the savagery of Indians, and graphically related that one victim had his windpipe "entirely cut out, his throat cut from ear to ear."[38] Federal marshals, troops, and militia from Missouri fanned out to apprehend Brown and his sons. These authorities found the abandoned family settlement of Brown's Station, burned it to the ground, and moved on. They seized John Jr. and tied him to a tent pole and beat him with their rifles. Jason Brown experienced a similar fate, although he, like John Jr., had nothing to do with the loathsome family business.

Over a week later some of the Missourians under the command of Henry Clay Pate drew near to John Brown at Black Jack Springs, about 20 miles south of Lawrence. But with help from local free-staters, Brown launched a preemptive attack, killing four of his pursuers. Pate hoped to stop the carnage then and there. Even though he had superior forces and arms, Pate unfurled a white flag and rode toward Brown to talk. Brown drew a revolver and aimed deliberately at Pate. "You can't do this," Pate later recalled, exclaiming, "I'm under a white flag; you're violating the articles of war."[39] Brown coolly replied that Pate was now his prisoner, marched him toward the Missourians with his gun planted firmly at Pate's head, and gave them the option of surrender or watching Pate's head getting blown off. They surrendered. Brown hoped to exchange these men for the release of the arrested Governor Robinson, but by June 5 federal cavalrymen surrounded him and successfully demanded the release of Pate and his men, although Brown eluded capture.

Brown and his sons remained on the lam for months, while other free-state forces commanded by would-be senator James Henry Lane conducted raids on proslavery settlements all over the region. On August 22, Brown reemerged, joined two more free-state guerilla units, and set off toward Osawatomie, near the site of the extinguished Brown's Station. Meeting proslavery forces at the Battle of Osawatomie, Brown's men were beaten badly and his son Frederick was killed by a shot through the heart.

Affairs in Kansas had sunk to such lows that they even moved President Pierce to act. In August he decided to remove Governor Shannon from office and replace him with John W. Geary, a Pennsylvania Democrat trained in law and engineering. Geary did not arrive in Kansas until September, but he then almost immediately worked to halt the chaos. He ordered the release of Governor Robinson and other free-staters, many of whom had languished in jails since May. Geary proved vigilant and competent in stopping guerilla fighting, pro- and antislavery alike, and effectively cut off the flow of ruffians from Missouri. Over 200 lives had already been lost and $2 million in property destroyed in a territory with just over 25,000 scattered settlers. Although free-staters had expected the worst—another "Northern man with Southern principles"— Geary quickly proved to all sides that he meant to stand disinterested and to stand strong. By favoring neither side in the cauldron called Kansas, Geary earned the enmity of both. By March 1857 death threats from both contending forces led to his resignation. He returned to Pennsylvania, went on to serve in the Union Army during the Civil War, and won election as governor of his state in 1867 as a Republican.

After moving along parallel paths for years, the drama in Kansas intersected with events in Latin America suddenly and fantastically. President Pierce had issued a proclamation against William Walker's invasion of Nicaragua and tried to take a stand against filibustering in general, despite support for Walker from Jefferson Davis. On the very day that Walker had executed his puppet president, Ponciano Corral, Pierce's secretary of state, William Marcy, directed the American minister in Nicaragua, John H. Wheeler, not to recognize Walker's regime. Furthermore, Marcy instructed Wheeler not even to engage Walker in official dialogue. The plan did not take into account John Wheeler. From North Carolina and steeped in racism that extended from African peoples to those in Latin America, Wheeler had already sided unofficially with Walker before the "grey-eyed man" made his pact with Corral. Over time, Wheeler not only met more frequently with Walker but also dined with him and attended parties with him. Wheeler had tried persistently to convince Marcy and Pierce to align officially with Walker; and, before receiving Marcy's specific instructions to the contrary, on his own authority Wheeler himself offered recognition of Walker's government.

Meanwhile, American support for Walker swelled, especially in the South. In Mobile and especially in New Orleans the docks buzzed with talk about Nicaragua and swarmed with adventurers ready to sail to Walker's aid. Now back from Spain and elected to the Senate, Pierre Soulé publicly solicited funds from merchants in New Orleans to help Walker. By spring, over 1,200 Americans had arrived in Nicaragua. In Congress a Texas representative called for recognition of Walker and the expulsion of Marcy. By May, President Pierce reversed himself and decided to receive Padre Vigil, Walker's minister to the United States, essentially recognizing the legitimacy of Walker's regime.

As Walker's power increased, so did opposition to him. Fearful that they would be his next victims, the nations of Costa Rica, Honduras, Guatemala, and San Salvador formed an alliance to depose Walker. A more immediate problem for the would-be leader came from his ill-advised confrontation with Cornelius Vanderbilt. Walker revoked the charter of Vanderbilt's Accessory Transit Corporation and seized its ships and property to open his own transit line. Vanderbilt, in turn, rendered his money and support to the allied central American nations and now worked to bring down Walker's regime.

In response, Walker took a more vigorous course in enlisting the aid of influential American expansionists, particularly from the South. He corresponded with former filibuster and now Congressman John Quitman of Mississippi to pressure Pierce for direct, formal recognition of his government. Quitman's efforts failed due to Secretary of State Marcy's dogged opposition. Later, Walker anointed John Heiss as a special commissioner to the United States and Great Britain, but Heiss possessed less diplomacy, tact, and common sense than did Walker himself. When the *Washington (DC) Evening Star* printed anti-Walker editorials, Heiss personally pummeled its editor. A great opportunity literally came to Walker when Pierre Soulé arrived in Nicaragua in August. After a series of parties to honor the Louisiana senator and repeated reassurances from Soulé that Southerners were anxious to support Walker, Soulé returned home to raise more men and money. But more important, Soulé also left a powerful impression on Walker.

With his enemies mounting in Central America, Walker made a calculated gamble to bolster his hold on the country. On September 22, 1856, he ordered the reinstitution of slavery. All five Central American republics had abolished slavery after winning their independence from Spain in 1821. Walker himself had not been a zealous proslavery advocate, and most of the Americans who had joined him to that point were Northerners. Clearly, though, Walker bet on Southern desire to expand slavery in Latin America at the very time that such expansion seemed blocked within the United States.

In the short term, the gamble proved effective. Already American slaveholders had set sail for Nicaraguan ports, and now the pace of that migration increased. Walker sent letters to several Southern newspapers, disingenuously explaining how he now helped lead the fight for the expansion of slavery. A Virginian in Nicaragua wrote to an Alabama newspaper that Walker had claimed this land "in the name of the white race, and now offers [it] to you and your slaves, at a time when you have not a friend on the face of the earth."[40] A member of Walker's government originally from

Kentucky wrote to the governor of that state also, urging the migration of slaveholders and their human property. And in New Orleans, Soulé and friends sold $43,000 in Nicaraguan bonds.

Walker's grip on power strengthened only momentarily. The combination of Vanderbilt's and neighboring nations' hostility rose simultaneously with Southern reinforcements. For the time, though, white Southerners believed that they had found an ally and source of hope and encouragement at the very period that they literally fought for slavery's expansion into Kansas.

Conversely, as antislavery forces struggled stoically against the proslavery forces in Kansas, they read in horror about the complicity of American political leaders in their seemingly successful effort to extend slavery to a place few Northerners ever dreamed it would go. Railroad baron John Murray Forbes spoke for multitudes to a friend of his in South Carolina. "The Slave Power" clearly was not content with forcing slavery into the territories of the United States, Forbes wrote, but now aimed to use "the whole power of the confederacy . . . for buying or conquering all the islands north of Panama for the mere extension of your institutions."[41]

The ongoing struggle for Kansas, the specter of slave expansion into the Caribbean, and the proslavery violence seemingly unchecked even on the floor of Congress all supercharged the defiant spirit of abolitionists. At the same time, however, for many opponents of slavery these same forces increased the tactical divisions between them. Lucretia Mott, a veteran women's rights advocate and abolitionist, stopped short of denouncing the Underground Railroad in 1856 when she proclaimed that aiding fugitive slaves was "not properly Anti-Slavery Work." Although standing firm on her pledge "to destroy the system [of slavery], root and branch, to lay axe at the root of the corrupt tree," Mott pointed out that every year vastly more human beings were born into slavery than the total number thus far who had escaped to freedom in the North or to Canada.[42] To Mott, limited financial resources dictated a different set of priorities, although she offered no specific alternative.

Black abolitionist Stephen A. Meyers, however, never worried about depleting resources or personal energy. A resident of Albany, New York, Meyers labored simultaneously as a manager of a local underground railroad, a temperance advocate, a journalist, and a lobbyist for all sorts of civil rights issues for African Americans— the very sort of combination of activities and causes that more and more white Southerners saw inextricably intertwined in Northern society and dreaded. Like many black abolitionists, Meyers steadfastly rejected activities of the American Colonization Society, a group founded in 1817 to promote black migration back to Liberia. Instead, he battled for equality of opportunity for free blacks in the North while continuing to work toward ending slavery. Therefore, as he said, "I am rather more favorable to Mr [Frederick] Douglass veiues [sic] and not to Mr Garrisons."[43]

In the spring of 1856, Meyers focused his efforts on equal voting rights and defeating state funding for colonization. The elective franchise remained a reserved right of states at the time, and most Northern states prohibited black voting outright. In New York free blacks could vote if they could prove ownership of at least $250 worth of property, a qualification that did not apply to whites in the Empire State. In a letter to white abolitionist Gerrit Smith, Meyers congratulated Smith for his electrifying speech at the statehouse on the Kansas question nine days before, an oration that helped spur Meyers's own efforts. Meyers gathered about 1,600 names on a petition to equalize voting and presented it to the assembly. The effort failed. Years later, after a renewed campaign by Meyers and others, the assembly presented the issue to voters in November 1860. Meyers, Frederick Douglass, Gerrit Smith, and others stumped the state, emphasizing blacks' role in winning American independence, their efforts at self-education and general social progress, and an appeal to natural rights arguments. Voters soundly rejected the bill.

Meyers fared better in combating colonization. The legislature entertained a petition from the New York State Colonization Society for a $10,000 appropriation to help purchase the freedom of slaves, provided they move to Liberia. Meyers reported to Gerrit Smith, "I hav[e] gotten about sixty members pledged to go against it on a final vote."[44] Meyers's efforts proved critical. The bill passed the lower house, but died in the state senate. A revised version of the bill quickly hit the floor of the assembly, containing an amendment mandating incarceration of all free blacks in New York if they did not leave the state in twelve months. Denounced as a proslavery bill, this version died as well, thanks again in part to the political operations of Stephen Meyers.

While Meyers struggled by the side of Frederick Douglass, Mary Ann Shadd struggled publicly against the famed former slave. From West Chester, Pennsylvania, this black abolitionist strongly supported Canadian emigration. In fact, during this decade not only had she and her family moved to Canada but her father, Abraham Shadd, had also become the only black man elected to public office in western Canada (Ontario) before the American Civil War. A supporter of Martin Delany and other black emigrationists, in July 1856, Mary Ann Shadd penned a scathing attack on Douglass in the *Provincial Freeman*: "Having been permitted so long to remain in our tub, we would rather that the great Frederick Douglass, for whose public career we have the most profound pity, would stay out of our sunlight."[45] Shadd had similarly harsh words for Harriet Beecher Stowe. Personal attacks such as these advanced her cause far less than they made Shadd herself a divisive force within the already contentious abolitionist movement.

Contentiousness reached another high—or low—in party politics as well. The presidential contest of 1856 received its formal debut on February 22—George Washington's birthday—as the Know-Nothing convention assembled in Philadelphia. It almost immediately split over slavery. Northern members called for a repeal of the Kansas-Nebraska Act; white Southerners demanded that the act be left alone. Many hoped the antidote to their problems lay in nominating a man who could provide unity within both the party and the country. For years, Know-Nothings had courted former president Millard Fillmore. A Whig who never had shared the American Party's stance on immigration and who had no enthusiasm for anti-Catholicism, Fillmore nevertheless offered impeccable unionist credentials, since he had played a vital role

Millard Fillmore
Library of Congress

in securing the Compromise of 1850. And Fillmore's sincere devotion to the Union overrode his serious personal reservations about Know-Nothing bigotry. As he explained to a friend, this party offered the "only hope of forming a true national party, which shall ignore this constant and distracting agitation of slavery."[46] After two days of acrimonious debate on their platform and the withdrawal of many Northern delegates, the American Party did nominate Fillmore along with Andrew Jackson Donelson of Tennessee, a nephew of a more famous former president. On September 17 these same candidates received the nomination of the moribund Whig Party.

On June 2, Democrats held their convention in Cincinnati. The embattled Stephen Douglas faced off against the equally assailed President Pierce, with both Northerners receiving their most severe criticisms from within their own section. For sixteen ballots they struggled, and on the seventeenth both withdrew for the sake of party harmony and unity in favor of James Buchanan. The 65-year-old Pennsylvanian had served his country in so many offices and in such lackluster fashion that he earned the nickname "Old Public Functionary." But in stark contrast to the liabilities that Douglas and Pierce presented to the North on account of their roles in Kansas-Nebraska, Buchanan had an ace up his sleeve unmatched by these men—availability. Throughout the unfolding horrors of Kansas, Buchanan served distantly and quietly as minister to Great Britain. Having no part whatever in the leading issue of the day, ironically, made him the perfect candidate.

In a conscious attempt not to alienate Northern voters, the Democratic Party platform spoke seldom of slavery. But where it did, it offered great assurance to the Southern portion of the party. It supported popular sovereignty in Kansas and blamed all troubles there on the Republican Party. Pierre Soulé authored two planks promoting slave expansion in Latin America. One supported the efforts of William Walker "to regenerate that portion of the continent," and the other more generally called for "American ascendancy in the Gulf of Mexico."[47] Both planks won adoption by commanding margins. For vice president the convention selected John C. Breckinridge, a slaveholder from Kentucky, to bring sectional balance to the ticket.

The Republicans gathered in their first-ever national nominating convention in Philadelphia on June 17. Ambitious and prominent party leaders such as Thurlow Weed and William H. Seward of New York and Salmon P. Chase of Ohio doubted that their new party could achieve victory in 1856, so they stepped aside to clear the way for a new face. Republicans selected John C. Frémont and William L. Dayton of New Jersey.

Frémont was born in Savannah, Georgia, in 1813, making him the youngest man yet nominated for president (at age forty-three). Frémont's wife gave him two great sources of political strength.

John C. Frémont
Library of Congress

Jessie Benton Frémont was the daughter of old stalwart Jacksonian Thomas Hart Benton of Missouri, who now stood resolute as an opponent of Atchison and his faction in that state. Having grown up steeped in her father's political world, Jessie Frémont possessed the political brains in the marriage rather than her husband. John C. Frémont's claim to fame came through his military career and reputation as "The Pathfinder" for his explorations of the Far West. His only political experiences came in California, where, for only three months, he served as a U.S. senator. His efforts to bring California into the Union in 1849 as a free state and his unequivocal support for free soil in Kansas earlier in 1856 made him acceptable to veteran party leaders. The party bosses also recognized that no one else could match "the romance of his life."[48]

Political veterans David Wilmot, George Julian, Joshua Giddings, Owen Lovejoy, John P. Hale, Henry Wilson, and Thaddeus Stevens crafted the platform. Republicans proclaimed that neither Congress, territorial assemblies, nor individuals had the legal authority to impose slavery in the national domain. Instead, they asserted, the federal government had both sovereign authority over territories and the duty to keep them free. The platform called for the admission of Kansas as a free state and condemned the Ostend Manifesto and any other attempt to annex Cuba. It also called for construction of a transcontinental railroad. But Republicans clearly focused on slavery and offered themselves and their candidate as pillars of morality. In fact, taking a stab at Mormons in Utah Territory as well, Republicans denounced "those twin relics of barbarism—Polygamy and Slavery."[49]

In an appeal to Northern voters, nativists and Free-Soilers alike, the *Springfield Republican* argued, "Those who work with their hands, who live and act independently, who hold the stakes of home and family, of farm and workshop, of education and freedom—these are, as a mass, enrolled in the republican ranks. . . . They form the very heart of the nation, as opposed to the two extremes of aristocracy and ignorance."[50]

This represented more than mere partisan rhetoric. Noting that in fact many Know-Nothings had begun switching over to the new party, the *Jamestown (New York) Journal* sympathized, "With every new concession on the part of the North comes new demands on the part of the South, until association in politics with southern men, is equivalent to stultification and disgrace."[51] The *Gettysburg Star and Banner* concluded, "The time has come for the North, with its superior numbers, intelligence, wealth and power, to take a stand . . . against the threatening, bullying, brow-beating, skull-breaking spirit of the South." The *Hartford Courant* proclaimed that a Frémont victory would result in "NO MORE NEGRO STATES TO DEGRADE FREEMEN AND WHITE LABOR."[52] Republican Hannibal Hamlin asserted that his old Democratic Party "has no basis but in the oligarchy of the South—we might well call it the BLACK OLIGARCHY." Radical congressman Benjamin Wade of Ohio called Frémont's nomination "the beginning of the second 'American Revolution'—the North is the band struggling for freedom—the South is the despotic power which wishes to enslave the North."[53] Henry Wilson echoed the call to Republicans to "overthrow the Slave Power of the country, now organized in the Democratic party."[54]

To a growing number of white Southerners it seemed as though Frémont's candidacy had ushered in a terrifying, revolutionary new era. A newspaper in Memphis, Tennessee, reported that a local plantation mistress "a few days ago went into her kitchen and gave some directions to the negro cook, who replied with a sneer, 'When Frémont's elected, you'll have to sling them pots yourself.' "[55] Outside of Baltimore some free black men got into a fight with several local whites, drove them off, and triumphantly offered three cheers for Frémont. Rumors of slave insurrections spread rapidly across the South, and publicly and privately white Southerners expressed concerns over their slaves' sudden interest in white men's politics. A chemistry professor at the University of North Carolina, Benjamin Hendrick, lost his job due to his open support of Frémont. Governor Henry Wise of Virginia planned to call up 150,000 troops if the Republican won, and rumors spread that the governor of South Carolina would add 75,000 more to resist a Frémont government.

In the November elections, Buchanan won 1,838,169 popular votes and 174 electoral votes, carrying fourteen slave states and five free ones. Frémont received 1,335,264 popular and 114 electoral votes, the latter exclusively from eleven free states. Fillmore's 874,534 popular votes translated into only eight electoral votes from Maryland. A closer look at the popular voting reveals a greater schism between the sections. Frémont had carried a whopping 60 percent of the Northern popular vote (to Buchanan's 36 percent and Fillmore's 4 percent). Buchanan carried the South by about 56 percent to Fillmore's 44 percent. Had Frémont won either Pennsylvania—Buchanan's home—or New Jersey, Illinois, and Indiana (he carried all other free states), he would have won a clear victory without a single ballot from slave states. Although Frémont and his party lost the presidency in 1856, they nevertheless signaled to the nation their strength and the overwhelming appeal of free-soil and free-labor sentiment to Northerners. Plus, despite having only two years to get organized, they racked up significant victories in congressional, state, and local elections across the North. They looked with great optimism toward the federal elections of 1858 and 1860.

Before his election, James Buchanan himself had said that if he were to win only "by the votes of the Southern States united with Pennsylvania & New Jersey alone, it might only be the beginning of the end."[56] And even before his first official test between his fidelity to the Union and his debt to the South, a songster wrote:

> No more I'm James Buchanan—I sold myself down South.
> Henceforth I'll do what my masters please
> And speak what they put in my mouth!
> But don't let that alarm you, forgive his slavish tone.
> Can you ask a man to stand up straight who was born
>   without a backbone?[57]

In the South, secessionists grew alarmed, and their cause was reinvigorated by the demonstrated Republican threat. Again they warned the South that the antislavery forces they had prophesied had arrived in the form of the Republican Party. In October, Laurence Keitt had warned white Southerners that if Republican John C. Frémont won the presidency in 1856, "*you have to choose between submission and dissolution.*"[58] Robert Barnwell Rhett, who had retired from politics in 1852 when a secessionist movement died, ended his self-imposed moratorium on public advocacy for disunion. At the hands of Republicans, a "complete revolution" had occurred in the North, Rhett warned, replacing free government with "a sheer despotism." The new Republican delegation in Congress was "vulgar and fanatical, hating us and hating our institutions." The solution, Rhett offered, lay in secession. "If we are true to ourselves, a glorious destiny awaits us, and the South will be a great, free and independent people!"[59] As though responding directly to Rhett and Keitt but in fact issuing a broad reaction to all new threats of disunion, Abraham Lincoln announced, "The Union, in any case, won't be dissolved. We don't want to dissolve it, and if you attempt it, *we won't let you.* With the purse and sword, the army and navy and treasury at our command, you *couldn't do it.*"[60]

NOTES*

1. Stephen Oates, *To Purge This Land with Blood: A Biography of John Brown* (New York: Harper & Row, 1970), 114.
2. Ibid.
3. Edward J. Renehan Jr., *The Secret Six: The True Tale of the Men Who Conspired with John Brown* (Columbia: University of South Carolina Press, 1996), 91.
4. Oates, *To Purge This Land with Blood*, 115.
5. Ibid., 116–17.
6. Ibid., 123.
7. Ibid., 125.
8. Kristen A. Tegtmeier, "The Ladies of Lawrence Are Arming! The Gendered Nature of Sectional Violence in Early Kansas," in *Antislavery Violence: Sectional, Racial, and Cultural Conflict in Antebellum America,* ed. John R. McKivigan and Stanley Harrold (Knoxville: University of Tennessee Press, 1999), 222–23.
9. Michael A. Morrison, *Slavery and the American West: The Eclipse of Manifest Destiny and the Coming of the Civil War* (Chapel Hill: University of North Carolina Press, 1997), 166.
10. C. Peter Ripley et al., eds., *Black Abolitionist Papers,* 5 vols. (Chapel Hill: University of North Carolina Press, 1985–1992), 4:340.
11. Carol K. Bleser, ed., *Secret and Sacred: The Diaries of James Henry Hammond, A Southern Slaveholder* (New York: Oxford University Press, 1988), 19.
12. John McCardell, *The Idea of a Southern Nation: Southern Nationalists and Southern Nationalism, 1830–1860* (New York: Norton, 1979), 224.

*Emphasis in all quotations is that of the original authors.

13. Ibid., 219–20.
14. Morrison, *Slavery and the American West*, 173.
15. Both in ibid., 174–75.
16. Ibid., 175.
17. *Congressional Globe*, 34th Cong., 1st sess., 639.
18. Morrison, *Slavery and the American West*, 166.
19. *Congressional Globe*, 34th Cong., 1st sess., 639.
20. Allan Nevins, *Ordeal of the Union*, 2 vols. (New York: Charles Scribner's Sons, 1947), 2:427.
21. *Congressional Globe*, 34th Cong., 1st sess., 587.
22. Ibid., 496.
23. Ibid., app., 530.
24. David Herbert Donald, *Charles Sumner and the Coming of the Civil War*, 1st ed. (New York: Knopf, 1960), 286.
25. *Congressional Globe*, 34th Cong., 1st sess., app., 543.
26. Frederick J. Blue, *Charles Sumner and the Conscience of the North* (Arlington Heights, IL: Harlan Davidson, 1994), 91.
27. *Congressional Globe*, 34th Cong., 1st sess., app., 547.
28. Ulrich B. Phillips, *The Course of the South to Secession* (New York: Appleton-Century Company, 1939), 128.
29. Blue, *Charles Sumner Conscience*, 93–94; Eric H. Walther, *The Fire-Eaters* (Baton Rouge: Louisiana State University Press, 1992), 173–74.
30. Donald, *Charles Sumner and Civil War*, 297.
31. William E. Gienapp, "The Crime against Sumner: The Caning of Charles Sumner and the Rise of the Republican Party," *Civil War History* 25 (1979): 230, 232.
32. Walther, *Fire-Eaters*, 174.
33. Gienapp, "Crime against Sumner," 221–22.
34. Blue, *Charles Sumner Conscience*, 95.
35. Walther, *Fire-Eaters*, 175.
36. Morrison, *Slavery and the American West*, 166.
37. Renehan, *Secret Six*, 95.
38. John Stauffer, "Advent among the Indians: The Revolutionary Ethos of Gerrit Smith, James McCune Smith, Frederick Douglass, and John Brown," in *Antislavery Violence: Sectional, Racial, and Cultural Conflict in Antebellum America*, ed. McKivigan and Harrold, 240.
39. Renehan, *Secret Six*, 101.
40. Robert E. May, *The Southern Dream of a Caribbean Empire, 1854–1861* (Athens: University of Georgia Press, 1989), 108.
41. Morrison, *Slavery and the American West*, 169.
42. Shirley J. Yee, *Black Women Abolitionists: A Study in Activism, 1828–1860* (Knoxville: University of Tennessee Press, 1992), 99.
43. Ripley, *Black Abolitionist Papers*, 4:328.
44. Ibid., 4:326–28.
45. Yee, *Black Women Abolitionists*, 127.
46. Tyler Anbinder, *Nativism and Slavery: The Northern Know Nothings and the Politics of the 1850s* (New York: Oxford University Press, 1992), 204.
47. May, *Southern Dream*, 101.
48. James M. McPherson, *Battle Cry of Freedom: The Civil War Era* (New York: Oxford University Press, 1988), 155.

49. Hans Trefousse, *The Radical Republicans: Lincoln's Vanguard for Racial Justice* (New York: Knopf, 1969), 100.

50. Bruce C. Levine, *Half Slave and Half Free: The Roots of Civil War* (New York: Hill and Wang, Noonday Press, 1992), 208.

51. Anbinder, *Nativism and Slavery*, 226.

52. Both in ibid., 227.

53. Both in Morrison, *Slavery and the American West*, 182.

54. Ibid., 183.

55. Levine, *Half Slave*, 208–9.

56. Morrison, *Slavery and the American West*, 185.

57. "Buck's Private Confession Publicly Revealed" (1856) in *Tippecanoe and Tyler Too: A Collection of American Political Marches, Songs, and Dirges* (Providence, RI: Newport Classic, 1992).

58. Walther, *Fire-Eaters*, 179.

59. Ibid., 147–48.

60. Roy P. Basler et al., eds., *The Collected Works of Abraham Lincoln*, 9 vols. (New Brunswick, NJ: Rutgers University Press, 1953), 2:354–55.

CHAPTER SIX

1857

"A Northern Man with Southern Principles"

ON JANUARY 15, 1857, in a segregated black neighborhood of Philadelphia, police arrested Henry Tiffney, a young, free black man. They charged him with theft, but in fact his apprehension was a ploy by slave catchers, and not a unique one. One of them, John Graham, worked for a detective agency in Baltimore. Graham received help from John Jenkins and James Crossin, deputy U.S. marshals in Philadelphia. Three times in recent years, Jenkins and Crossin had defended themselves in court against charges of assault and battery with deadly intent, stemming from attempts to detain fugitive slaves, and three times they won acquittal. Tiffney's captors brought him before a federal slave commissioner, claiming that he was really Michael Brown, a slave who had run away from his master, William H. Gatchell Sr. of Maryland. Black abolitionist William Still rushed to Tiffney's hearing, both to witness it and to report it in the black press. Tiffney's captors refused to let him speak to anyone but his court-appointed lawyer. Over the two-day trial, local black citizens testified that Tiffney was who he claimed and that he had lived in Philadelphia for six years, but the slave commissioner refused to let any black observers enter the courtroom and finally ordered Tiffney "returned" to his supposed master in Baltimore in accordance with the Fugitive Slave Act of 1850.[1]

The same day that Tiffney's doom was set, radical abolitionists led by William Lloyd Garrison held a Disunion Convention in Worcester, Massachusetts, proclaiming, "No Union with Slaveholders." Thomas Wentworth Higginson, who had led the mob in Boston that tried to stop the rendition of Anthony Burns in 1854, returned from Kansas to participate. He concluded that "the disease [of slavery] is too deep to cure without amputation."[2] On his way, Higginson met up with John Brown, who had returned to Boston to raise money for more weapons. Brown fired Higginson's hope for an imminent conflagration. Brown also met George Luther

Stearns, a wealthy lead-pipe manufacturer and philanthropist in Boston. Stearns's life changed the moment he heard of the Fugitive Slave Act. He armed himself and used his mansion as a safe house for the Underground Railroad. Stearns, too, looked for anything—anything at all—that promised to end slavery. John Brown's audacity and fanaticism appealed to Stearns.

Before Brown left Boston he paid a visit to another local luminary, Charles Sumner. The senator was still slowly recovering from his assault eight months before. Even walking caused pain. But Sumner received the notorious John Brown, who asked the senator if he could see the coat Sumner was wearing on the day of his beating. Sumner limped slowly to a closet and retrieved the coat, stiff with his own blood. Brown gazed at the relic but said nothing.

James Buchanan
Library of Congress

While radical abolitionists encouraged disunion and armed their peers in Kansas for more bloodshed, President-elect James Buchanan prepared to take office and work for peace. After his election he had told a Southern senator that he would strive "to arrest, if possible, the agitation of the Slavery question at the North and to destroy sectional parties."[3] Significantly, Buchanan said nothing about Southern agitation.

If his electoral vote total or his private statements about slavery did not convince most Americans that, like Pierce, Buchanan was yet another "Northern man with Southern principles," or "doughface," his cabinet appointments clearly did. Most of Buchanan's informal advisers, such as his late friend William R. King of Alabama, were Southerners or had strong ties to the section. John Slidell of Louisiana replaced King as Buchanan's chief adviser, and the governor of Virginia, Henry A. Wise, matched Slidell's proslavery enthusiasm and also had the ear of the next president. Even Senator Jesse D. Bright of Indiana, another close associate, owned land and slaves across the Ohio River in Kentucky. Another old friend, John Appleton of Maine, told Buchanan that with Minnesota and Kansas Territories likely to soon enter the Union as free states, Buchanan ought to "yield pretty generously to the weaker portion," the South.[4] These and others like them helped Buchanan select the men who would lead the country.

An old Democratic standard-bearer, Lewis Cass of Michigan, got the nod for the State Department. John B. Floyd of Virginia, a close friend and associate of Governor Wise, headed the War Department. Howell Cobb of Georgia, a unionist during the crisis that ended with the Compromise of 1850, was selected for the Treasury Department. Jacob Thompson of Mississippi, who had opposed that compromise, now served as secretary of the Interior. Aaron V. Brown, a proslavery expansionist from Tennessee, headed the Post Office Department and the tremendous patronage opportunities that came with it. Isaac Toucey of Connecticut took over the Navy Department, and Jeremiah Black, a friend from Pennsylvania, accepted the post of attorney general.

Buchanan's cabinet was neither as talented as Pierce's had been nor particularly weak, but it was decidedly pro-Southern, and all politicians knew it. It had not only a majority of four Southerners but also three other members who offered little balance. Toucey supported the Fugitive Slave Law and, while on the Senate committee that investigated the Sumner-Brooks affair, never spoke out against the assault. In fact, the assembly of his home state voted to remove Toucey's portrait from a gallery dedicated to its former governors. Cass was mostly a figurehead. Now seventy-four, Cass accepted his post under the conditions that he renounce his well-known Anglophobia and take on an assistant secretary who would actually handle most of the responsibilities of the department. Jeremiah Black began his service innocently enough, but over time he revealed himself as an outspoken defender of slavery in the territories.

All of that lay in the future, however. Americans came together for a joyful inauguration ceremony on March 4. On a clear and balmy early spring day, a cannon blast from the Navy Yard signaled the start of festivities. Congressman John A. Quitman, elected recently from Mississippi to take his place among the proslavery leadership in Washington, led a parade down Pennsylvania Avenue to the National Hotel, where Buchanan lodged. Buchanan, with his niece, Harriet Lane, then joined Franklin Pierce in an open carriage that rode toward Capitol Hill past tens of thousands of cheering citizens.

Buchanan spoke what he very likely believed in his heart and what most Americans wanted to hear. After all the turmoil of the recent elections, "the tempest at once subsided and all was calm," he said. Buchanan directly addressed the question of slavery in Kansas, endorsing Douglas's popular sovereignty and affirming that "the will of the majority shall govern." He planned to leave the people of that embattled territory "perfectly free to form and regulate their domestic institutions in their own way, subject only to the Constitution of the United States."[5]

After a brief appearance at his own inaugural ball that evening, Buchanan immediately threw himself into his work: meeting with his cabinet, conducting correspondence, and entertaining official guests. Members of the cabinet got along extraordinarily well with one another and with their boss, especially the jovial and proficient Howell "Fatty" Cobb. Harriet Lane, at twenty-six years of age, served as de facto first lady in her bachelor-uncle's White House, managing both social events and a major interior renovation for the presidential mansion. But lightness and mirth ended abruptly.

Buchanan, his niece's brother Elliott E. Lane, John Quitman, and perhaps 100 others who had lodged at the popular National Hotel all became quite ill. Poor ventilation and bad sewers set the stage for what Americans soon called National Hotel Disease, similar, if not identical, to Legionnaire's Disease experienced in the twentieth century. Quitman never fully recovered, and he died the next year. The *New York Herald* claimed that thirty others died from the same cause. Buchanan himself remained ill until the middle of April, but Elliott Lane succumbed to the malady and died that month.

Before manifestations of this ailment started to take their grim toll, a political firestorm broke out that unleashed a new dimension in the sectional crisis. On March 6 the Supreme Court announced a decision in the much anticipated case of *Dred Scott v. Sandford*. Scott was born in Virginia and moved by his master, Peter Blow, to Alabama in 1830 and then to St. Louis, Missouri. Blow died in 1832, and around that time, John Emerson, a local physician, purchased Scott. Two years later, Dr. Emerson entered the army as a surgeon and moved to his first assignment at Fort Armstrong, Illinois, with Scott going along as a personal servant, a common enough practice for Southerners in the armed forces. Two years later the two moved again, this time to Fort Snelling, near St. Paul, in what was then Wisconsin Territory. There Scott met another slave named Harriet Robinson. They fell in love. Scott's master purchased Robinson so she and Scott could "marry" (a legal fiction, of course, since slaves, as property, could neither marry nor divorce). They had two daughters. Off they all went again in 1837 when the army assigned Emerson to Fort Jesup, Louisiana. There the doctor fell in love with and married Eliza Sanford. In 1843, Dr. Emerson died.

Dred Scott
*Courtesy of the Missouri
Historical Society*

Legal title to the Scott family fell to his widow, whose father, Alexander Sanford, served as executor of Emerson's estate.

Some details remain murky, but by 1846, Dred Scott and his wife had begun a long, arduous legal battle for their freedom. Working with white lawyers, they based their claim on the fact that they had resided for some time in both a free state and a free territory. A local judge granted their petition. Then the Scotts filed charges against Mrs. Emerson in Missouri for enslaving them and for beating them. Their case had precedents; other slaves in Missouri had successfully gone to court and won their freedom after their masters had taken them to free portions of the country. But delays and appeals dragged their case along year after year, all the way through the state's legal system. Meanwhile, the Scotts were held in custody by a sheriff who rented them out, with the proceeds going to Mrs. Emerson.

By 1853 one of the Scotts' attorneys had died, and the other had moved out of state. Mrs. Emerson remarried, and her brother took over legal custody of the hapless Scott family. A new lawyer emerged with a strategy to take the Scotts' case to the U.S. Circuit Court in Missouri. The new suit argued that Scott was a citizen of Missouri and that he and his family were being held illegally as slaves. They lost but appealed to the Supreme Court in 1854. There, as before, more delays prevented the case from proceeding until 1856. By then, official records misspelled the defendant's name in the case of *Dred Scott v. Sandford*.

Old Democratic and Southern justices dominated the Supreme Court in 1856. Chief Justice Roger Taney, a former slaveholder from

Maryland, was seventy-nine, an appointee of Andrew Jackson dating from 1835. John A. Campbell of Alabama, John Catron of Tennessee, Peter V. Daniel of Virginia, and James M. Wayne of Georgia all had solid credentials as proslavery, states' rights justices, and all had owned slaves for various periods of time. Daniel even avoided stepping on Northern soil and went on record stating that he was "prepared for any extremity" to keep Yankees from ban-

Roger B. Taney
Library of Congress

ning slavery in the territories.[6] Two of the Northern justices, Benjamin Curtis of Massachusetts and Robert Grier of Pennsylvania, had long supported both slave expansion and the Fugitive Slave Act. The Scotts' case finally received the full attention of the court on December 19, 1856, but more delays postponed matters until February 14, 1857, eleven years after their legal ordeal began.

James Buchanan had perhaps as great an interest in the outcome of this case as anyone in the country, except for the Scott family. Since the heart of this case had to do with the question of slavery and freedom in the Western territories, if Buchanan was lucky, the Supreme Court might settle everything once and for all, immediately before or after his inauguration. On February 3 the president-elect, oblivious to matters of ethics and propriety, began to correspond with Justice Catron, who just as mysteriously responded to each letter. Buchanan wanted to know when the country might learn about a decision. Catron could not say but did reveal that the territorial question would almost certainly be involved, in turn involving a ruling on the Missouri Compromise of 1820 that prohibited slavery north of that state. On February 23, Justice Grier finally answered an earlier inquiry by Buchanan that completely tipped off the coming result. There would be "six if not *seven* . . . who will decide the compromise law of 1820 to be of *non-effect*."[7]

Buchanan knew what was coming. In his inaugural address, he simply referred to a pending Supreme Court decision that would "speedily and finally" resolve all questions about slavery in the territories and vowed to submit to that decision, whatever it might be. Much later, speculation suggested that Buchanan had either already seen a copy of Chief Justice Taney's decision or that Taney, before issuing the oath of office, had whispered something to Buchanan about the case.

On March 6, Roger Taney and his associates announced their decision. The chief justice declared that Scott had no right to sue in an American court. Neither slaves nor free blacks, Taney explained, were included "and were not intended to be included, under the word 'citizens' in the Constitution." The Founding Fathers, according to Taney, regarded these "as a subordinate and inferior class of beings, who . . . had no rights or privileges but such as those who held the power and the Government might choose to grant them." He considered all blacks "altogether unfit to associate with the white race" and so inferior "that they had no rights which the white man was bound to respect."[8]

Taney then addressed the issue of transporting the Scotts into territory established as free by the Missouri Compromise and whether or not that act effectively freed them. Taney attempted to demolish that in two distinct ways. Citing the Fifth Amendment, Taney asserted that one could not be deprived of one's property— slave or other—without due process of law and that taking property into an American territory absolutely did not mean automatic forfeiture of that property. He backed up this argument by stressing that "if Congress cannot do this—if it is beyond the powers conferred on the Federal Government—it will be admitted, we presume, that it could not authorize a Territorial Government to exercise them."[9] As far as the Scotts' residence in Illinois, Taney ruled that their legal status depended upon Missouri law, not the law of the free state.

The Scott family's fate seemed sealed, but in May a member of the Blow family, an early owner of Dred Scott, purchased him, Harriet, and the girls and set them free. Dred Scott only enjoyed his liberty until September 17, 1858, when he died, leaving his wife and children to pass their days in obscurity.

Among Democrats, especially in the South, reactions to this case were decidedly satisfied and only occasionally joyful. After all, by 1857 most white Southerners had agreed that the Missouri Compromise had been unconstitutional all along and that Congress could not prohibit slavery from any territory of the United States. The *Dred Scott* ruling simply confirmed those beliefs, and for most in the South it ended the controversy once and for all. Speaking through his newspaper, the *Charleston Mercury*, secessionist Robert Barnwell Rhett explained, "We have been simply a step in advance of the highest tribunals in the country, in declaring what was the law of the land, and seeking honestly and faithfully to enforce it."[10]

Northern reactions to the *Scott* decision came quickly and ferociously, especially from Republicans. After all, by ruling that Congress had no power to prohibit the spread of slavery into the territories, the Supreme Court effectively denied the legitimacy of the core issue of this young and growing party. To many the decision represented no less than the nationalization of slavery, if Congress truly had no power over slavery in the territories and if masters could bring their slaves into free states and territories without consequence.

Northern public opinion vehemently denounced the court's pronouncement. The *New York Independent* declared, "The Decision of the Supreme Court is the Moral Assassination of a Race and Cannot be Obeyed."[11] The *New York Journal of Commerce* declared that *Dred Scott* "dissipates the mist in which we have been enveloped for years; it exposes in all their deformities the slavery heresies by which we have been disturbed for more than half a century." The *Ohio State Journal* claimed that Taney's judgment rendered the territories "one great slave pen." Republican senator Hannibal Hamlin insisted angrily that the high court "had no more authority to decide a political question for us [in Congress], than we had to decide a judicial question for them. . . . We make the laws, they interpret them."[12] Abraham Lincoln lambasted Taney's assertion that the Founding Fathers denied the fundamental equality of all people, regardless of race, and that their statement of inalienable rights pertained only to white men—a contention fully endorsed by Stephen A. Douglas. No, Lincoln insisted, the Founders "meant to set up a standard maxim for free society, which should be familiar to all, and revered by all; constantly looked to, constantly labored for, and even though never perfectly attained, constantly approximated, and thereby spreading and deepening its influence, and augmenting the value of life to all people of all colors everywhere."[13]

Talk led to action. The state assemblies of New York, Massachusetts, Maine, Connecticut, Vermont, and Pennsylvania all rebuked the Supreme Court. In Pennsylvania the legislature declared the ruling inoperative. New York went further. The state that had originated the infamous Lemmon case back in 1852, which allowed slaveholders to bring slaves into New York for short periods of time, now decided to stop instantly any imposition of slavery whatsoever and passed legislation forbidding even sojourners to bring their slaves into the Empire State for any amount of time at all, punishable by jail for the master and instant freedom for the slave. New Hampshire responded by explicitly bestowing citizenship upon all blacks within its borders (just over 500 people).

If whites in the North reacted to the decision with indignation, blacks responded with horror, outrage, and anger. On May 12 the American Anti-Slavery Society held a meeting in New York City that drew 2,000 people. William Lloyd Garrison chaired the gathering, but no one expressed his fury more eloquently than Robert Purvis, an African American. Purvis gave voice to the convictions of those who had determined to work for black freedom within the law of America but who now, after the *Dred Scott* decision, believed that African Americans had no allegiance whatsoever to those laws: "Are we to clank the chains that have been made for us, and praise the men who did the deed? Are we to be kicked and scouted, trampled upon and judiciously declared to '*have no rights which white men are bound to respect*,' then turn round and glorify and magnify the laws under which all this is done? Are we such base, soulless, spiritless sycophants as all this? Sir, let others do as they may, I will never stultify or disgrace myself by eulogizing a government that tramples me and all that are dear to me in the dust."[14] And with Buchanan so quickly fixing himself in the minds of Northerners as another doughface, or a Northern man with Southern principles, many abolitionists, black and white alike, resumed their agitation for disunion.

In May, Buchanan's appointee as governor for Kansas, Robert J. Walker, arrived there to replace John W. Geary, President Pierce's surprisingly fair-minded and tough executive. Walker was born in Pennsylvania but had moved to Mississippi, where he built up a thriving law practice and stocked his plantation with slaves. He had a great interest in the territories and had personally invested in land, mining, and railroad ventures in the West. At 5 feet 2 inches and about 100 pounds, Walker had a diminutive appearance that belied his energy and determination to meet any political challenge. He had already made quite a name for himself in 1856 when he published a pamphlet called "An Appeal for the Union," in which he argued that the soil and climate of Kansas were not conducive to the spread of slavery—that an "isothermal" line prevented the institution from reaching so far north.[15] Before he accepted Buchanan's nomination, Walker laid down clear conditions: he would personally select the territorial secretary (he chose Frederick P. Stanton, a Tennessean whom he trusted); he insisted on acquiring a force of 1,500 federal troops, for obvious reasons; and he demanded that only "actual, *bona fide* residents" could participate in "a fair and regular vote, unaffected by fraud or violence."[16]

Buchanan agreed. Walker's appointment stood out conspicuously as among the best Buchanan had ever made. Of course, Southern extremists were irate. One Georgian grumbled, "*We are betrayed.*"[17] Jefferson Davis termed Walker's words and acts "treachery."[18] Democrats in Alabama held an anti-Walker protest in June, condemning Walker's actions as "dangerous to the institutions of the South," in violation of Buchanan's policies, and contrary to the *Dred Scott* decision.[19] More moderate Southerners, however, decided they had lost nothing with a fair-minded slaveholder in charge. And, surprisingly although Republicans suspected that behind Walker's "honeyed words" lay another proslavery plot, a fair number adopted a wait-and-see stance.[20]

By the time Walker arrived in Kansas, however, only weeks remained for the previously scheduled election on the Lecompton proslavery constitution. In the first two months of 1857 the territorial assembly had ordered a census enumeration for March that favored the proslavery settlers of eastern Kansas; they also set elections in June for delegates to a constitutional convention. On March 10, free-staters gathered in Topeka and denounced these election procedures as fraudulent, claiming that a majority of people in Kansas favored their own proposed constitution instead. When Walker arrived on the scene in late May, a quick canvass of the territory convinced the new governor that few free-staters would take part in the selection of representatives to the Lecompton constitutional convention, which was weighted toward the counties with the strongest proslavery sympathies. Walker then strived to convince free-staters to disband their illegal Topeka government and to turn out and vote in the fall referendum on Lecompton to defeat it.

In the June elections, proslavery delegates won control of the convention because the free-state majority chose instead to boycott the election. Only a few hundred antislavery men turned out, with 1,800 proslavery voters taking the day. But over 7,000 registered voters, mostly free-staters, had not turned out. Walker convinced the free-staters to disband a convention they had called for Topeka in July. Territorial elections would have to wait until October 5, giving Walker and his aides plenty of time to settle in and ensure a fair vote.

An old, familiar face with gray eyes reemerged in the Southern states late in the spring of 1857. William Walker, erstwhile president of Nicaragua, returned to an enthusiastic welcome from 10,000 people in New Orleans on May 27. With Commodore Vanderbilt against him, his troops succumbing to disease, and the neighboring countries of El Salvador, Costa Rica, Guatemala, and Honduras rallying together against their common foe, Walker was driven out of Nicaragua by opposition forces. He came back to the United States determined to gather more men and supplies for a renewed effort to claim Nicaragua. William Walker crisscrossed the slave South, quickly taking the pulse of a people who pinned their hopes on the now embattled Lecompton regime in Kansas. Walker fused together slave expansion into Kansas and Nicaragua and offered himself as the leader. More than that, Walker vowed that his Latin American effort signified to white Southerners no less than the "only means, short of revolution, whereby they can preserve their present social organization."[21]

As William Walker stirred the cauldron of Southern radicalism, so, too, did an ostensibly nonpolitical meeting in Knoxville, Tennessee, in August—the annual meeting of the Southern Commercial Convention. These assemblies began in 1839 as gatherings of mostly businessmen to discuss and advance agricultural, commercial, and industrial information, trends, and developments. But with every chapter of the sectional conflict, these meetings became more and more politically charged, and delegates to them knew far better than most that the relative lack of economic diversification in the South boded ill should secession and war ever become realities.

A meeting in Memphis in 1845 helped convince James D. B. De Bow to move from his native Charleston to New Orleans, the great commercial entrepôt of the South, and to publish his influential *De Bow's Review*. His tenure at the Census Bureau in 1853 and brief academic career as chair of commerce, public economy, and statistics at the University of Louisiana (now Tulane University) helped secure his selection as president of the Knoxville meeting. By now a confirmed secessionist, De Bow used his presidential address to call for disunion.

De Bow insisted that Republican "task masters" truly meant to shut the West to slave expansion and in the process denounced white Southerners as "cowards and robbers . . . unfitted to share with them in christian communion." If Republicans cut off slave expansion, De Bow promised that they would next abolish the institution of slavery itself, and following that would come a race war with free blacks. If the Union was no longer safe nor honorable for white Southerners, De Bow demanded, "it is to be crushed." And to De Bow the Union as it stood was, at best, a "festering corpse."[22]

De Bow and others also raised the tantalizing—or terrifying, depending upon one's viewpoint—issue of the Atlantic slave trade. De Bow added his voice to a small but significant number of Southern radicals who had recently begun promoting a renewal of the African slave trade, a practice outlawed by Congress in 1807 with the strong support of slaveholders like President Thomas Jefferson and his secretary of state, James Madison. Most slaveholders, whatever their commitment to the peculiar institution, had an aversion to raiding the African continent, kidnapping free people, destroying their families, and forcing them to endure the historically catastrophic Middle Passage across the Atlantic. But faced with the unrelenting opposition of abolitionists and Free-Soilers, some proslavery advocates latched onto this explosive issue.

This campaign began in 1853, when Leonidas W. Spratt, owner of the *Charleston Southern Standard*, argued that because slavery was morally and socially beneficial to all, no one could consider any aspect of it to be bad. If it was all right for masters to purchase slaves in Virginia and take them to Texas, why not purchase more of them, more cheaply, from Africa? Spratt also set up the debate for others by arguing that whether or not the South revived the African slave trade, the federal prohibition on it represented a moral stigma and condemnation of the institution, an insult that no honorable Southerner ought to accept. Venerable secessionist Robert Barnwell Rhett supported the notion in the columns of his *Charleston Mercury*, Governor James H. Adams of South Carolina threw his support to the movement in 1854, and delegates to the Commercial Convention in 1856 in Savannah began serious deliberation of the idea.

At Knoxville and in his *Review*, De Bow spoke out boldly on behalf of renewing the nefarious trade. De Bow promised others that reopening the trade would yield an abundance of inexpensive slaves that would help populate "Texas, New Mexico, Southern California, Northern Mexico, and Central America," despite the little details that California already had proclaimed itself free and that the United States did not possess some of the regions he spoke of.[23] A related issue at Knoxville called for Congress to repeal a portion of the Webster-Ashburton Treaty of 1842 that committed a U.S. naval squadron to help Britain patrol the African coast to stop illegal shipments of kidnapped Africans to the Americas. The latter motion won approval by a vote of 66 to 26, and De Bow's more radical measure was referred to a committee for preparation for debate at the next annual meeting, in Montgomery, Alabama, in 1858.

The *Philadelphia Public Ledger* complained, with good reason, that the Knoxville meeting was not, in fact, a commercial convention, but rather, "a political club . . . of secessionists in disguise."[24] Even the governor of Georgia, Hershel V. Johnson, urged his state's assemblymen to refrain from delving into serious discussion over this issue, which was "adverse to the sentiments of the civilized world" and more likely to divide rather than unite the South.[25]

By 1857 voices of moderation in the South—and in much of the country—found themselves overwhelmed by extremists. Two important books made their way into print that year that helped widen the growing chasm between the sections. One came from the pen of George Fitzhugh, the Virginian who had published *Sociology for the South* in 1854. His new volume took proslavery into new dimensions. In *Cannibals All! or Slaves Without Masters*, Fitzhugh built upon previous publications by himself and others and took their reasoning to a logical extreme. Insisting that slavery provided order for society, that it was essentially humane, that the personal relationship between master and slave elevated the enslaved far above the status of a mere wage worker, and that cash and profit were not the bottom line for masters who cared for the sick, disabled, and elderly, Fitzhugh concluded that *all* workers should be enslaved, white as well as black. Fitzhugh observed how industrialists in the North terrorized factory workers and discarded those maimed in workplace accidents as easily as worn-out machinery, and he feared imminent social chaos and workers' revolt if society did nothing to address the situation. By emulating Southern slaveholders, Fitzhugh explained, labor and capital no longer vied against each other but instead became literally bound together in the person of a slave.

Even other proslavery advocates denounced this work as "incendiary & dangerous" and called Fitzhugh a "great egoist" and "absurd."[26] And no wonder. Fitzhugh admitted to a friend, "Confessing myself the greatest egoist in the world," he self-consciously made his writings "odd, eccentric, extravagant, and disorderly."[27] And yet, Fitzhugh simply extended the reasoning of others who, agreeing that slavery had only benefits and no ills, advocated reopening the African slave trade.

Proslavery had long had a grasp of the scientific mind of the South, and in 1857, Dr. Josiah Nott of Mobile added yet another astonishing volume to the growing literature of intolerance. Educated in medical schools in New York, Philadelphia, and Paris, Nott stood with many in the transatlantic world who studied ethnology, the supposed science of ethnic and racial characteristics. After years of lecturing and publishing essays in medical journals, Nott gathered together his most important pieces in a book titled *Types of Mankind*. Nott argued that Africans were an entirely different species than whites; that they had not descended from Adam and Eve; that they had shorter physical endurance, shorter lives, and were less prolific than whites; and that intermarriage only led to the destruction of both races. By an "immutable law of nature," Nott concluded, blacks could not be civilized and they were "better off in slavery [in] the South than in freedom elsewhere."[28]

Although working independently from Nott and Fitzhugh, at the same time they published their efforts, a very peculiar Southerner produced the most powerful volume for the antislavery camp since *Uncle Tom's Cabin*. In 1857, Hinton Rowan Helper published *The Impending Crisis of the South: How to Meet It*. Helper used statistical data from the 1850 census to show how slavery had retarded the entire South. He blamed the institution of slavery for the region's relative dearth of cities, commerce, industry, and manufacturing as well as its high illiteracy and paucity of schools, libraries, and newspapers.

Helper was born in Davie County in the North Carolina Piedmont (in the foothills of the Appalachians) in 1829. Reared in a yeoman family by a German father who owned a few slaves, Helper received his education at a private academy and took a job as a clerk in a local store. He was accused of embezzling $300, which he most likely had done, and decided to do what so many Americans did when they washed out or committed crimes back East: he went west. In 1850, Helper took a ship to California, but his experiences in the raucous, wild West embittered him for the rest of his life. Helper hated blacks as much as he hated slavery. The specter of free blacks moving about California, combined with his economic failure there, helped launch his publishing career after he returned to the more orderly East Coast.

In 1855, Helper published *Land of Gold*, titled sarcastically as a warning to other fortune seekers to stay put or at least to avoid California. In this work, Helper vented his xenophobia toward Indians, Latinos, Africans, Asians, and Jews. Helper agreed with ethnologists such as Josiah Nott that African people were a different species from Europeans and called for the colonization of all African Americans to Liberia within six months, whether or not they wished to go and no matter how brutal the conditions would be aboard another forced Middle Passage.

When his publisher for *Land of Gold* expressed objections to portions of the manuscript that made unfavorable comparisons between slavery and free labor, Helper decided to assault slavery. He later claimed that he had written *Impending Crisis* to attack censorship in the South. Through a Northern publisher, Helper presented highly selective data from the federal census, omitting much in the process, to draw extreme and spectacular conclusions. Helper often left precise, causal factors implicit to the point of invisibility; for example, he claimed that hay from the North was worth more than Southern cotton, tobacco, sugar, and rice combined. He conveniently ignored the facts that little need existed in the warm South to purchase dry grass when green forage remained available much of the year and that corn was cheap and abundant. Imports and exports were each much greater in the North, but only if one counted exclusively industrial goods: cotton led the nation in total value of exports. Helper claimed that the average value of land in the North in 1850 stood at $28.07 per acre, as opposed to only $5.34 in the South, and mystically concluded, "Emancipate your slaves on Wednesday morning, and on the Thursday following the value of your lands, and ours [non-slaveholders] too, will have increased to an average of at least $28.07 per acre."[29]

Helper saved his harshest words for slaveholders. He suggested banning them from public office; boycotting slaveholding merchants, editors, lawyers, ministers, hotel keepers, and the like; and taxing slaveholders $40 annually per slave, with the proceeds going to colonize blacks in Liberia or Central or South America. He called those who hired slaves "lickspittles" and suggested that most slaves "would be delighted with an opportunity to cut their masters' throats" and join an army of white non-slaveholders.[30] Helper proclaimed that not only are "the lords of the lash . . . absolute masters of the blacks . . . but they are also the oracles and arbiters of all non-slaveholding whites, whose freedom is merely nominal, and whose unparalleled illiteracy and degradation is purposefully and fiendishly perpetuated."[31]

This book sold 100,000 copies in its first printing, mostly to sympathetic, righteously indignant Northerners. Republicans rejoiced that such a powerful, if eccentric, Southern voice joined their cause. A Washington newspaper proclaimed that *Impending Crisis* would "open the eyes of the blind" and ought to be "scattered broadcast throughout the country." Many Northerners believed— or made themselves believe—that Helper represented the muted voice of multitudes of ordinary Southerners, who were "emancipationists at heart, and free-soilers secretly."[32] Amid the furor that was the year 1857, Helper's book got noticed, but its real impact did not manifest itself for two more years.

Anyone who believed Helper's outrageous economic contrast between North and South must have had a tough time reconciling that with events of the last months of the year, when the bustling economy that characterized most of the 1850s hit a sharp reversal. Thousands of miles of railroad construction had helped fuel the boom, particularly in the North, although great construction projects also took place in the South, most notably the beginnings of a transcontinental route linking New Orleans and the West Coast. In part due to this building boom, the number of banks in the country nearly doubled between 1850 and 1857, with a disproportionate number again in the North. A constantly increasing flow of settlers expanded the agricultural production of the West. Some skeptics pointed out that too much investment in reality was reckless speculation, involving heavy borrowing at high interest rates for poorly thought-out schemes.

The bottom fell out suddenly. Grain exports from the North to Europe ebbed quickly in 1857, after a brief spike in demand during the Crimean War, but production increased nevertheless, further depressing the market value of these crops. Most banks had printed and circulated far more paper notes than the value of specie (gold and silver) they had to back them. On August 24 the Ohio Life Insurance and Trust Company (actually a bank) suspended payments on its notes. It had capital assets of about $2 million but liabilities of $5 to $7 million. The suspension started a cascade effect. Several New York banks had served as creditors for Ohio Life and now called in their loans. By August 27 other banks had failed, one in Virginia and five in New England, and within days, more followed suit as far west as Nebraska. The process repeated itself with ever greater scope through the autumn. Anywhere and everywhere that banks closed, depositors were left holding worthless paper notes and therefore had trouble paying their bills, let alone repaying debts or purchasing anything at all. Starved for capital, businesses collapsed one after another, with hundreds of thousands of people losing their jobs in the process. Multitudes of people lost their homes. It was the Panic of 1857.

Across the North—in New York, Providence, Philadelphia, Newark, and other cities—officials appropriated funds to feed the hungry and to hire the unemployed in public works projects. One newspaper complained that these efforts had "a flavor of communism about them."[33] Faced with layoffs or reduced wages, many factory workers turned to unions for help. Business owners invariably reacted to strikes by closing down their own operations, generally receiving great public support in the process. The scope of the Panic overwhelmed charitable and humanitarian efforts through benevolent societies, churches, and philanthropy. By November angry unemployed workers in New York City marched menacingly toward Wall Street and City Hall, resulting in such great apprehension that the mayor called out his police force in large numbers. After one protester announced that they must either get jobs or "get bread by violence," the mayor called for both state militia and federal troops to stem the growing confrontation.[34]

The Panic manifested itself differently in the South. People there generally had displayed great hostility to banking institutions—local and national alike—from the beginnings of the Republic. In each major panic to date, most Southerners had focused their wrath on these institutions as the culprits for drying up capital, calling in loans, and ignoring the needs and the pain of ordinary people while protecting the interests of wealthy investors who dominated these establishments. Although plenty of Southern banks had practiced the same ruinous policies as Northern ones—and failed right along with them—most Southerners aimed their anger at Northern institutions and centers of commerce.

Other phenomena in the South gave this panic a peculiar twist. Despite some notable bank failures and contractions of cash, the economy of the region weathered this setback far better than did that of the North. In part because cotton prices remained stable— incredibly—despite increased production, and in part because monied interests in the South tended to roll over profits into the acquisition of land and slaves rather than into more speculative investments, the economic storm proved quite limp and short-lived there. This fact fed the collective conscience of many, who concluded irrationally that the South's superior, slave-based social and economic systems showed their might in this time of crisis. No mutinous, unemployed factory hands roamed Southern city streets. For masters, capital and labor stood united and harmonious in the person of a slave—a worker never cast out during hard times, never left hungry or abandoned like George Fitzhugh's "wage slaves" of the North. While the North suffered through chaos and a slow recovery, white Southerners felt stronger than ever.

Even as the developing panic worried those in the North and offered a smug sense of superiority for many in the South, one of the last sources of national unity before the Civil War occurred in a most unusual way in the summer of 1857 in far-off Utah Territory. Since their inception in New York in 1830, Mormons—members of the Church of Jesus Christ of Latter-Day Saints—had faced ferocious persecution for their belief that they represented a new chosen people of God, vested with a mission to spread the word of His teachings as contained in the Book of Mormon. Driven from one settlement to another, Mormons reached a temporary haven in Nauvoo, Illinois. There Joseph Smith, the church's founder, had a revelation that polygamy was divine, a concept that took even many believers by surprise. Mormons were already known for tight, communal living arrangements—and hated for that, by and large, by "gentiles" (nonbelievers)—but this proved the last straw for the mob that kidnapped and murdered Smith.

Brigham Young emerged as the new leader of the Mormons. Starting in 1846, Young organized a mass migration of the faithful to what became Salt Lake City, and by 1849 church leaders held a constitutional convention to create the sprawling State of Deseret. The Compromise of 1850 and the federal government overrode local desires and interests, instead creating a new territory called Utah, and by 1852, Young had received a federal appointment as its governor. At that point, Young was effectively leader of both spiritual and secular concerns, and he governed accordingly. Whenever federal agents arrived in Salt Lake City, they found themselves unwelcome and ineffectual, and they quickly retreated eastward. After bad crops afflicted the area in 1856, religious revivals, called the Reformation by Mormons, resulted in a wave of popular zeal and renewed commitment to the faith, particularly the "plurality of wives."

Gentiles demanded action. The self-professed champion of popular sovereignty, Stephen Douglas, lashed out, calling Mormons "outlaws and alien enemies" and demanding that Congress "apply the knife and cut out this loathsome, disgusting ulcer." Republicans, who had never subscribed to popular sovereignty and had always believed that Congress could regulate institutions in the territories, enjoyed taunting the Little Giant for his hypocrisy but agreed fundamentally with his sentiments. And even slaveholders considered Mormon practices "revolting alike to civilization and law."[35] From all quarters, Americans demanded that President Buchanan do something about the Mormons.

Buchanan acted promptly and vigorously. He appointed a replacement for Governor Young as well as three new territorial judges and other agents. He also prepared 2,500 well-supplied troops to protect these officials. The War Department only notified Brigham Young of these actions on July 28, after this force had left eastern Kansas for Utah. Mormons reacted quickly and angrily, gathering over 2,000 troops of their own and vowing to fight to the death. At an initial encounter between contending forces on September 7, federal officers assured Mormons that they did not intend to attack, and although both sides averted violence then, over the next several days Mormon raiders attacked federal supplies, burned scores of wagons, and drove off hundreds of cattle and horses. The "Mormon War" ended almost immediately and without any pitched battles when federal forces set off to their winter camp over 100 miles from Salt Lake City.

On September 11, however, a horrible incident occurred in southern Utah, at a place with the bucolic name of Mountain Meadows. An unsuspecting party of about 140 emigrants heading toward California stumbled into the path of overzealous Mormons who were determined to stop incursions by any gentiles. Fate played into the hands of the Mormons as the emigrant party fell victim to an Indian attack. The Mormons offered the besieged travelers safe passage if they would give up their weapons and supplies to the Indians and follow the Mormon group to the nearest city. The sojourners agreed but found themselves escorted directly into a prearranged Indian ambush. Mormons shot the men, and Indians cut down the women and older children with knives and hatchets. Only eighteen infants survived, with 120 adults and children killed. The Mountain Meadows massacre had a profound impact on Brigham Young. During the next few months he concluded that continued conflict would not likely end without tremendous loss of life, so he allowed his successor to assume the governorship the following summer. As spiritual leader of the Mormons, however, Young remained the power behind the throne in Utah, and Buchanan's show of force resulted in only a pyrrhic victory.

Shortly after the bloodshed in Utah, territorial elections took place in Bloody Kansas. On October 5 the free-staters won a decisive victory at the polls, one secured by the vigilance of Robert Walker and his deputies, who threw out thousands of fraudulent proslavery ballots. Having come so far, however, proslavery settlers refused to give up now. On October 19 they met at Lecompton and drafted their own constitution, knowing full well that it could not survive a fair up or down vote. So they rigged the election. Voters could opt for the constitution "with slavery" or for the "constitution without slavery" that nevertheless explicitly stated that the right to slaves already in Kansas, and their descendants, would remain in effect. Free-state advocates saw the impending fraud for what it was, as did the intrepid Governor Walker. He dashed back to Washington, DC, and personally told Buchanan about the looming deception. The president, buckling again to his Southerner-heavy cabinet and to his own perception of Democratic Party interests, withdrew his public pledge of support for Walker, who reacted by resigning his office on December 17. Without his steady hand few free-staters even bothered to turn out on election day, December 21. It did not matter. The constitution "with slavery" received 6,226 votes (2,720 of which later proved fraudulent); the constitution "without slavery" gained but 569.

Free-staters had already convinced acting governor Frederick P. Stanton to convene the assembly early, on December 7. The legislature scheduled their own constitutional election for January 4, 1858. On that date, and with renewed support for honest voting by Stanton, 138 men cast their votes for the constitution "with slavery," twenty-four for the one "without slavery," and a resounding 10,226 rejected the Lecompton constitution altogether.

Buchanan, straining to end the chaos in the West and bowing yet again to the Southern wing of his party, announced his support for the Lecompton constitution. Stephen Douglas spurned his president and party leader by rejecting it. Douglas, the champion of popular sovereignty, explained that whether a territory voted slavery up or down "is none of my business and none of yours." But he could not watch passively as a minority, meeting without congressional approval or by authority of a territorial governor, tried to impose its will on a majority. That was not democracy. "If this constitution is to be forced down our throats, in violation of the fundamental principles of free government, under a mode of submission that is a mockery and insult, I will resist it to the last," he vowed.[36]

Radical Republican congressman Benjamin Wade of Ohio captured the moment for many in his party. Wryly commenting on Douglas's defiance of Buchanan, Wade said, "I have never seen a slave insurrection before." Some moderate Republicans suddenly considered creating a fusion

Benjamin F. Wade
Library of Congress

party with their erstwhile adversary, Douglas, but all Republicans relished the significant and damaging cleavage that had emerged in the other party. Most Republicans also saw in the Democratic split over Lecompton the logical absurdity of Douglas's "great principle"—that the people in territories, rather than Congress, should make the decisions about slavery. But for the time, Wade explained to Salmon P. Chase, Douglas "seems just now to be doing a good business for us [so] we think it best to let him have the field & fort."[37]

The absurdities and chaos associated with Lecompton and the split in the Democratic Party caused some Southerners—even a few radical ones—to pause. Albert G. Brown of Mississippi feared that Lecompton "will establish a principle which may be carried out to the utter destruction of all popular government."[38] James Henry

Hammond, recently elected to the U.S. Senate from South Carolina, decided to both "vote with *indifference*" for Lecompton and to "*repudiate* the question as a test on slavery."[39]

Southern extremists, of course, cried foul. Determined to have Lecompton and slavery prevail, they abandoned Douglas more quickly than they had rallied toward him in 1854, for what they considered his betrayal on Kansas. Hammond's close friend, author and political radical William Gilmore Simms, scolded Hammond for his willingness to bend. "You *cannot* vote with indifference upon a subject which, you admit, involves the honour, if not the safety of the South," Simms demanded.[40] Senator Judah P. Benjamin of Louisiana concluded that the real lesson of Lecompton was that "Kansas shall never be admitted as a slaveholding State ... not even ... if the whole people of the territory should establish a Constitution recognizing that institution."[41] Just before his death, House member John Quitman told a young new colleague from South Carolina, "The test struggle is before us. . . . It will soon be seen whether we will maintain our equality [in the Union] or sink into a degrading subserviency to political masters."[42]

As a friend and confidant of President Buchanan, Governor Wise of Virginia was deeply troubled in the waning days of 1857. Wise explained to Douglas, "I know that a conspiracy exists to drive the northern Democracy from the Administration on the Kansas [issue] and the Southern from it on the filibustering Walker affair."[43] Sure enough, as though both sectional tensions and conspiracy theories had not spread apprehension enough, in November 1857, William Walker again set sail for Nicaragua, this time with 270 men from Mobile. But before Walker's ship made its way to the interior of Nicaragua via the San Juan River, Commodore Hiram Paulding of the U.S. Navy stopped him and, citing American neutrality laws, arrested Walker and sent him to New York. There authorities escorted Walker to Washington and delivered him to Secretary of State Lewis Cass. Reasoning that Paulding had no jurisdiction on foreign soil, Cass dropped all charges. President Buchanan, as always trying to please everyone, criticized Paulding for his "grave error" while simultaneously suggesting that patriotic motives had led the commodore to try to save Nicaragua from "a dreaded invasion."[44]

Across the South, anger and protests broke out in response to Walker's apprehension. Public meetings denounced Buchanan and Paulding while they lauded William Walker, who now truly seemed a man of destiny. In New Orleans one protest turned violent; in Alabama, Tennessee, Texas, and Virginia, state assemblies passed anti-Paulding resolutions; and in Washington, DC, senators from Dixie defended Walker and denounced Paulding.

As for William Walker, he looked forward to 1858 with plans for yet another regional tour and recruiting effort for his third try to take and keep Nicaragua. For Buchanan, his stance on *Dred Scott*, Lecompton, Robert J. Walker, and William Walker—and just about everything that he touched—had severely crippled his effectiveness as president in his first nine months in office. One of his early supporters ended the year complaining, "I had considerable hopes of Mr. Buchanan—I really thought he was a statesman—but I have now come to the settled conclusion that he is just the d—dest old fool that has ever occupied the Presidential chair. He has deliberately walked overboard with his eyes open—let him drown, for he must."[45] Despite the fears of Henry Wise, Southern Democrats would rally toward Buchanan in 1858, if only for lack of another choice, while Republicans finally saw brighter days ahead and a chance to break the Democrats' control of Congress.

NOTES*

1. C. Peter Ripley et al., eds., *Black Abolitionist Papers*, 5 vols. (Chapel Hill: University of North Carolina Press, 1985–1992), 4:358–61.

2. Stephen Oates, *To Purge This Land with Blood: A Biography of John Brown* (New York: Harper & Row, 1970), 190.

3. Kenneth M. Stampp, *America in 1857: A Nation on the Brink* (New York: Oxford University Press, 1990), 48.

4. Ibid., 49.

5. Ibid., 64.

6. Ibid., 87.

7. Ibid., 92.

8. Ibid., 95.

9. Ibid., 96.

10. Michael A. Morrison, *Slavery and the American West: The Eclipse of Manifest Destiny and the Coming of the Civil War* (Chapel Hill: University of North Carolina Press, 1997), 194.

11. David M. Potter, *The Impending Crisis, 1848–1861* (New York: Harper & Row, 1976), 284.

12. Morrison, *Slavery and the American West*, 189, 191.

13. Roy P. Basler et al., eds., *The Collected Works of Abraham Lincoln*, 9 vols. (New Brunswick, NJ: Rutgers University Press, 1953), 2:406.

14. Ripley, *Black Abolitionist Papers*, 362–65; 364 (quote).

*Emphasis in all quotations is that of the original authors.

15. Morrison, *Slavery and the American West*, 196.

16. Stampp, *America in 1857*, 161.

17. Morrison, *Slavery and the American West*, 196.

18. James M. McPherson, *Battle Cry of Freedom: The Civil War Era* (New York: Oxford University Press, 1988), 164.

19. *Montgomery Advertiser*, July 1, 1857.

20. Stampp, *America in 1857*, 161.

21. Robert E. May, *The Southern Dream of a Caribbean Empire, 1854–1861* (Athens: University of Georgia Press, 1989), 113.

22. *De Bow's Review* 23 (September 1857): 230–31.

23. Ibid. 22 (June 1857): 663–64.

24. Stampp, *America in 1857*, 189.

25. Ibid., 117.

26. George Frederick Holmes and Edmund Ruffin, quoted in Drew G. Faust, ed., *The Ideology of Slavery: Proslavery Thought in the Antebellum South, 1830–1860* (Baton Rouge: Louisiana State University Press, 1981), 18.

27. Faust, *Ideology of Slavery*, 18.

28. Charles Reagan Wilson et al., eds., *Encyclopedia of Southern Culture* (Chapel Hill: University of North Carolina Press, 1989), 1355.

29. Clement Eaton, *The Mind of the Old South* (Baton Rouge: Louisiana State University Press, 1964), 157.

30. Ibid.

31. Stampp, *America in 1857*, 140.

32. Ibid., 140–41.

33. *Washington National Era*, quoted in ibid., 227.

34. Stampp, *America in 1857*, 229.

35. Ibid., 200.

36. Ibid., 302.

37. Hans Trefousse, *The Radical Republicans: Lincoln's Vanguard for Racial Justice* (New York: Knopf, 1969), 112–13.

38. Morrison, *Slavery and the American West*, 202.

39. Drew Gilpin Faust, *James Henry Hammond and the Old South: A Design for Mastery* (Baton Rouge: Louisiana State University Press, 1982), 344–45.

40. Ibid., 345.

41. Morrison, *Slavery and the American West*, 202.

42. Eric H. Walther, *The Fire-Eaters* (Baton Rouge: Louisiana State University Press, 1992), 110.

43. Craig M. Simpson, *A Good Southerner: The Life of Henry A. Wise of Virginia* (Chapel Hill: University of North Carolina Press, 1985), 165.

44. May, *Southern Dream*, 114.

45. B. B. French, quoted in Allan Nevins, *The Emergence of Lincoln*, 2 vols. (New York: Scribner, 1950), 1:239.

CHAPTER SEVEN

1858

"It Is an Irrepressible Conflict"

ON JANUARY 18, William Walker arrived in Montgomery, Alabama, to seek support for his third effort to take Nicaragua. Pandering directly to the supporters of slavery in the very heart of the Cotton Belt, the charismatic and outrageous "president" enthralled a large crowd for over an hour with harrowing accounts of his deeds in the sultry tropics. As he concluded, the crowd called upon their hometown hero, fire-eater William Lowndes Yancey, to add some remarks. Obliging as always, Yancey condemned Commodore Hiram Paulding's recent arrest of Walker as "tyrannical and unjustifiable" and defended Walker's "enterprise as the cause of the South." In his harshest public criticism of President Buchanan, Yancey attacked the "old woman policy of the administration in apologizing for Paulding" and concluded that, however valuable Buchanan remained as a friend of slavery in Kansas, his arrest of William Walker proved "a fatal blow" to his ability to help the South.[1] For the next few weeks, as Walker continued his Southern tour, Yancey remained steadfast in his public declarations that the fates of Kansas and Nicaragua were one and that Buchanan had lost the trust of the South. "The time has passed for little men to lead and control great parties," he demanded. "The mighty interests at stake have attracted the attention of the people, and parties of late shriveled up under the burning indignation of the Southern masses."[2]

In Congress all signs pointed toward victory for the Lecompton constitution in January. When the Thirty-fifth Congress had assembled for its first session the month before, it selected two slaveholders as its leaders, Benjamin Fitzpatrick of Alabama as president pro tempore of the Senate and James L. Orr of South Carolina as House Speaker. Democrats had a strong majority in both houses—128 to 92 Republicans (and four Know-Nothings) in the House, 39 to 20 to 5 in the Senate. Plus, the president of the United

States endorsed Lecompton. On February 2, James Buchanan sent the Lecompton bill and his support to Capitol Hill. The president asserted that Kansas Territory, with its mere 200 or so slaves, was "at this moment as much a slave state as Georgia or South Carolina."[3]

Irate antislavery Northerners rallied behind Stephen A. Douglas, the man whom they despised and did not trust from 1854 until December 1857. The assemblies of New Jersey, Michigan, and Rhode Island passed resolutions condemning Lecompton, and the Ohio legislature actually instructed one of the state's senators to vote against it. Rumblings against the measure appeared across the North in newspaper editorials, and even the governor of Buchanan's home state, Pennsylvania, joined the war cry against him. Buchanan's old friend, Governor Henry A. Wise of Virginia, publicly turned against the president and toward Douglas. Like Wise, even scattered Southern newspapers now opposed Lecompton, if only out of the fear that if it passed it could make the Republican Party the big winner by drawing to it more discontented Northern Democrats. This all took a toll on the embattled president, whose health began to suffer.

When Douglas spoke on the Senate floor, he centered his case around his "great principle" of popular sovereignty, of local, democratic rule. He challenged Lecompton's mostly Southern supporters directly and with impeccable logic. "Reverse the case," he posited. "Would Southern men, if a convention of freesoilers should make a constitution, and allow you to vote for it, but not against it, and then attempt to force that constitution on a slaveholding people against their will, would Southern gentlemen have submitted to such an outrage?"[4]

Jefferson Davis and other Southerners now considered the Democratic Party all but destroyed as a national institution and placed the blame squarely on the shoulders of Douglas. To Davis popular sovereignty had proven "a siren's song . . . a thing shadowy and fleeting, changing its color as often as the chameleon." Senator James Mason of Virginia agreed, saying of Douglas and his popular sovereignty, "You promised us bread, and you have given us a stone; you promised us a fish, and you have given us a serpent; we thought you had given us a substantial right, and you have given us the most evanescent shadow and delusion."[5]

James H. Hammond gave himself more time to reply to Douglas. On March 4 the Carolinian delivered the most memorable speech of his life. In contrast to Douglas, Hammond argued that the legitimacy of the Lecompton constitution did not truly make up the central issue of the debate. "The true object of the discussion . . . is to agitate the question of slavery" and thereby destroy the unity of the Democratic Party by antagonizing its Northern members. Hammond warned that Republicans' actions belied their assurances of Southern rights and that their growing strength boded ill for the South. "We cannot rely on your faith when you have the power," he said. But the political power of the North, according to Hammond, paled in comparison to sources of strength in the South. With all whites supposedly unified in their mastery over happy and productive slaves, a combined militia force of one million, and

James M. Mason
Library of Congress

the tremendous productivity of her plantations, the South's economy and society proved superior to those of the North in every way. And if push came to shove, all the South had to do was withhold shipments of cotton from the factories of the North—or from Europe, for that matter—and utter destruction of their economies would rapidly ensue. Defiantly, Hammond declared, "No, you dare not make war on cotton. No power on earth dares make war on it. Cotton *is* King."[6]

Facing united Republican opposition and Stephen Douglas's spirited stand against Lecompton, President Buchanan used every weapon he had in order to prevail, especially political appointments to reward friends and hurt foes. The few Southerners who faced the fact of Lecompton's illegitimacy, such as the staunch unionist from Texas, Senator Sam Houston, in the end capitulated to his state assembly's directive to support the administration bill. Enough Northern Democrats toed Buchanan's line so that on March 23 the Senate accepted the proslavery constitution by a vote of 38 to 25.

In the House, Alexander H. Stephens, a former Whig from Georgia who had helped shepherd the Kansas-Nebraska Bill into law in

1854, again served as the floor leader for the administration. He had plenty of help. William Porcher Miles, a newly elected representative from the Charleston district of South Carolina, leaped into the fray. He acknowledged that climate and soil likely forbade a significant development of slavery in Kansas, where few slaves now resided, but explained that "the issue has been made, the battle joined; and though it be on an abstract principle which does not at present promise to result in any practical advantage to us, I am willing to stand by the guns and fight it out." Should the North defeat Lecompton, Miles predicted, Southerners would be forced to see "that they have no hope in the future of maintaining their equality in the Union. It will then compel them to ponder the question whether they will choose subjugation or resistance, colonial vassalage or separate independence."[7]

On February 4 the House debate grew so superheated that thirty or more congressmen actually came to blows, literally fighting it out over Kansas, divided precisely along sectional lines. "All things here are tending to bring my mind to the conclusion that the Union cannot or will not last long," Stephens penned sadly to his brother. The diminutive and sickly Georgian muttered, "I am wearing out my life for nothing."[8]

The brawl left an atmosphere of hostility that lingered in the House chamber for days. On February 6 at 2:00 A.M., as the interminable debate continued, a Republican from Pennsylvania named Galusha Grow wandered the quiet but tense House floor to confer with a Pennsylvania Democrat, separated from Grow by the center aisle. Probably not thinking at that late hour about the congressional etiquette that called for Republican and Democratic members to address the Speaker from their respective sides of the chamber, when Grow heard another colleague issue a motion he did not like, he stated his objection.

Laurence Keitt, the South Carolina Democrat who had aided Preston Brooks in his assault on Sumner two years before, had been sleeping restlessly, stretched across two desks, one shoe dangling from his toes. Awakened and groggy but aware of Grow's breach of protocol, Keitt asked angrily, "What business have you on this side, anyhow?" Grow responded, "This is a free hall and I have a right to object from any part of it, when I choose." Taking the challenge, Keitt retorted, "I'll show you, you d—d Black Republican puppy!" Taking the dare, Grow shouted back, "You may think me what you please, Mr. Keitt; but let me tell you that no nigger-driver shall come up here from his plantation and crack his lash about *my* ears!" An infuriated Keitt snarled, "We'll see about that!" as he leapt toward Grow, grabbing his victim's throat.[9] Six other congressmen joined the tumult, which finally ended in laughter when one member tried to lift another by the hair, the better to punch him in the face, only to fall back, clutching his colleague's wig.

Although this incident ended without lasting harm to life or limb of the combatants, the violence that Brooks and Keitt had brought to the Senate now established its potential for the same in both houses of Congress. In fact, over the next two years, congressmen and senators began arming themselves on the very floor of the national legislature, a body designed to protect liberty and mitigate conflict. During one contentious debate a pistol fell out of the pocket of a congressman from New York. Iowa senator James W. Grimes reported, "The members on both sides are mostly armed with deadly weapons, and it is said that the friends of each are armed in the galleries." South Carolina's James H. Hammond concurred, telling a friend, "The only persons who do not have a revolver and a knife are those who have two revolvers."[10]

Despite the bitter hostility, President Buchanan insisted upon ramming the Lecompton constitution through the House "naked."[11] Northern public opinion left no mistake in the minds of House members that the people of that section had no taste for Lecompton and that most demanded its defeat. The *Pittsburgh Morning Post* complained, "We have had to swallow many things which are disgraceful to us, for the sake of preserving the first great principle of democratic unity." A desperately ill Thomas Harris of Illinois was determined to defeat the bill, even if it meant his life; he had friends carry him onto the House floor and lower him into his seat for the vote (he died nine months later). Some twenty other Northern Democrats vowed to stand resolutely with him and work with Republicans to stop Lecompton. On March 23 these Democrats offered to support Lecompton if Buchanan and the others agreed to add a provision to the bill allowing the people of Kansas to change their constitution at any time (the original bill proscribed that until 1864). Buchanan refused to budge.

Before the victory of Lecompton in the Senate, Kentucky's John J. Crittenden, the successor to Henry Clay, had tried his own hand at compromise by offering an amendment that would have resubmitted the constitution to the people of Kansas under meticulous, watchful supervision to avoid fraud. Although the Senate had rejected the plan, House members, under the leadership of Democrat William Montgomery of Pennsylvania, now championed the idea. On April 1 the Crittenden-Montgomery resolution passed the House, 120 to 112. Because the two chambers passed different measures, the issue remained unresolved.

As though Kansas had not already grown complicated enough, yet another complex transmutation occurred. William H. English, a Democratic representative from Indiana, tried to break the impasse. A quirk in the original Lecompton proposal stated that the federal government should grant Kansas 23 million acres of public land, roughly six times the normal allocation to a new state. English proposed that Congress accept the proslavery Lecompton constitution but append a provision that linked keeping slavery with forfeiting the larger land grant. Furthermore, should Kansans reject the congressional version, they would not be allowed to apply again for statehood until a census revealed that their population reached 90,000—which meant waiting for 1860 at the earliest.

The *Illinois State Journal*, a Republican paper, blurted out, "This project is the biggest swindle yet." Radical Republican Benjamin Wade of Ohio agreed, calling the English bill "a fraud" and "trickery" because it made the only immediate option for statehood one that included slavery. Even Stephen Douglas recoiled in horror. William H. Seward derided it as "an act of immorality in legislation, deserving of severe censure."[12]

Enough Northern Democrats finally caved in to the pressures of party politics to pass the English bill on April 30, by 31 to 22 in the Senate and 112 to 103 in the House. Kansans voted yet again on August 2, theoretically on a referendum on the land grant, but for most, in fact, this was perhaps their last chance to reject slavery. They annihilated the Congressional bill and slavery with it, 11,300 to only 1,788. Although violence in the territory remained simmering, resolution had come at last. By 1860 only two slaves lived in the territory. In 1861, Kansas entered the Union as a free state, shortly after eleven slaveholding states seceded and formed a new republic.

As with so many prior compromises, the end of the Kansas debate satisfied few. Buchanan not only claimed victory but also actually wrote to Representative English to thank him for shepherding the bill through Congress. Free-Soilers and abolitionists rejoiced that matters had not become worse, yet they had to wait three more years to finally eradicate slavery in Kansas. Southern extremists tried desperately to claim that slavery had not in fact faced rejection and only the land grant issue had, but privately most gave up on Buchanan and his ability to protect their interests. Even after all was said and done, William Porcher Miles wrote to Senator Hammond that battling over slavery in the arid plains of Kansas "was a bad way . . . of preparing the Southern mind for a war to the knife." Then he groaned, "Eternal and infernal Kansas—Kansas—Kansas!"[13]

When it came to waging war in Kansas and refusing to give up, one of the most conspicuous characters in the drama remained "Old Osawatomie," or John Brown. Back in 1857 he had begun discussing a plan to deliver a death blow to slavery in the states, rather than simply continuing guerrilla efforts at keeping it from spreading to Kansas. He told one supporter of his idea to take twenty to fifty men and "beat up a slave quarter in Virginia," probably near the federal arsenal at Harpers Ferry.[14] From there, Brown reasoned, slaves would flock to him and in turn he would arm them for nothing less than a race war against Southern whites. After destroying slavery in Virginia, Brown imagined that this black army would continue to grow as it moved steadily southwest along the Appalachian Mountains through Tennessee and into northern Alabama. His inspiration, he freely told any who listened, came directly from God.

On January 28, 1858, Brown paid a visit to Frederick Douglass, staying in Douglass's home in Rochester, New York. There Brown composed a constitution for a new political order that would rise from the ashes of the old United States of America, destined and damned in Brown's mind for extinction when the race war he would start fully developed. He needed money again, for the purchase of weapons and supplies, so he turned once more to his associates Gerrit Smith, Thomas Wentworth Higginson, Franklin Sanborn, Samuel Gridley Howe, Theodore Parker, and George Luther Stearns. They responded eagerly and without any concern for detail. Sanborn explained to Higginson that Brown had a plan "but does not say what it is. Still I have confidence enough in him to trust him with the moderate sum he asks for . . . without knowing his plan."[15] Once fully apprised of the details, Sanborn labored in vain to dissuade Brown from a plot clearly doomed to fail. Unable to persuade Brown to give up his scheme, Sanborn grumbled that Brown left him and his other five associates "the alternatives of betrayal, desertion, or support. We chose the last."[16]

Brown wound his way through New York, back west to Iowa, and eventually to St. Catherines, a town in Canada with a large population of fugitive slaves. He gathered men, money, and arms as he went. Upon his arrival north of the border, he met Harriet Tubman and persuaded the famous leader of the Underground Railroad to support his effort. From there Brown traveled to Chatham, about 45 miles east of Detroit in what was called Canada West (Ontario), arriving on May 8. He hoped that his six financial backers would turn up as well as Frederick Douglass and Tubman, all of whom he had invited, but none of them came. To those who did attend, including several black leaders from the area and from Detroit, Brown provided copies of his "Provisional Constitution and Ordinances for the people of the United States." All present approved the document, selected Brown as commander in chief, and adopted as their own the flag of the revolutionaries of 1776.

When Brown explained his plan to Frederick Douglass, the famed abolitionist recoiled. Although he was philosophically opposed neither to slave insurrection nor to violence in general, Douglass could not help but grasp both the insanity of the plot and the madness of his brutal houseguest. Through his own experiences as a slave in Maryland and information he had gathered ever since, Douglass did not doubt the willingness or the ability of African Americans to strike a blow for their own liberation, but he understood two critical factors that Brown had never even contemplated. For one, after hundreds of years of oppression, occasional raised hopes, and countless broken promises by whites, many blacks had become distrustful of white people's plans for blacks. Second, and more important to Douglass, any sane slave could see that Brown's maniacal plan must fail and result in the deaths of all who joined him.

Generally, most black abolitionists fully stood with Douglass, sympathetic but unwilling to support Brown's scheme. Two exceptions were James N. Gloucester, a minister in Brooklyn, and his wife, Elizabeth. Gloucester enthusiastically endorsed Brown's plan to attack "that *hellish system*, against which every honest man and *woman* in the Land should be combined," and sent $25 to Brown for his war against "*the all damnable foe*." Elizabeth Gloucester, the breadwinner in the marriage with her own furniture store and real estate dealings, shared her husband's zealousness. Director of the Colored Orphan Asylum of Brooklyn and an advocate for adult education for blacks, Elizabeth Gloucester sent her own $25 contribution to Brown for "the good of your cause."[17]

While Brown plotted in the North and Canada to create some sort of new nation, Southern radicals gathered in Montgomery, Alabama, to stage a rally of sorts for disunion and Southern nationhood. The Southern Commercial Convention for 1858 assembled as planned in the hometown of secessionist William L. Yancey. Other fire-eaters, including James D. B. De Bow, the main speaker from the previous meeting, labored doggedly to make the Montgomery convention the most politicized and radicalized yet. To De Bow from George Fitzhugh came the injunction, "Stick to the [African] Slave Trade." Yancey wrote to De Bow stating that the single theme he wished to address was "the federal statutes that outlawed the slave trade."[18]

Yancey stood alongside Robert Barnwell Rhett as the premier disunionists of the South. Like Rhett, Yancey had led the secession efforts that emerged during debates concerning the Compromise of 1850, and he was also bitterly disappointed in the failure of secession and disgusted in general by political parties and their compromises on principle. After spending portions of two terms in Congress before the Mexican War, Yancey had abandoned seeking public office in favor of working in state and local organizations to fan the fires of resistance to any Northern attack on slavery. The Commercial Convention served as a perfect forum for him, especially after De Bow's efforts at Knoxville in 1857. Rhett traveled to Alabama for the occasion, as did Virginia's foremost fire-eater, the old, long-haired Edmund Ruffin, and scores of other radicals from far and near, numbering 710 delegates by May 10. And the next day, as though the affair were not radical enough already, William Walker returned and received an invitation to join the proceedings.

As Yancey began his two-day oration, any semblance of a commercial convention vanished, and instead a great secession rally began. Yancey denounced "this eternal cry of Union." In a rare public critique of Lecompton, Yancey explained that Kansas had proven that politics in the Union had degenerated to the point that "we have to get by trick what we ought to demand as freemen." Party politics and forced alliances with Northerners like Douglas and Buchanan had brought ruin to the South. "We have been degraded, sorely degraded," Yancey lamented, since the time they had accepted the Missouri Compromise of 1820 that banned the spread of slavery to most of the Louisiana Territory.

Yancey remained focused on degradation and dishonor as he turned to the African slave trade. He logically argued, "If slavery be right, it is right to buy and sell slaves, and to buy where we can make the purchase most profitable." And yet, current federal laws now forced Southerners in the federal navy into the position of "catching, imprisoning, and degrading a southern man who shall dare to buy a negro upon the coast of Africa." Yancey cunningly denied calling for a reopening of the slave trade—even while promising untold riches and power for the South should the trade resume—and carefully kept honor at the center of his speech. He argued that "the system of slavery is founded upon high and immutable laws" and that the remarks of those who condemned the Atlantic slave trade as a violation of Christendom instead represented "the opinion of devildom." The solution was obvious to Yancey. "Let us then wipe from our statute book this mark of Cain which our enemies have placed there," he cried, to thunderous applause and cheers.[19]

Edmund Ruffin was thrilled. The iconoclastic Virginian who had published endless articles promoting both slavery and secession had just witnessed firsthand Yancey's famous ability to sway the masses through his voice. The soft-spoken Ruffin addressed the convention himself to call upon "all true and patriotic men of the South" to avoid "unprincipled demagogues and greedy and interested office seekers" and instead to remain in touch with one another "for consultation, for concert, and for combined action."[20]

Official business of the convention ended with resolutions to address the slave trade again at next year's meeting in Vicksburg, Mississippi, but several of the most radical delegates joined Yancey at his home for dinner and more political conversation. There Ruffin learned from William Walker that he had 700 men armed and ready for his next foray into Nicaragua. But more important to Ruffin was ample confirmation that Yancey could fulfill an old idea of his —to unite ordinary Southerners, beyond the confines of partisan institutions, to achieve secession. In person and by mail the two quickly devised their scheme for a League of United Southerners, modeled after citizens' committees of correspondence prior to the American Revolution.

The two launched the effort in June, from Virginia and Alabama, respectively. Southerners would form leagues across the region, and Ruffin and Yancey sketched out plans for a general council with delegates from each league. Members would support no politician who found party allegiance more important than absolute dedication to Southern interests. As Yancey explained to a comrade, James Slaughter, "No National Party can save us; no Sectional Party can do it. But if we could do as our fathers did, organize Committees of Safety all over the cotton States . . . we shall fire the Southern heart—instruct the Southern mind—give courage to each other, and at the proper moment, by one, organized, concerted action, we can precipitate the cotton States into a Revolution."[21]

Slaughter allowed the press to publish Yancey's letter, and it produced a tidal wave. Extremists like Rhett hailed the Slaughter letter in the *Charleston Mercury*. Stephen Douglas blasted it on the floor of the Senate as a design to destroy both the Democratic Party and the Union. Newspaper editor Horace Greeley called it the Scarlet Letter in his influential *New York Tribune*, and Northerners who had already suspected a Slave Power conspiracy to destroy the country now found horrible confirmation of their nightmare.

Although Edmund Ruffin's interests and participation with the league waned, Yancey spent months traveling through Alabama to help start new league chapters. By early summer, Yancey and the league drew the anger of Roger A. Pryor, editor of the influential *Richmond South*. Pryor viciously attacked Yancey and the League of United Southerners, both because Pryor considered it a thin disguise for secession and because in the Slaughter letter Yancey expressed his willingness to leave Virginia behind once the Southern "revolution" had begun. Yancey fired back on the stump and in long public letters to Pryor. Then, less because of the newspaper attack from Virginia than from a sudden illness, Yancey abruptly curtailed his activities, and the whole league movement fizzled.

Several other Virginia newspapers took up a crusade of their own in June, targeting Anthony Burns, the fugitive slave apprehended in Boston in 1854. Some of the same Bostonians who had violently defied efforts to apprehend Burns later raised money to purchase Burns from his master in Virginia and set him free. Burns then studied diligently at Oberlin College until 1857 and continued his education at the Fairmount Theological Seminary outside Cincinnati. There a shocked Anthony Burns learned that several newspapers in Virginia had printed stories claiming that he recently was arrested for robbery, convicted, and jailed in Massachusetts. It was all a lie without the slightest substance, doubtless told by proslavery men who believed that all free blacks, sooner or later, would turn to vice or crime, poverty or insanity, as James De Bow had strived to prove in 1853 with his *Compendium* to the Census report.

Seeking help to refute this fantasy, Burns turned to William Lloyd Garrison. Through Garrison's *The Liberator*, Burns fired back. He called white Southerners "liars, Cradlerobbers, Thieves, Murderers, Idolators and Whoremongers" and argued that it was they who ought to be arrested and jailed. Meanwhile, Burns continued his studies and prepared to launch a tour during the coming fall, the "Grand Moving Mirror of Slavery," a traveling exhibit designed both to inform Northerners about "Startling and Thrilling Incidents, degradation & Horrors of American Slavery" and to help sell copies of his autobiography so that he could pay for the remainder of his education.[22] Burns in fact completed his studies and obtained a pastorate in Indianapolis, but racial prejudice there convinced him to leave the United States altogether. In 1860 he moved to St. Catherines in Canada West, where he worked at the Zion Baptist Church until his death in 1862.

During the summer a chronically ill Jefferson Davis took his doctor's advice and left the oppressive heat of the Deep South for the coolness of New England. The Mississippi senator, former congressman, war hero, and secretary of war received a proper celebrity's welcome as he ventured from New York to Boston and on to Portland and Augusta, Maine. He even received an honorary degree from Bowdoin College, known for its antislavery atmosphere and alma mater to men like Free-Soil senator John P. Hale and African American abolitionist John Brown Russworm. His health and spirits revived, Davis publicly remarked, "The whole Confederacy is my country, and to the innermost fibers of my heart I love it all, every part. . . . I could not if I would, and would not if I could, dwarf myself to mere sectionality. My first allegiance is to the State of which I am a citizen, and to which by affection and association I am personally bound; but this does not obstruct the perception of your greatness."[23]

When Southern newspapers got wind of this, they went berserk. "Jefferson Davis gone to Boston," the *Charleston Mercury* reported with double meaning. Its editors called Davis a "pitiable spectacle of human weakness" and "a signal example of Southern defection. . . . The Jefferson Davis that we loved to honor is no more," they concluded, suggesting that Davis "not only go to Boston but stay there." A Georgia newspaper asserted that "the fleshpots of place have seduced [Davis] from the paths of States Rights." One Mississippi newspaper sneered that Davis "loves the yankees, calls abolitionists brothers," and another from his own state charged that Davis had become one of the "can't-be-kicked-out-of-the-Union-gentlemen." As Daniel Webster had learned in 1850, so now Jefferson Davis learned that moderation and brotherhood could endanger one's political career.[24]

On June 16 a man whose destiny was linked with Jeff Davis found his fortunes suddenly rising. After bowing out to Lyman Trumbull in 1855, Abraham Lincoln now accepted the nomination of Illinois Republicans to challenge Stephen Douglas for the U.S. Senate. He announced his candidacy with the "House Divided" speech. Referring to growing sectional conflict, Lincoln predicted:

> In *my* opinion, it will not cease, until a *crisis* shall have been reached, and passed. "A house divided against itself cannot stand." I believe this government cannot endure, permanently half *slave* and half *free*. I do not expect the Union to be *dissolved*—I do not expect the house to *fall*—but I *do* expect it will cease to be divided. It will become *all* one thing, or *all* the other. Either the *opponents* of slavery, will arrest the further spread of it, and place it . . . in [the] course of ultimate extinction; or its *advocates* will push it forward, till it shall become alike lawful in *all* the States, *old* as well as *new*—*North* as well as *South*.[25]

Lincoln explained that a vast Slave Power conspiracy existed, one that involved Northern accomplices, determined to impose slavery upon the free states and territories. Had not Douglas sponsored the Kansas-Nebraska Bill, which allowed slavery the potential to spread as far north as the Canadian border, and had not the Northerner Franklin Pierce signed that into law? Lincoln pointed out that in the *Dred Scott* decision, Southerner Roger Taney had effectively affirmed the right of slaveholders to travel to free states and territories with their slaves and denied Congress the authority to stop it from spreading, and that Buchanan had supported these judgments. Lincoln concluded, "We find it impossible not to *believe* that Stephen and Franklin and Roger and James all understood one another from the beginning, and all worked upon a common *plan* or *draft* drawn up before the first lick was struck."[26] Just as the *Dred Scott* decision simultaneously upset Republicans and energized white Southerners, the House Divided speech became a source of Republican unity and a lightning rod for the gravest fears of whites in the South.

Douglas remained by far the most famous politician in the West, if not in the entire country. He had little to gain in a direct challenge with any opponent, but the democratic politics of the nation—

and especially Illinois—virtually demanded some head-to-head campaigning. Although state assemblies still selected senators, candidates could often count on popular pressure on legislators to influence their selection. Both Lincoln and the Little Giant agreed to participate in seven debates across the state between August and October. Douglas remained the champion of popular sovereignty. Lincoln stood ready to attack him and his "great principle" as well as to continue to convince the public that Douglas played a pivotal role in the vast Slave Power conspiracy. Lincoln also had the burden of proving to voters whether, in the wake of the English bill and rejection of slavery in Kansas, the Republican Party still had any purpose left. Douglas happily attacked Lincoln and his party as superfluous and as friends of African Americans and advocates of racial equality, the latter a flatly false charge. Most people in Illinois simultaneously opposed both slavery and emancipation, the latter mostly out of fear of a mass migration of free blacks moving northward and "amalgamating," socially and sexually, with whites.

The first debate took place at Ottawa, a staunchly Republican town that had helped elect an abolitionist to Congress. But Douglas came out fighting, striving to depict Lincoln and his party as extremists who endangered a peaceful resolution of the territorial question. Douglas pounded away relentlessly, asking if his opponent rejected the admission of new states "with such a Constitution as the people of that state may see fit to make." Douglas also asked if Lincoln favored repeal of the Fugitive Slave Act and if he desired abolishing slavery in the federal capital.[27] A defensive and tentative Lincoln did not even answer many of Douglas's queries. At one point, in an effort to prove his moderation, he read lengthy excerpts from a speech he gave in 1854 in which he declared that if he had all the power in the world, he simply would not know what to do about ending slavery. The off-balance Lincoln even finished his speech with fifteen minutes to spare. The Democratic press spared Lincoln nothing. The *Chicago Times* wrote, "Lincoln's Heart Fails Him! Lincoln's Legs Fail Him! Lincoln's Tongue Fails Him!" Although more impartial observers concluded that the event was more balanced, and most Republicans felt some satisfaction, Lincoln himself, frequently modest and always demanding of himself, penned an editorial to the *Urbana Union*: "Douglas and I, for the first time this canvass, crossed swords here yesterday; the fire flew some, and I am glad to know I am yet alive."[28]

Appearances did nothing to help Lincoln. While Douglas toured the state on a train specially equipped for entertaining, and the senator dressed immaculately in a blue suit with silver buttons and a crisp linen shirt, the tall, gangly Lincoln traveled simply and wore, according to a staunch supporter, "a rusty frock-coat with sleeves that should have been longer" and black pants that "permitted a very full view of his large feet."[29] Simply put, Douglas *looked* like a powerful and accomplished senator, while Lincoln looked like the self-made prairie lawyer that he was.

Lincoln's supporters adamantly urged him to take a more aggressive approach for the next debate, at Freeport. One group of Republicans advised him, "Don't act the *defensive* at all . . . hold Doug up as a traitor and conspirator, a proslavery, bamboozling demagogue."[30] Lincoln agreed, turning the table on the Little Giant by demanding that Douglas answer several of his own questions, the most important of which was, in light of *Dred Scott*, how people of any territory could prohibit slavery if Congress had no power to do so.

Douglas answered precisely as Lincoln had expected. "Slavery cannot exist a day or an hour anywhere, unless it is supported by local police regulations," Douglas replied coolly. "Mr. Lincoln has heard me answer [that question] a hundred times from every stump in Illinois."[31] In fact, Douglas argued a valid legal point. Without local support—slave patrols, legal protection for owners of human property, and the like—slavery faced a tough time establishing a foothold. But by forcing Douglas to unequivocally state this principle—henceforth known as the Freeport Doctrine—Lincoln could pound away on him later as well as dramatize the fact that Douglas was out of step with his own party, which agreed with Buchanan that *Dred Scott* had destroyed popular sovereignty and ended the territorial question altogether. Moreover, the Freeport Doctrine finished off any chance Douglas had to regain Southern support, since he now clearly provided the formula for Free-Soilers to override the Southern version of popular sovereignty. Momentarily rattled, Douglas attempted to incite the crowd by calling them all "Black Republicans," but the strongly partisan audience shouted back, "White, white." Douglas then, as in Chicago in 1854, turned on his own electorate, shouting, "I have seen your mobs before, and defy your wrath."[32]

At the southern Illinois town of Jonesboro, the next debate venue, Lincoln took on the Freeport Doctrine in front of a strongly pro-Southern and pro-Douglas assembly. With the reality of Kansas in mind, Lincoln explained that Douglas's doctrine did not match history. There was, Lincoln argued, "vigor enough in slavery to plant itself in a new country even against unfriendly legislation."[33] On they went, battling throughout Illinois. Morality, the Constitution, the intentions of the Founding Fathers, and, of course, race relations pervaded each encounter. At Charleston, Lincoln rebutted one of Douglas's many accusations that Republican policies would inevitably lead to the end of slavery and then to racial amalgamation by stating simply enough, "I do not understand that because I do not want a negro woman for a slave I must necessarily want her for a wife. My understanding is that I can just let her alone."[34] But Douglas never shied away from the race card, proclaiming once, "I do not question Mr. Lincoln's conscientious belief that the negro was made his equal and hence is his brother, but for my own part, I do not regard the negro as my equal, and positively deny that he is my brother or any kin to me whatever."[35]

With the debates concluded and ballots tallied in November, the Democratic Party held a solid majority in the Illinois assembly, and on January 5, 1859, they selected Douglas over Lincoln by a vote of 54 to 46. But despite his bitter disappointment, Lincoln knew one thing. The campaign, he wrote to a friend, "gave me a hearing on the great and durable question of the age, which I could have had in no other way; and though I now sink out of view, and shall be forgotten, I believe I have made some marks which will tell for the cause of civil liberty long after I am gone."[36] The chronically depressed Lincoln, smarting over his defeat, probably had little idea that despite the loss, newspaper coverage of the contest had launched him into national importance. He had gone toe-to-toe with one of the most successful and prominent politicians of his day and proved himself a force within his still-infant Republican Party.

Among the topics that Lincoln had used to attack Douglas before the debates was a not-so-logical link between Douglas's position on popular sovereignty and the volatile issue of reopening the African slave trade. Lincoln explained that Douglas had long "labored to prove it a *sacred right* of white men to take negros into the new territories. Can he possibly show that it is *less* a sacred right to *buy* them where they can be bought cheapest? And they can unquestionably be bought *cheaper* in *Africa* than in *Virginia*."[37] It was a shrill accusation that Lincoln subsequently abandoned, and wisely so. But in the midst of his debates that summer, the abstract discussion of renewing the Atlantic slave trade got a sudden dose of reality.

On August 21 the USS *Dolphin* apprehended the *Echo*, a slave ship off the coast of Cuba. The *Echo* had set out from New Orleans with a mostly Portuguese and Spanish crew and sailed for Kabenda on the Guinea coast of Africa. It took on a human cargo of 470, over a third of whom died on its 47-day voyage west across the Atlantic toward its destination back in Cuba. The *Dolphin* intercepted the ship and brought it, its crew, and the captives to Charleston harbor. Another thirty-eight Africans perished in captivity at the unfinished Fort Sumter, victims of the rigors of the Middle Passage that had led the United States to outlaw the nefarious trade to begin with.

"The great topic of conversation, the great theme of interest, are the new niggers," a columnist wrote for Rhett's *Charleston Mercury*.[38] The fate of the Africans and their captors fell into the hands of a grand jury in Columbia, South Carolina, and the federal circuit court in Charleston. Under a statute from 1820, the prosecution in both cases pressed its case for piracy with a penalty of death for the captain and crew if convicted. Through the *Mercury*, Rhett now mimicked Yancey's assertions that slave trading at home was not significantly different from the international trade and therefore that the piracy law stigmatized "every buyer and seller of slaves in the South."[39] Rhett also harped upon antislavery aggression by pointing out that the *Dolphin* had seized her prize beyond the limits of American authority on the seas, and therefore the federal ship and crew were the real lawbreakers. Rhett then wrote to President Buchanan, disingenuously offering his services to resolve the situation. In fact, Rhett hoped to snatch the slaves from the military authorities guarding them and have them sold to Carolina planters. Buchanan turned down Rhett's offer, instead ordering the captives to be returned home to Africa.

Meanwhile, the captain and crew awaited their fate. In the federal court the defendants won acquittal, and the grand jury in South Carolina never brought an indictment. Furthermore, the state assembly subsequently declared the federal piracy law unconstitutional, null, and void, just as they had done over tariff issues in 1832. The *Echo*'s Captain Townsend went to trial at a federal court in Key West, Florida, early in 1859, where he, too, won acquittal when the Southern judge rejected all evidence that Townsend had bought and registered the ship. Defiant Southerners had their victory. Northerners wondered if any federal law could restrain slaveholders.

Just as the *Echo* captain and crew neared the end of their saga, another slaver made the news. The *Wanderer*, built in Long Island, was a 114-foot yacht designed for speed. After its completion in 1857 the *Wanderer* sailed to Charleston and Savannah, where it gained the attention of Charles A. L. Lamar, an entrepreneurial cotton trader, banker, and planter. Through a third party, Lamar purchased the ship and refitted it with drastic changes below deck. After its arrival in Charleston in 1858, Lamar gathered a special crew for its first voyage; its destination, Africa. A British ship patrolling for slavers intercepted the craft, but the captain of the *Wanderer*, William C. Corrie, talked his way out of the situation, landed on the coast, and loaded over 500 people for the voyage home. Roughly half died at sea and were tossed overboard, sharing the same watery grave as some two million others through 450 years of systematic human plunder. At night in late November, the survivors reached Jekyll Island near Brunswick, Georgia, to find themselves sold immediately to waiting, prearranged buyers.

The vastness of the *Wanderer* enterprise prevented information from remaining secret for very long. A federal marshal in Savannah learned about it and began his investigation. He seized the yacht in early December and worked with U.S. Justice Department officials to build a case for prosecution. Lamar, concerned that "things are in a hell of a fix," decided he must bribe witnesses to escape punishment.[40] In fact, he offered two key witnesses $5,000 each to keep quiet. A grand jury in Charleston acquitted Captain Corrie, and the officiating judge refused to permit Corrie's removal for trial in Georgia. In Savannah a federal attorney remained determined to convict Lamar, but the jury at Lamar's trial proved even more obstructionist than the Carolinians involved in the *Echo* and *Wanderer* cases. The grand jury there initially returned indictments against Lamar, Captain Corrie, and others but later recanted and actually published a protest against the entire process: "We feel humbled, as men, in the consciousness that we are freemen but in name" and living under despotism and tyranny created by "sickly sentiment of pretended philanthropy and diseased mental aberration of 'higher law' fanatics."[41] Early in 1859, Lamar even regained possession of his yacht, having learned his own, peculiar lesson. "I have been in it for 'grandeur,' and have been fighting for a principle," Lamar explained to a friend. "Now I am in it for the dollars."[42]

Proponents of slavery had no monopoly on lawlessness in the name of their interests. In September the people of Oberlin, Ohio, staged a massive attack on the Fugitive Slave Law in their successful effort to save local resident John Price. A fugitive from his master near Maysville, Kentucky, John P. G. Bacon, Price and his cousin, Dinah, together with a friend of theirs, Frank, owned by a nearby farmer, made their escape over the frozen Ohio River in the winter of 1855–56, in a scene right out of *Uncle Tom's Cabin*. They eventually settled in Oberlin. The college in that town and the town itself were unique. Founded by a utopian Presbyterian minister, the college prohibited gambling, smoking in public, selling or possessing alcohol, and even wearing "unwholesome fashions of dress, particularly tight dressing and ornamental attire"—anything, in short, that might have distracted students from their training to spread the Gospel.[43] But from the start, Oberlin College welcomed women as well as men; it graduated the first three women in the United States to receive baccalaureate degrees. Even more startling, the town of Oberlin welcomed African American men and women, both to the college and into its racially integrated public schools.

In the summer of 1858, Price was too ill to work very much and depended upon the town's funds for paupers. He even told a friend that he missed his home in Kentucky. In late August, Anderson Jennings, a neighbor of Price's master in Kentucky, came to Oberlin in pursuit of his own runaway slave, where he happened to notice both Price and Dinah. Jennings notified Bacon, who began preparations for apprehending his slaves. On September 13 three slave catchers lured Price and his friend Frank into a carriage and continued southward to Wellington, waiting for a train to speed the fugitives back to Kentucky. Word quickly spread through Oberlin.

"They can't have him!" several people cried, and dozens of people, black and white, raced quickly on horseback toward Wellington.[44] Hundreds of local townsfolk gathered as well, forming a determined, angry, and unorganized mob gathered around the hotel where Price and the others waited for their train. John Copeland Jr., a freeborn black man from Oberlin, drew a gun on one of Price's captors and whisked the fugitive to safety. For a few days, Price stayed at the home of James Fairchild, an Oberlin College faculty member, and then, at last, he made his way to Canada. The citizens of Oberlin celebrated their victory.

White Southerners and the Buchanan administration were irate. The people of Oberlin—the embodiment of all sick "isms" to so many in the South—had already thwarted attempts to apprehend fugitives twice earlier that same year. But this massive resistance to federal law had to be dealt with. Federal authorities indicted thirty-seven of Price's rescuers and obtained two convictions in 1859, barely enough "justice" to placate the South but not enough retribution to further infuriate the North.

Oberlin Rescuers
Courtesy of the Ohio Historical Society

In 1850, William H. Seward had made himself famous (or infamous) when he announced from the Senate that Northerners should invoke a "higher law" than the Constitution whenever and wherever slavery was concerned. On September 25, days after the people of Oberlin exercised that very doctrine, Seward added another rhetorical salvo while stumping in Rochester on behalf of a Republican candidate for governor of New York. America had developed two distinct systems of labor, he explained, one free and one enslaved, which collided with greater ferocity and frequency both in the territories and among the states. "It is an irrepressible conflict between opposing and enduring forces," he said, "and it means that the United States must and will, sooner or later, become either entirely a slaveholding nation, or entirely a free-labor nation." Seward practically restated Lincoln's theme from the House Divided speech of June. But the New Yorker went further: "I know, and you know, that a revolution has begun. I know, and the world knows, that revolutions never go backward." And now, the senator announced, the free North stood poised "to confound and overthrow, by one decisive blow, the betrayers of the Constitution and Freedom forever."[45] While Lincoln had explained that one side or the other must prevail, Seward sounded the call of Northern revolution.

Even many Northerners—Republicans included—recoiled from Seward's manifesto. Southerners reacted predictably. James Hammond reported to a friend, "It is glorious. We have got them dead." Seward's careless word selection had resulted in more clarity for Southern extremism than any fire-eater could have supplied. Hammond continued, "But the true issue is now made. The South is to be Africanized and the elections of 1860 are to decide the question. In other words it is emancipation or disunion after 1860, unless Seward is repudiated."[46]

The November elections provided yet another signal to both North and South that the party of Seward and Lincoln was the party of the future. Republicans gained eighteen seats in the House of Representatives, but among Democrats elected or reelected, the solid majority supported Douglas and opposed Buchanan. Michigan, Wisconsin, and Indiana went Republican, and all of New England remained firmly in with them. In Ohio, Republicans took eighteen house seats, but the four they lost went to Douglas men, with similar results in New Jersey and New York. In many ways the Little Giant's victory over Lincoln proved as much a rebuke to President Buchanan as if Lincoln had won, and Republicans and Douglas Democrats even made significant inroads in the president's home state, Pennsylvania. Buchanan's rickety power had crumbled. Coupled with the victory of so many Douglas Democrats, the results boded ill for Southern interests.

After over a generation of public service, Buchanan knew at once that he had been trounced. The president dined with close friends as election results came to the White House. Powerless to do much else, as he wrote to Harriet Lane, "we had a merry time of it, laughing among other things at our crushing defeat. It is so great that it is almost absurd."[47]

A few days after the election, Senator Jefferson Davis made an appearance in the Mississippi assembly. Still smarting from the Southern critics of his summer trip to New England, Davis labored to vindicate himself, to regain some of his damaged reputation. He insisted that he had never before advocated secession "except as the last alternative," but now intimated that this alternative might soon arrive. Seward's recent speech, Davis announced, proved that the New Yorker was a "dangerously powerful man," and with the

Republicans in the ascendance, Davis now urged his fellow Mississippians to prepare for a possible separation from the Union.[48]

A different sort of Southern defiance occurred early in December, in neighboring Alabama, when William Walker finally launched his latest effort to recapture Nicaragua. Having learned some lessons from previous failures, Walker decided to avoid a landing in Nicaraguan ports, knowing full well that opponents—likely the British Royal Navy—would be looking for him. Instead, he would enter via Honduras and this time send men ahead to secure a base of operations. With 120 men and ample supplies, the schooner *Susan*, under the command of Henry Maury, set out from Mobile with enthusiastic backing from the locals:

> To Nicaragua Walker's bo[u]nd,
>   He scorns your mean frustration,
> Impartial Judges, Northern Spies
>   And Buck's Administration
> Success to Maury and his men,
>   They'll safely cross the water;
> Three cheers for Southern enterprise,
>   Hurrah for General Walker[49]

The voyage of the *Susan* mirrored the pathetic, persistent, and simultaneously doomed efforts of Southerners to maintain slavery in Kansas. It struck a coral reef about 60 miles from the coast of Belize. Its crew survived, stranded for days on a tiny island, until a British warship found them and carried them back to Mobile. Walker's latest effort failed, but like those Southerners whose determination to spread slavery to the West would never subside, he would try yet again in 1859.

NOTES*

1. *Montgomery Advertiser*, January 20, 1858.
2. Ibid., February 3, 1858.
3. Allan Nevins, *The Emergence of Lincoln*, 2 vols. (New York: Scribner, 1950), 1:270.
4. Ibid., 1:278.
5. Bruce C. Levine, *Half Slave and Half Free: The Roots of Civil War* (New York: Hill and Wang, Noonday Press, 1992), 213.
6. Drew Gilpin Faust, *James Henry Hammond and the Old South: A Design for Mastery* (Baton Rouge: Louisiana State University Press, 1982), 346.

*Emphasis in all quotations is that of the original authors.

7. Eric H. Walther, *The Fire-Eaters* (Baton Rouge: Louisiana State University Press, 1992), 282–83.

8. William C. Davis, *The Union That Shaped the Confederacy: Robert Toombs and Alexander H. Stephens* (Lawrence: University Press of Kansas, 2001), 72.

9. Walther, *Fire-Eaters*, 180–81.

10. David M. Potter, *The Impending Crisis, 1848–1861* (New York: Harper & Row, 1976), 389.

11. Ibid., 323.

12. All from Michael A. Morrison, *Slavery and the American West: The Eclipse of Manifest Destiny and the Coming of the Civil War* (Chapel Hill: University of North Carolina Press, 1997), 205.

13. Walther, *Fire-Eaters*, 284.

14. Edward J. Renehan Jr., *The Secret Six: The True Tale of the Men Who Conspired with John Brown* (Columbia: University of South Carolina Press, 1996), 126.

15. Ibid., 141.

16. Ibid., 144.

17. James N. Gloucester to John Brown, March 9, 1858, and Elizabeth Gloucester to Brown, August 18, 1859, both in C. Peter Ripley et al., eds., *Black Abolitionist Papers*, 5 vols. (Chapel Hill: University of North Carolina Press, 1985–1992), 4:378–79.

18. Fitzhugh to De Bow, January 26, 1858; Yancey to De Bow, March 25 [1858], both in James D. B. De Bow Papers, William R. Perkins Library, Duke University, Durham, North Carolina.

19. *Montgomery Advertiser*, May 19, 1858.

20. *De Bow's Review* 25 (October 1858): 459–60.

21. Walther, *Fire-Eaters*, 71.

22. Burns to Garrison, July 1858, in Ripley, *Black Abolitionist Papers*, 4:395–96.

23. Dunbar Rowland, ed., *Jefferson Davis, Constitutionalist: His Letters, Papers and Speeches*, 10 vols. (Jackson: Mississippi Department of Archives and History, 1923), 3:331.

24. Lynda Lasswell Crist and Mary Seaton Dix, eds., *The Papers of Jefferson Davis*, 10 vols. to date (Baton Rouge: Louisiana State University Press, 1971–), 6:207–8, notes.

25. Roy P. Basler et al., eds., *The Collected Works of Abraham Lincoln*, 9 vols. (New Brunswick, NJ: Rutgers University Press, 1953), 2:461–62.

26. Ibid., 2:466.

27. David Herbert Donald, *Lincoln* (New York: Simon & Schuster, 1995), 216.

28. Both in David Zarefsky, *Lincoln, Douglas, and Slavery: In the Crucible of Public Debate* (Chicago: University of Chicago Press, 1990), 55–56.

29. Carl Schurz, quoted in Donald, *Lincoln*, 215.

30. Zarefsky, *Lincoln, Douglas, and Slavery*, 56.

31. Donald, *Lincoln*, 218.

32. Ibid., 219.

33. Ibid., 220.

34. Donald Fehrenbacher, ed., *Abraham Lincoln: A Documentary Portrait through His Speeches and Writings* (Stanford, CA: Stanford University Press, 1964), 106.

35. Ibid., 105.

36. Donald, *Lincoln*, 228–29.

37. Fehrenbacher, *Abraham Lincoln*, 102.

38. William C. Davis, *Rhett: The Turbulent Life and Times of a Fire-Eater* (Columbia: University of South Carolina Press, 2001), 370.

39. Ibid., 371.

40. Nevins, *Emergence of Lincoln*, 1:436.

41. Ibid.

42. Ibid., 1:437.

43. Nat Brandt, *The Town That Started the Civil War* (Syracuse, NY: Syracuse University Press, 1990), 31.

44. Ibid., 73.

45. Nevins, *Emergence of Lincoln*, 1:409–10.

46. Ibid., 1:412.

47. Ibid., 1:400.

48. Crist and Dix, *Papers of Jefferson Davis*, 6:588.

49. Robert E. May, *The Southern Dream of a Caribbean Empire, 1854–1861* (Athens: University of Georgia Press, 1989), 129.

CHAPTER EIGHT

1859

"When I Strike, the Bees Will Swarm"

THE NEW YEAR began calmly enough. The Thirty-fifth Congress, which had commenced in December, met in a Capitol that finally had new chambers for both the House and the Senate, although it still required completion of its immense new dome. The White House required significant interior improvements. Its curtains and rugs were frayed; furniture desperately needed new upholstery; and without enough pictures and decorative objects to fill its vast rooms and walls, the presidential mansion mirrored the deterioration and hollowness of its occupant's leadership. Some in Congress favored appropriating money for its refurbishment, but Northerners were not amenable to making James Buchanan's surroundings more pleasant, and, for different reasons, most Southerners also preferred to wait until the current president left office. At least Buchanan's cabinet continued to get along well with one another, and Harriet Lane and Stephen Douglas's wife, Martha, hosted a series of social events that winter. On February 17 the greatest soiree in Washington that season involved over 1,200 people in the grand ballroom of the Willard Hotel, in honor of Lord Napier, the retiring British minister to the United States. Laurence Keitt of South Carolina seemed to enjoy the company of a congressman from Massachusetts, and Texan Sam Houston danced with a woman from the same Yankee state. Even the cantankerous William Seward hit the dance floor.

The peacefulness of the new year ended abruptly only ten days later with an episode of celebrity sex and murder soon known as The Washington Tragedy. Daniel E. Sickles, a congressman from New York City and close friend of the president, had just learned that his wife of five years, Teresa, had spent most of the past year having an affair with a friend of his, Philip Barton Key, a local U.S. attorney for the District of Columbia and son of Francis Scott Key, author of "The Star Spangled Banner." (Key was also a nephew of Chief Justice Roger B. Taney.) Sickles had already confronted Teresa about rumors he had heard of her infidelity, but she had assured him that they were not true. Then Sickles received a letter that detailed the exact location of the townhouse that Key had rented for his trysts with Mrs. Sickles. The popular Key often greeted admirers as he and Teresa publicly and brazenly entered their love nest together. On Sunday, February 27, Sickles found Key sitting quietly on a bench in Lafayette Park across the street from the White House. He pulled a pistol from his pocket and announced, "Key, you scoundrel, you have dishonored my house—and must die," and fired repeatedly.[1] Key's body was taken to the nearby home of Attorney General Jeremiah Black, and at a friend's urging, Sickles immediately turned himself in to local police. Allowed to visit his wife briefly after swearing not to harm her, Sickles came back to jail with her wedding ring and his dog. An unfounded rumor had it that the president visited Sickles in his jail cell. Not even James Buchanan was that inept, but the gossip reflected how little the public respected his judgment. Sickles's murder trial occurred in May, grabbing headlines in *Harper's Weekly* and *Frank Leslie's Illustrated*, the only two national newspapers. The jury unanimously returned a verdict of not guilty, to the delight of the cheering audience in the courtroom. One juror suggested that Sickles should have avenged himself with a howitzer instead of a handgun. Ten jurors joined the celebration for Sickles, which spilled outside, and accompanied the aggrieved husband to his hotel.

Daniel Sickles
Library of Congress

The murder of Key and trial of Sickles eclipsed anything that occurred in Congress that winter. Having dispatched with the English bill and the admission of Minnesota and Oregon as states in December and February, respectively, nothing particularly menacing occurred. Sectionalism hardly vanished; it still popped up everywhere. Congressmen divided along regional lines over issues such as further discussion of a transcontinental railroad (each region continued to hope that it would gain the eastern terminus) and tariffs (the South stood resolutely opposed, the North in favor). Southerners continued in vain to lobby for the annexation of Cuba and its valuable slave population. Northerners promoted a homestead bill, a measure to help free men acquire land from the national domain provided only that they occupy it and improve it (with a dwelling, a fence, a well, or the like). Senator Robert Toombs of Georgia voiced Southern apprehensions that Northerners' real design with the homestead bill was to populate the West with Free-Soilers. Toombs denounced William H. Seward, a homestead proponent, as a demagogue and a coward and shoved his chair against the seat of Republican Benjamin Wade of Ohio in the process. Wade seized the floor and took on Toombs directly, and in reference to both the Cuba and homestead proposals demanded crudely, "The question will be, shall we give niggers to the niggerless or land to the landless?"[2] Jefferson Davis, Judah P. Benjamin, and other Southern senators began to challenge Douglas directly for his Freeport Doctrine in much the same way that Abraham Lincoln had the year before, but with entirely different motives: they demanded positive federal protection for slavery in the territories. Douglas defied these men as well, who responded in turn by promising to rend the Democratic Party at the 1860 national convention if Douglas got his way. In the midst of this battle, word arrived in the chamber that the assembly of Kansas had just voted to outlaw slavery immediately. Congress managed to avoid both bloody confrontation and passing any substantial legislation by the time the session came to a close on March 5.

In the Deep South, summer heat sets in early, and fire-eaters there helped warm things up quickly at the 1859 Commercial Convention in Vicksburg, Mississippi, May 9–19. Picking up where the Montgomery meeting had left off a year before, James De Bow resumed his agitation for renewal of the African slave trade. Even though only a minority of Southerners favored this, the *Echo* and *Wanderer* incidents remained fresh in the minds of most, and the Vicksburg assembly had, as did most of these meetings in the 1850s, a disproportionate number of radicals. De Bow himself asked the delegates, quite logically, if African slavery were "very right and very proper," how the transportation of more slaves from Africa to the South could be "immoral, irreligious, wicked, and inexpedient." He pointed to the steady increase in prices for slaves, suggesting that demand exceeded current supply, especially in the

Southwest, and argued that natural reproduction could never make up the difference. De Bow also asserted that if more new slaves lowered prices enough, then vastly more whites would and could purchase slaves and use them to toil on land or in industry. De Bow concluded by agreeing with William L. Yancey's position, the year before, that regardless of whether or not the trade resumed, current federal proscriptions placed an intolerable "brand upon the institutions of the South."[3] His arguments proved persuasive; the meeting voted 44 to 19 in favor of urging each state and Congress to repeal all laws prohibiting the trade.

Encouraged by the outcome of the Vicksburg Convention, Southern radicals headed into the summer determined to prepare the public for the federal elections of 1860, a contest that many fire-eaters hoped would provide the final straw for the Union. On the Fourth of July, 1859, veteran Robert Barnwell Rhett made his first public speech since his abrupt resignation from the U.S. Senate in 1852. With the steady rise of the Republican Party in mind, Rhett taunted his South Carolina audience, "To submit to this vulgar crew of plunderers and fanatics, is a degradation no other free people than the people of the South ever endured, but to submit to their *rule* will be the desperation of a weak and conquered race—conquered without a fight."[4] With the power of her agricultural staples to back the will of her people, Rhett assured his listeners, an independent South had a glorious future ahead of her. He promised territorial expansion the likes of which no one had seen—to the southern tip of Brazil and everything in between. With nothing but danger within the Union and glory outside of it, Rhett promised on this Independence Day, "Let this election be the last contest between the North and the South; and the long, weary night of our dishonor and humiliation be dispersed at last, by the glorious dayspring of a Southern confederacy."[5]

On the heels of this pronouncement, South Carolina received a visit from a longtime associate of Rhett, William L. Yancey of Alabama. He addressed an audience in Columbia and reinforced the need to take an unequivocal stand in Charleston during the Democrats' national convention there in April 1860. The South should negotiate no longer, Yancey insisted. They must reject Douglas and stand on their right to take slavery to the territories no matter the consequences. If Northern delegates blocked them, Yancey said that Southern ones should leave the convention. Rhett endorsed this position a few months later through his *Charleston Mercury*.

While fire-eaters strove to lay the groundwork for disunion, in Ohio, composer Daniel Decatur Emmett published a new song destined to secede as well. Somewhat of a prodigy, at age fifteen Emmett first performed his composition "Old Dan Tucker." With the music bug established within him, at age sixteen he ran away and joined a traveling circus as a fiddler. The next year he enlisted in the army and became leading fifer at Jefferson Barracks, Missouri, before his discharge in 1835, when army officials discovered he had lied about his age to enlist. Emmett spent the next several years traveling with circus bands and started to incorporate elements of African American music into his own works. By 1843, Emmett created the "Original Virginia Minstrels," the first performers in the United States to use blackface (burned cork applied to the face to create a black caricature, complete with oversized pants and other gaudy, poorly fitting clothing). They instantly became a hit. Other songs credited to Emmett include "Turkey in the Straw" and "Jimmy Crack Corn." By 1858 he had joined Bryant's Minstrels in New York and continued to both compose and perform, especially "walk-arounds," songs sung at the end of a production while a single entertainer walked around the stage. The story goes that on a cold, rainy evening in 1859 the manager of Bryant's told Emmett to compose a lively new tune, one that everyone would whistle in the streets after they heard it. The next morning, still damp and chilly, Emmett sat uninspired and unable to begin. When his wife entered his room, Emmett supposedly exclaimed, "What a morning! I wish I was in Dixie."[6] Within an hour he completed his composition, and he later sold the publication rights for $500 to a company in New York—all he ever received for it. The African American Snowden family in Knox County, Ohio, musicians who performed for both black and white audiences in that state, claimed that Emmett had learned "Dixie" from them. At any rate, in the summer of 1859, Emmett and Bryant's Minstrels played at the Montgomery Theater in Alabama. The theater's conductor asked Emmett for a copy of the score for "Dixie." Emmett did not have one, so as he hummed the tune the conductor scribbled out the score in charcoal on a wall of the theater. Its popularity spread as state after state seceded from the Union during the winter of 1860–61, much to the chagrin of its unionist Yankee composer.

Abraham Lincoln watched the latest rising swell of Southern radicalism with his usual melancholy and hypersensitivity to a supposed Slave Power conspiracy. As foreboding as the future appeared to him, Lincoln's driving ambition and his personal commitment to stop the spread of slavery led him to seriously consider and finally actively pursue a presidential nomination for the very election that fire-eaters had vowed to make their last in the United States. He launched a series of public speeches in Kansas, Iowa, Illinois, Indiana, Wisconsin, and Ohio both to promote his candidacy and to keep his party's focus on restricting the spread of slavery. At Columbus, Ohio, Lincoln asked his audience to recall the condition of the country on January 1, 1854. The African slave trade was prohibited by Congress; most states had outlawed slavery; the Missouri Compromise prohibited slavery in the bulk of the national domain. But when Douglas passed his Kansas-Nebraska Act, slavery instantly began to spread; the *Dred Scott* decision stated that Congress could not stop it; and, according to Lincoln, if pushed to its logical conclusion, that ruling "would decide that the constitutions of the Free States, forbidding slavery, are themselves unconstitutional." Lincoln asserted that proslavery advocates who found that "there is no wrong in slavery, and whoever wants it has a right to have it" had set the stage for the next step. "They will be ready for Jeff. Davis and [Alexander] Stephens and other leaders of that company, to sound the bugle for the revival of the slave trade . . . for the flood of slavery to be poured over the free States, while we shall be here tied down and helpless and run over like sheep." After tackling Southern extremism, Lincoln added that Stephen Douglas's popular sovereignty held that "the people of the territories have the right, by his principle, to have slaves, if they want them. Then I say the people of Georgia have the right to buy slaves in Africa, if they want them, and I defy any man on earth to show any distinction between the two things." [7] Clearly, Lincoln presented Republicans—men like himself—as the only way to stop this onslaught.

In September, James Buchanan announced that he would not seek a second term as president, which was pretty much a foregone conclusion as far as most Americans were concerned. But his public statement opened the floodgates for ambitious Democrats. Despite Douglas's checkered record on slavery in the territories, the Little Giant had towered over all other prospective candidates from the free states ever since he defied his president on Lecompton. Few other Northern Democrats seriously considered challenging him, but more and more Southerners vowed to stop him. Dozens of Southern Democrats sensed the opportunity for one of their own to take the White House for the first time since James K. Polk's election back in 1844. The Southern press speculated with some accuracy about men like Howell Cobb, Jefferson Davis, James H. Hammond, Vice President John C. Breckinridge, and Virginia's governor, Henry A. Wise. In the case of the latter, no one needed to guess. Wise wrote a public letter to the *New York Herald* in which he boldly asserted that after Southerners denied the nomination of Douglas the senator would run as an independent candidate. In a shameless display of egotism, Wise concluded that if Douglas did that "and Seward runs, and I am nominated at Charleston, I can beat them both."[8]

An early indication of how volatile elections would prove in 1860 came on September 7, 1859. Over 100,000 Californians turned out to vote for assemblymen who, in turn, would select their state's senator. David C. Broderick, a Douglas Democrat, squared off against William M. Gwinn, a Buchanan ally, in the most bitter political contest yet in the Golden State. Gwinn won by a narrow margin, much too narrow for his partisans in these superheated times, and Broderick still had four years to serve in his term before Gwinn would replace him. This was all too much for David S. Terry. A hotheaded Southerner who had already wounded a man in a fight with a bowie knife, Terry challenged Senator-elect Broderick to a duel, a rarity on the West Coast. In front of a sizeable crowd, Terry's shot ripped into Broderick, who slumped to the ground. Like a Shakespearean actor, Broderick moaned, "They have killed me because I was opposed to the extension of slavery and a corrupt Administration." With Broderick's death, Gwinn and his pro-Southern forces were able to lead California Democrats to the upcoming ill-fated Democratic Party National Convention, to be held in Charleston, South Carolina, in April 1860.[9]

Violence, death, and the specter of slavery resulted in the one act of 1859 that overwhelmed all others and lingered longer and more powerfully than anything before, and this time it happened not by accident but with careful planning and calculation. Through the end of 1858 and into 1859, John Brown continued raising money and purchasing weapons for his attack on slavery, relying on his six prestigious backers, the "Secret Six": Thomas Wentworth Higginson, Samuel Gridley Howe, Theodore Parker, Franklin Sanborn, Gerrit Smith, and George Luther Stearns. By July 1859, Brown had rented a small farm in Maryland at the narrowest portion of that state, between Pennsylvania and Virginia, only 5 miles from his target, the federal arsenal at Harpers Ferry, Virginia. In August he sent to New York for Frederick Douglass, who met Brown at Chambersburg, Pennsylvania, at an abandoned quarry where Brown had already stashed his considerable cache of weapons: 200 rifles, 200 revolvers, and nearly 1,000 iron pikes (medieval weapons with a barbed spearhead mounted on a long shaft so that once they penetrated a human body, pulling them back out would extract an even larger amount of flesh). Against this grim backdrop, Brown asked Douglass once more for help. Referring to his hope that once his invasion began, slaves would flock toward him, Brown explained, "When I strike, the bees will begin to swarm, and I shall want you to help hive them." Douglass repeated his belief that Brown's plan was doomed and stated that the federal arsenal was a "perfect steel trap," that Brown and his men "will never get out alive," and that the act would pit the entire country against the abolitionist movement.[10] Brown did not waver for a moment.

Just after midnight on October 17, five of Brown's men, each armed to the teeth, pounded on the door of the unsuspecting Lewis W. Washington, a small farmer and slaveholder near Harpers Ferry. Brown figured that taking hostage the great-grandnephew of George Washington would aid his designs if the going got rough. Brown's men also helped themselves to some relics of President Washington. They forced Lewis Washington, along with several of his slaves, into a wagon, then stopped at another farmer's home, kidnapping his son and several more slaves. Before 3:30 A.M., Brown easily captured the armory at Harpers Ferry, protected as it was by a single sleepy guard. A little later Brown and eighteen of his men and their hostages walked up to the gate of the arsenal. A sentry approached them and, when one of Brown's men said, "All's well," casually, mysteriously, let them in. Brown entered that easily; several million dollars' worth of weapons and ammunition now belonged to him. By 5:00 A.M., Brown ordered three of his forces to return to the Maryland side of the Potomac River and to wait there with his stash of weapons from Chambersburg—including the pikes—to distribute them to the slaves who Brown knew would rush to his side. As dawn approached and the officers and craftsmen trickled in to work at the arsenal, they found themselves taken prisoner each in turn. Everything worked perfectly.

After sunrise the townsfolk quickly realized that something terribly wrong had occurred, and to their horror they discovered that abolitionists had planned and begun a massive slave insurrection. Many prudently abandoned their homes and sought refuge behind the town or across the river in the steep hills that surrounded their community. And therein lay the folly of Brown's plan: getting in was one thing, but now he and his small force were trapped at the base of a narrow river valley and surrounded on all sides by an angry citizenry that had exclusive access to communication from the hinterlands. Locals kept up their fire until militia forces and federal troops arrived and quickly took over. One militia company charged swiftly across the Potomac on the Harpers Ferry bridge, effortlessly dispatching Brown's two guards—a son, Oliver, and a mulatto, Dangerfield Newby. Both were shot. Oliver Brown escaped back to the armory, but Newby died from a bullet that literally slit his throat. One furious Southerner then dragged Newby's body through the streets and cut off his ears to keep as souvenirs; others beat the lifeless body and drove hogs to devour the corpse.

More troops arrived by the hour, some from as far away as Baltimore, totaling up to 1,000, but no slaves swarmed to help Brown. The people of Harpers Ferry yelled for the soldiers to kill all of the invaders. Brown sent a man out to negotiate under a flag of truce, but a mob seized him and held him under arrest. Brown sent one of his sons, Watson, and another man to try again; both were gunned down instantly. Brown's efforts to fight back proved worse than futile; the first man his forces killed was a free black man. One by one, more of Brown's men were shot or captured. The savagely wounded Oliver Brown lay in a corner of the engine house where the remnant abolition force remained, near his dying brother Watson. Desperately, Oliver Brown begged his father to shoot him in the head and end his agony, but the reproachful father only replied, "If you must die, die like a man." A little later, as night fell, John Brown called out to Oliver, who did not reply. "I guess he is dead," he said blandly to Lewis Washington.[11] Brown tried sending out a note offering to release his hostages if the Southerners would let the rest of his men go; he received no reply.

The next morning federal army troops arrived, sent under orders by President Buchanan and commanded by Colonel Robert E. Lee. As dawn broke, Brown and his four surviving raiders faced an awesome sight: hundreds of marines, armed with firearms, battering rams, and cannon, in front of 2,000 locals who demanded death to the invaders. Now Lee's messenger approached Brown to offer safety if his squad surrendered, but with Brown's refusal the federal forces pounded their way into the engine room. Two federal troops died in the assault, but the group captured the last of Brown's men and stabbed Brown and beat him until he lay unconscious. The spectators demanded the immediate execution of the few survivors. Colonel Lee refused to let the mob have its way, instead turning over the prisoners to local police authorities, who quickly indicted Brown and his four living accomplices for treason, murder, and conspiracy to incite a slave insurrection. Each man had his own trial in nearby Charles Town.

As soon as Brown was in custody, he faced interrogation by a committee that included Governor Henry A. Wise, Robert E. Lee, Lewis Washington, and Senator James Mason. They tried every way they could to force Brown to name his accomplices, supporters, and financial contributors—anyone who in any way had aided his crime. Brown refused to betray a soul but defiantly told his inquisitors that many in the North supported him. His stoicism would have had a far greater impact had not Brown been so careless with hundreds of letters between himself and his backers—the Secret Six— that he had left in the rented farmhouse in Maryland, discovered days after the raid by local authorities. The names were published throughout the country. The *New York Herald*'s headline read, "THE EXPOSURE OF THE NIGGER-WORSHIPING INSURRECTION-ISTS."[12] Higginson, Howe, Parker, Sanborn, Smith, and Stearns understandably panicked when they read other newspaper accounts about Brown's stupendous failure and arrest, and their own implication. Sanborn sought legal counsel, received the advice to flee the country, and did so immediately, setting off for Canada. Howe frantically raced to the home of George L. Stearns when his wife, Julia Ward Howe, told him the news. They consulted the same attorney Sanborn had, but with a little time to ponder matters, the lawyer now advised that while all of the six were accessories to treason and therefore could be tried for treason, they could only face trial in Massachusetts, not in Virginia. Relieved, these two decided to stay put, and men of no less status than Ralph Waldo Emerson wrote to Sanborn urging him to come home.

John Brown's trial began on October 27, with the wounded defendant lying on a cot on the floor of the courthouse. It ended three days later with convictions on all counts and a death sentence set for December 2. From his jail cell, Brown penned in a letter to his wife, "I have been *whipped* as the saying *is*, but am sure I can recover all the lost capital occasioned by that disaster, by only hanging a few moments by the neck; & I feel quite determined to make the utmost possible out of a defeat."[13] Rumors abounded in both the North and South that other abolitionists were conspiring to form a rescue party and swoop down from Pennsylvania to rescue their hero from the gallows; Sanborn and Higginson actually discussed the possibility but then dismissed it. Virginia's veteran secessionist, Edmund Ruffin, actually hoped for such an effort: "I wish that the abolitionists of the north may attempt a rescue. If it is done, & defeated, every one engaged will be put to death like wolves."[14] But well before the appointed day arrived for the execution, John Brown knew better than most that the best thing for his cause was now for slaveholders to kill him. Other radicals agreed. The Rev. Henry Ward Beecher, veteran gun smuggler to Kansas, announced from his pulpit, "Let no man pray that Brown be spared! Let Virginia make him a martyr! Now, he has only blundered. His soul

John A. Copeland
Library of Congress

was noble; his work miserable. But a cord and a gibbet would redeem all that, and round up Brown's failure with heroic success." When a jailor showed Brown a copy of that sermon, the condemned man wrote "good" near the word "martyr."[15]

Some of Brown's surviving accomplices received the news of their fate the same way. John Copeland, one of the African American students at Oberlin who had violently resisted slave catchers the year before, sat calmly through his two-day trial. His attorney, a Bostonian who volunteered for the impossible defense, tried arguing that according to the *Dred Scott* decision, blacks were not citizens and therefore could not commit treason. Prosecutors actually agreed but focused on other charges to gain Copeland's conviction and death sentence. As the student waited through the last few days of his young, defiant life, he assured his parents, "I am not terrified by the gallows. Could I die in a more noble cause? Could I die in a manner and for a cause which would induce true and honest men more to honor me, and the angels more ready to receive me to their happy home of everlasting joy above?"[16] No less than his leader had done, Copeland faced death fearlessly.

Partly out of fear of a last-minute rescue effort and partly to present watchful Northerners with a display of Southern military capacity and determination, Governor Wise came to the execution site at the end of November to personally administer the proceedings. Wise authorized $250,000 to pay for the thousands of troops he ordered to patrol the area. He repeatedly demanded of his old friend James Buchanan that federal troops supplement the local forces, and at last the president submitted, again sending Robert E. Lee and some artillery. The Virginia Military Institute (VMI) in nearby Lexington contributed its corps of cadets under the command of their professor of mathematics, Thomas J. Jackson (who would earn the nickname "Stonewall" early in 1861). The 65-year-old Ruffin talked his way into the teenage corps from VMI to get himself a good, close view. A member of a famous family of actors, John Wilkes Booth grabbed a uniform and pretended to represent part of the Richmond militia so that he, too, could witness Brown's death. Even with the many military precautions, Governor Wise issued a proclamation that strenuously advised local citizens to stay home in case trouble erupted.

A pleasant, late-autumn breeze warmed the morning of December 2 as John Brown arrived at the gallows riding on a wagon, sitting upon his own coffin. He never showed the slightest fear or trepidation and walked alone and unaided up to the scaffold. Brown's last message to the outside world, written that morning and delivered to his executioners, pledged defiantly, "I John Brown am now quite *certain* that the crimes of this *guilty, land: will* never be purged *away*; but with Blood."[17] A rope dangled from a beam above; the noose was placed around his neck, his arms pinioned together behind his back, and his ankles bound to each other as Brown stood over a trapdoor. Upon the executioner's signal the door opened and Brown's body dropped nearly a foot. After about a minute his body suddenly convulsed and then swayed lifelessly in the breeze.

After all the wild schemes and bizarre deeds that failed during his life, ironically, the impact of John Brown's death might have surpassed his wildest hopes. It was overwhelming and seemingly immutable across the entire country. His death inspired Walt Whitman to write, "I would now sing how an old man, tall, with white hair, mounted the scaffold in Virginia / (I was at hand, silent I stood with teeth shut closed, I watched / I stood very near the old man when cool and indifferent, / but trembling with age and your unheal'd wounds / you mounted the scaffold.)"[18] Henry David Thoreau joined Emerson and others at a prayer service in Concord, Massachusetts, on the day of Brown's hanging, announcing, "Some eighteen hundred years ago Christ was crucified. This morning . . . Brown was hung. These are two ends of a chain which is not without its links."[19] Author Louisa May Alcott attended that service and later wrote: "No monument of quarried stone / No eloquence of speech / Can grave the lessons on the land / His martyrdom will teach."[20] In *The Liberator*, William Lloyd Garrison exhorted, "Let the day of his execution . . . be the occasion of such a public moral demonstration against the bloody and merciless slave system as the land has never witnessed."

Elizabeth Cady Stanton
Library of Congress

Fellow abolitionist Wendell Phillips announced that "John Brown has twice as much right to hang Governor Wise as Governor Wise has to hang him."[21] The *Boston Post* offered that "John Brown may be a lunatic," but if that was true, "then one-fourth of the people of Massachusetts are madmen."[22] Elizabeth Cady Stanton wrote to Susan B. Anthony that "the martyrdom of that great and glorious John Brown" made her regret "my dwarfed and perverted womanhood. In times like these, every soul should do the work of a grown man."[23] Novelist and radical abolitionist Lydia Maria Child of Massachusetts did not condone Brown's violent intentions, but she shared others' admiration for the old warrior. She sent Brown a letter of sympathy and support before his execution and published a letter to Governor Wise blaming the whole affair on "the continual, and constantly-increasing aggressions of the Slave Power."[24]

Elected officials weighed their public statements more carefully. Even the most radical of Republicans, men like Thaddeus Stevens, believed that Brown deserved hanging. Many feared that the association of Brown with the Secret Six and those men's ties to free soil, the Republican Party, and abolitionism combined to threaten the steady progress and popularity of their party, just in time for the presidential election of 1860. William H. Seward denounced Brown and called his execution "necessary and just," despite understanding the motives that had impelled Brown to act.[25]

Northern Democrats did not shy away from public judgments either. The *Indianapolis Locomotive* described Brown's raid as "this most fiendish plot . . . having for its object plunder, violations of female chastity, and an indiscriminate slaughter of all who should oppose its fearful march."[26] From Lincoln's home state, the *Springfield State Register* published an error-filled report on the raid, claiming, "Under the lead of the most infamous of the Kansas crew of black republican marauders, Ossawatomie [*sic*] Brown, the insurgents, to the number of five or six hundred, attacked and took possession of the whole town of Harper's Ferry [*sic*]." It then placed the blame squarely upon the Republican Party leadership: "Their open-mouthed treason, which culminates in precisely such outrages as that at Harper's Ferry [*sic*], is but the logical sequence of the teachings of Wm. H. Seward and Abraham Lincoln—the one boldly proclaiming an 'irrepressible conflict' between certain states of the Union . . . and the other declaring from stump and hustings . . . that the Union cannot continue as the fathers made it—part slave and part free states."[27]

Despite loud criticism by Democrats and a pervading abhorrence for violence, the general public in the North overwhelmingly sympathized with Brown for his motivation—to do something about the evil of slavery. And that proved almost as shocking and ominous to white Southerners as Brown's raid itself. Margaretta Mason spoke for a multitude. The wife of Virginia senator James Mason read Lydia Maria Child's letter and sent her a terse reply. "Do you read your Bible, Mrs. Child?" she asked, condemning her for offering to console "the hoary-headed murder of Harper's Ferry [*sic*]."[28] The *Richmond Whig* announced, "If this Union is to last, and civil war averted, the masses of the northern people must . . . set their seal of eternal condemnation upon these bold, bad men, and their dangerous, incendiary counsels. If they do not, and that promptly, the Harper's Ferry [*sic*] conspiracy will constitute the beginning of an *'irrepressible conflict'* between the North and the South, *which can only end in an utter destruction of the Federal Govern-*

ment, and in oceans of fraternal blood."[29] In North Carolina the *Asheville News* exclaimed, "Now . . . we see what the irrepressible conflict of Seward means . . . we see the feast of blood to which [Republicans] will invite the South," and urged preparations for further conflict with the North.[30] Many Southern states passed emergency appropriations bills to bolster their state militias. An ad appeared in a Richmond newspaper offering $50,000 for the head of William H. Seward. On December 20 all 395 Southerners at the Jefferson Medical College in Philadelphia—over 60 percent of the student body—and those at the University of Pennsylvania Medical College resolved to "secede" and return to the South. Within a few weeks, over 300 of them fulfilled their threat. When the first trainload arrived in Richmond they received heroes' greetings, complete with local dignitaries and a band playing "Carry Me Back to Old Virginny." Others saw Harpers Ferry as unequivocal proof that slaves were happy and content. The *Wilmington Daily Herald*, for instance, complained loudly, " 'Twas no insurrection, and it is a libel upon the slave in designating it as such. They had nothing whatever to do with it. *There was not a single slave engaged but what was drawn in by compulsion.*"[31] Abraham Lincoln later suggested that Brown's plan was so poorly conceived and executed that "the slaves, in all their ignorance, saw plainly enough it could not succeed."[32]

Unlike the variance in the North between mainstream Democrats, Republicans, and abolitionists, the line in the South between moderation and extremism all but vanished among their elected officials. Naturally, the senators from Virginia were particularly livid. R. M. T. Hunter demanded that his Northern colleagues explain what was "the real state of northern feeling in regard to these matters."[33] James Mason shared his wife's outrage and publicly asserted that among Republicans, "John Brown's invasion was condemned only because it failed." Georgian Robert Toombs vowed that the South would never allow the federal government "to pass into the traitorous hands of the black Republican party." Jefferson Davis agreed that the core of that party was "organized on the basis of making war" on the slave states.[34] Albert Gallatin Brown of Mississippi refused to believe the words of Northerners who claimed to criticize John Brown: "No, gentlemen, disguise it as you will, there is throughout all the non-slaveholding states of this Union, a secret, deep-rooted sympathy with the object which this man had in mind."[35]

Of course, not all Southerners condemned Brown's raid or Northern sympathy toward it. Late in 1859 in Baltimore, Maryland, police burst into an annual ball held by free blacks of that city. They found the assembly hall filled with Brown's image emblazoned on banners and a bust of John Brown inscribed "The martyr—God bless him."[36]

For many in the South, Brown's raid for the first time made them question the value of remaining in the Union. Robert Barnwell Rhett's *Charleston Mercury* put matters simply enough: "The Union shall be dissolved, or slavery shall be abolished." Rhett believed absolutely "that there is no peace for the South in the Union, from the forbearance or respect of the North. The South must control her own destinies or perish."[37] Abraham Lincoln responded both to Brown and to the renewed Southern threats of secession in the wake of Harpers Ferry, on December 5 in Leavenworth, Kansas: "Old John Brown has just been executed for treason against a state. We cannot object, even though he agreed with us in thinking slavery wrong. That cannot excuse violence, bloodshed, and treason." But then Lincoln applied the same lesson to those who vowed to dissolve the Union if a Republican won the presidency eleven months in the future: "So, if constitutionally we elect a President, and therefore you undertake to destroy the Union, it will be our duty to deal with you as old John Brown has been dealt with."[38]

Only days after Brown's execution, the Thirty-sixth Congress assembled in Washington, DC. To say the least, the atmosphere was palpably tense. Although still ailing, in part because of the shabby medical treatment he had received for years, Charles Sumner finally felt ready to return to the Senate. He vowed, "If health ever returns I will repay to slavery and the whole crew of its supporters every wound, burn, . . . ache, trouble, grief which I have suffered." Southern anger toward Sumner had only increased during his absence, and upon his return new threats streamed his way. "We plainly see that you are fast spoiling for another licking," one forewarned, assuring the senator that neither his bad health nor Northern threats of reprisal offered any deterrence. "What the Hell do we care for the Vengeance of the Yankees. Why, a dissolution and a fight is what we are after. And if giving you *another pummeling* will be the means of bringing it about then here go[e]s it."[39]

From the House side, Congressman Laurence Keitt of South Carolina, one of Preston Brooks's accomplices in the assault on Charles Sumner, was enjoying his honeymoon in Europe when he learned of Harpers Ferry, prompting him to cut short the excursion. His young bride complained, "Disappointed, disappointed. And the cause *Politics*. How I *hate* the word." After Representative Keitt returned and caucused with fellow Southerners, he announced, "There is an indissoluble connection between the principles of the Republican party . . . and their ultimate consummation in blood and rapine on the soil of Virginia." Then, suddenly, Keitt learned that his brother, while lying in a sickbed on his Florida plantation, had had his throat slit by one of his slaves. The brother died, and vigilantes hanged the accused slave on the spot. Laurence Keitt customarily left his new wife alone on his plantation of over 100 slaves while he tended to his duties in Washington, DC. The combination of events and circumstances proved as alarming to Keitt as it did to countless other slaveholders: "Our Negroes are being enlisted in politics. I confess, this new feature alarms me."[40] He vowed to promote secession just as vehemently as Sumner had pledged his might to stop the Slave Power.

As though the atmosphere was not grim enough, old Edmund Ruffin paid a visit to Washington with a frightful souvenir. Before he had left Harpers Ferry, the fire-eater had managed to obtain a quantity of the iron pikes that Brown's men had intended to distribute to slaves. He sent one to each of the fifteen governors of the slave states with a tag attached, reading *"Samples of the favors designed for us by our Northern Brethren."*[41] He now personally brought one into the Capitol.

The Senate quickly turned its attention to the creation of a committee to investigate the Harpers Ferry affair. While Brown and most of his men were either dead or in captivity, angry Southerners resumed their insistence that anyone who had aided the raid must be ferreted out and brought to justice. James Mason of Virginia chaired the committee along with Jefferson Davis and pro-Southern Indiana senator Graham N. Fitch; Jacob Collamer of Vermont and James R. Doolittle of Wisconsin, both Republicans, constituted the minority. They questioned leading Republicans William H. Seward, Henry Wilson, and Joshua Giddings, but contrary to the innuendo published in the Southern press, they concluded that none had any involvement with Brown.

Among the scores of individuals anticipating subpoenas by the committee, several of the Secret Six anxiously corresponded with one another. Theodore Parker had already fled to Italy, and on May 10, 1860, he died from tuberculosis before the age of fifty. Gerrit Smith had friends check him into an insane asylum in New York in early November 1859. Before the year's end, when it seemed unlikely that he would be arrested, Smith regained his sanity and returned home. To the end of his life, in 1874, he denied having had any knowledge of Brown's raid until he read about it in the press. Howe, Stearns, and Sanborn decided that any testimony they gave would occur in Massachusetts, not Washington. As Sanborn explained, "I, an avowed abolitionist, and friend of Brown, cannot be safe in a city so near Virginia." However, no one ever forced him to testify, either at home or in Washington.[42] Howe and Stearns both decided to flee to Canada for a while. Higginson alone stood firm, refusing to deny his role in the affair or to run: "Henry [Thoreau] told me that . . . civil disobedience, in the pure form, required staying in place, a certain willingness to suffer the consequence—whatever that might be—of refusing to participate in an immoral act, statute, or investigation."[43] Ironically, Higginson was never subpoenaed. And never one to forgo violence for the cause of freedom, on November 10, 1862, Colonel Thomas Wentworth Higginson took command of the First South Carolina Volunteer Infantry—one of the many segregated black units within the federal army during the Civil War—in his continued efforts to destroy slavery.

By January 1860 it appeared obvious to Howe and to Stearns that Mason's committee lacked focus and that those who testified easily wriggled out of any incriminating connection to Brown. By February, both testified and steadfastly denied any direct or indirect knowledge of Brown's exact intentions before the raid actually occurred. After Stearns finished his testimony, he and a skeptical Senator Mason found themselves alone together for a moment. According to Stearns, the Virginian handed him a rifle and asked if his conscience bothered him for helping send such weapons to Kansas. Stearns replied that the South had sent off the Buford Expedition before New Englanders started sending arms. Mason snatched back the gun and said, "I think when you go to that lower place, the old fellow will question you pretty hard about this matter, and you will have to take it." Stearns replied calmly, "Before that time comes, I think he will have about two hundred years of slavery to investigate, and before he gets through with that will say 'We have had enough of this business, better let the rest go.'"[44] The committee completed its inquiry on June 15, 1860, concluding that all of those directly involved with John Brown either died in the effort or were apprehended at Harpers Ferry.

While the Mason committee captured the attention of the Senate, the House faced its most acrimonious contest ever for the speakership. Republican candidate John Sherman had supported a plan by other party members early in 1859 to produce an abbreviated compendium of Hinton R. Helper's inflammatory *Impending Crisis of the South*. Wishing to spread the word of this Southern foe of slavery among others in the South who they supposed would take courage by reading it—if they could afford it—sixty-eight leading Republicans signed a circular letter endorsing the book and its message. Sherman stood with that company. "You ask why I signed the recommendation of the Helper book," he wrote to his brother, William Tecumseh Sherman. "It was a thoughtless, foolish, and unfortunate act."[45] It was especially reckless after the compendium appeared in print with a heading that read "Revolution—Peaceably if we can, Violently if we must," words that sent chills down white Southerners' spines ever since October 16 and Harpers Ferry.[46]

All hell broke loose. Day after day, physical confrontation and bloodshed seemed inevitable, especially with so many congressmen now armed with guns and knives. From the Senate, Alfred Iverson of Georgia summed up the thoughts and emotions of multitudes of Southerners. Even while Republicans denied that their party encouraged the likes of John Brown, they simultaneously "propose to elevate to a high office a man who has . . . attempted to circulate a pamphlet containing the most treasonable and the most insurrectionary sentiments . . . exciting insurrection and advising our slaves to fire our dwellings and put their knives to our throats,"[47] Iverson stated. A Mississippi representative called for the hanging of William H. Seward. An Illinois Democrat actually grappled with a Republican from his own state. People on the House floor and throughout the building openly discussed the possibility of secession and war over this issue. Governor William Gist of South Carolina wrote to his state's representatives to tell them that the people of the Palmetto State would fully support their withdrawal from Congress should Sherman win the speakership. Gist himself preferred ousting Sherman by force, if necessary, and assured his delegation that if they agreed, "write or telegraph me, & I will have a Regiment near Washington in the shortest possible time."[48] Even as the debate continued, Governor Gist sent a special representative to Virginia in order to convince that state to secede immediately and join South Carolina as the core of a new Southern Confederacy.

The speakership controversy did not end until January 30, 1860. Sherman finally withdrew his candidacy and in turn supported a compromise candidate. William Pennington of New Jersey, a former Whig, had only recently won his first election to Congress by the meager majority of 117 votes, but he proved satisfactory enough to end the prolonged contest. With tension in the House relieved, if only by a little, and with Virginia politely declining South Carolina's invitation to destroy the Union, it seemed as though the high drama of 1859, which had spilled over into the new year, had diminished enough for Americans to try yet again to regroup and go about their lives. But the ghost of John Brown rendered that impossible.

NOTES*

1. "A National Morality Play: The Trial of Daniel Edgar Sickles for the Murder of Philip Barton Key," http://www.assumption.edu/HTML/Academic/history/Hi113net/sickles/default1.html, accessed July 29, 2003.

2. Hans Trefousse, *The Radical Republicans: Lincoln's Vanguard for Racial Justice* (New York: Knopf, 1969), 127.

3. Eric H. Walther, *The Fire-Eaters* (Baton Rouge: Louisiana State University Press, 1992), 218.

4. William C. Davis, *Rhett: The Turbulent Life and Times of a Fire-Eater* (Columbia: University of South Carolina Press, 2001), 377.

5. Ibid., 378.

6. http://www.fortunecity.com/tinpan/parton/2/dixie.html, accessed July 16, 2002.

7. Donald Fehrenbacher, ed., *Abraham Lincoln: A Documentary Portrait through His Speeches and Writings* (Stanford, CA: Stanford University Press, 1964), 122, 124, 126.

8. Allan Nevins, *The Emergence of Lincoln*, 2 vols. (New York: Scribner, 1950), 2:42.

9. Ibid., 2:68–69.

10. Edward J. Renehan Jr., *The Secret Six: The True Tale of the Men Who Conspired with John Brown* (Columbia: University of South Carolina Press, 1996), 190.

11. Ibid., 202.

12. Ibid., 222.

13. David M. Potter, *The Impending Crisis, 1848–1861* (New York: Harper & Row, 1976), 376.

14. Walther, *Fire-Eaters*, 258.

15. Stephen Oates, *To Purge This Land with Blood: A Biography of John Brown* (New York: Harper & Row, 1970), 318–19.

16. Ibid., 338.

17. Ibid., 351.

18. Renehan, *Secret Six*, 234.

*Emphasis in all quotations is that of the original authors.

19. Ibid., 230.

20. Wendy Hammond Venet, " 'Cry Aloud and Spare Not': Northern Antislavery Women and John Brown's Raid," in *His Soul Goes Marching On: Responses to John Brown and the Harpers Ferry Raid*, ed. Paul Finkelman (Charlottesville: University Press of Virginia, 1995), 105.

21. Potter, *Impending Crisis*, 378–79.

22. C. Vann Woodward, *The Burden of Southern History* (Baton Rouge: Louisiana State University Press, 1968), 48.

23. Venet, " 'Cry Aloud and Spare Not,' " 105–6.

24. Ibid., 107.

25. Potter, *Impending Crisis*, 380.

26. Furman University, Secession Era Editorials Project; Harper's Ferry/John Brown Editorials (1859), http://history.furman.edu/~benson/docs/iniljb59a22a.htm, accessed July 16, 2002.

27. Furman University, Secession Era Editorials Project; Harper's Ferry/John Brown Editorials (1859), http://history.furman.edu/~benson/docs/ilsrjb59a20a.htm, accessed July 16, 2002.

28. Venet, " 'Cry Aloud and Spare Not,' " 108.

29. Peter Wallenstein, "Incendiaries All: Southern Politics and the Harper's Ferry Raid," in *His Soul Goes Marching On*, ed. Finkleman, 152.

30. John C. Inscoe, *Mountain Masters, Slavery, and the Sectional Crisis in Western North Carolina* (Knoxville: University of Tennessee Press, 1989), 212.

31. Furman University, Secession Era Editorials Project; Harper's Ferry/John Brown Editorials (1859), http://history.furman.edu/~benson/docs/ncwhjb59a26a.htm, accessed July 16, 2002.

32. Roy P. Basler et al., eds., *The Collected Works of Abraham Lincoln*, 9 vols. (New Brunswick, NJ: Rutgers University Press, 1953), 3:541.

33. Wallenstein, "Incendiaries All," 159.

34. All in Potter, *Impending Crisis*, 383.

35. Wallenstein, "Incendiaries All," 161.

36. Bruce C. Levine, *Half Slave and Half Free: The Roots of Civil War* (New York: Hill and Wang, Noonday Press, 1992), 233.

37. *Charleston Mercury*, November 1, 1859.

38. Basler, *Collected Works of Abraham Lincoln*, 3:502

39. David Herbert Donald, *Charles Sumner and the Coming of the Civil War*, 1st ed. (New York: Knopf, 1960), 347, 349.

40. Walther, *Fire-Eaters*, 184–85.

41. Ibid., 259.

42. Renehan, *Secret Six*, 240.

43. Ibid., 241.

44. Ibid., 250–51.

45. Nevins, *Emergence of Lincoln*, 2:123.

46. Wallenstein, "Incendiaries All," 163.

47. Ibid., 165.

48. Walther, *Fire-Eaters*, 286.

EPILOGUE
The 1860s and Beyond

JOHN BROWN'S GHOST haunted the South for months. When extreme heat and drought helped spark a series of fires in far-off Texas in the summer of 1860, many there blamed abolitionist emissaries and supposed black allies. After Dallas burned, white vigilantes whipped every single adult slave in the county in their frenzied efforts to get confessions. Suspicious Northerners residing in the South found themselves whipped, beaten, or banished. In Kentucky twelve entire families involved with Berea College were driven from the state; three seamen from Maine were pummeled when they came ashore in Georgia; the new president of the University of Alabama, a New Yorker, had to flee to save his life. To growing numbers, secession suddenly seemed the only way not just to protect slavery but also to save their own lives. And every day, more clamored for disunion.

Abraham Lincoln never let threats of secession and war alter his commitment to the Republican Party, its pledge to stop the spread of slavery, or his desire now to lead the nation. He heard loud and clear the Southern accusations of Republican complicity in the John Brown affair but met that challenge just as directly as he had faced the warnings of disunion. As he explained emphatically at the Cooper Institute in New York on February 27, 1860, "Neither let us be slandered from our duty by false accusations against us, nor frightened from it by menaces of destruction to the Government nor of dungeons to ourselves. LET US HAVE FAITH THAT RIGHT MAKES MIGHT, AND IN THAT FAITH, LET US, TO THE END, DARE TO DO OUR DUTY AS WE UNDERSTAND IT."[1]

William Lowndes Yancey entered the Democratic National Convention in Charleston in April equally resolved not to let Stephen Douglas and his popular sovereignty get that party's backing for the presidency. Instead, Yancey continued to demand, as Jefferson Davis now did, active federal government support to promote slavery in the national territories. He reminded all Americans about what Harpers Ferry meant: "Ours is the property invaded; ours are the institutions which are at stake; ours is the property to be destroyed; ours is the honor at stake." In his attempt to court Northern delegates, Yancey offered, "If we beat you, we give you good servants for life and enable you to live comfortably," and so invited all white men to join him "among the master race and put the negro race to do the dirty work which God designed they should do."[2] Delegates pledged to Douglas stood their ground as well, so Yancey kept his promise to walk out of the convention. In his wake so did the delegates from most of the slave states and even some sympathetic Northern Democrats. The party split in two, just as many politicians had promised or predicted in 1859. Douglas got the nomination from Northern Democrats, and Vice President John C. Breckinridge accepted the presidential nomination of Southern Democrats.

A few weeks later in Chicago, after three rounds of ballots, Abraham Lincoln prevailed in the Republican National Convention, defeating party luminary and favorite William H. Seward. Although Southerners had expected Seward to prevail and prepared to assail him for his "higher law" and "irrepressible conflict," once the news spread they instantly shifted their wrath to Lincoln and his conviction that the nation could not long stand "half slave and half free." For a growing number of Americans a grim inevitability emerged, with the Republican Party both determined and poised to win without a single vote from the South and the South threatening to dissolve the Union should that occur. Against this backdrop a new party emerged. It called itself the Constitution Union Party, and it nominated John Bell, a Unionist slaveholder from Tennessee, for president. Bell and his party consciously decided to avoid all substantial issues and to cling religiously and myopically to the sanctity of the Constitution and the Union. It was a party of desperation in the face of disaster, and it drew its considerable support mostly from voters in Kentucky, Virginia, Tennessee, Missouri, and North Carolina—the very states most likely to host contending armies if secession materialized and led in turn to war between the sections.

In October 1860 several states held their elections for statewide and local positions. All eyes turned to Pennsylvania: the state with the largest electoral vote in the North, the state that Republicans had failed to carry in 1856, and the state they had to win along with two others from the North to elect Lincoln. Republicans won there in a landslide, giving everyone a clear idea of how things

would unfold in November. Even Stephen Douglas saw the implications and decided to do something extraordinary and heroic. The
Little Giant abandoned his long quest for the presidency and, literally at the risk of his life, made a speaking tour in the Deep South
to try and stem secession. He assured the few who listened that
Lincoln had no intention of destroying slavery in the states, just to
stop it in the territories. Douglas urged Americans to continue de-
bating that issue and begged them not to destroy the country. His
labors, of course, proved futile.

Lincoln won. The governor of South Carolina called a special
convention for his people to consider their reaction. On December 20
the convention agreed unanimously to dissolve its compact with
the other states and thereby dissolved the Union. Robert Barnwell
Rhett composed an address to the other slave states, inviting them
to join South Carolina in a slaveholding republic. He suggested
Yancey's hometown, Montgomery, Alabama, as the new capital.
After a tense lull for the holidays, in rapid order, Mississippi,
Florida, Alabama, Georgia, Louisiana, and Texas each seceded by
February 1 and sent delegates to Montgomery to create a provisional government for the Confederate States of America. Ironically,
in 1859, Lincoln had accused Jefferson Davis and Alexander H.
Stephens of leading the forces of the "Slave Power," and now these
very two became president and vice president of a slaveholding
republic.

Until March 4, 1861, James Buchanan remained president in title
and in fact. Before South Carolina's convention assembled in December, the president issued a bold proclamation clearly condemning secession as unconstitutional. Yet in the same message,
Buchanan meekly conceded that the Constitution gave him no
power to stop it. As militia units started to confront federal troops
in various locales in the seceded states and threats piled up high
upon other threats, the president, too afraid to precipitate conflict
and bloodshed, did nothing. Only weeks after Buchanan turned
over the command of the ship of state to Lincoln, America's bloodiest war began. After the events of the previous ten years, it was
remarkable that the Union held together as long as it did.

The same forces that drove politics during the 1850s—animos-
ity, paranoia, the certainty among so many Americans that only
people in their section of the country truly understood what
America represented and what God's will was—now came to the
battlefield, with horrific results. Each side initially expected a quick

victory and either restoration of the Union or Confederate independence, but neither occurred for a long time. Instead, after four
years of brutal combat, the North had mustered into service some
two million troops, the South about 900,000; of these, over 405,000
Northern men died, with another 385,000 wounded, and the South
suffered 260,000 killed and 320,000 more wounded. It was a level
of sustained violence and bloodshed that has enthralled Americans
ever since. If the United States were to experience the same magni-
tude of slaughter in proportion to the total population of the country according to the 2000 federal census, that would leave us with
over 10,457,000 casualties. This, in turn, would average a stagger-
ing 6,925 killed and wounded—more than twice the toll of September 11, 2001—every day for slightly over four years.[3] Whole towns
and villages in both the North and South lost virtually every young
man they sent off to war. Hundreds of thousands of widows and
orphans joined the sea of wounded soldiers in dealing with the
scars of war for the rest of their lives.

As the war progressed and grew more bloody, Abraham Lincoln
struggled against many in his own party to stick to his campaign
promise not to touch slavery where it already existed and to only
prevent it from spreading into the territories. Frederick Douglass,
Charles Sumner, William Lloyd Garrison, and others criticized
Lincoln's war aim of simply restoring the old Union; they argued
that as long as the source of conflict—slavery—remained, the entire human sacrifice of the war would prove in vain. That argument made sense to Lincoln, who had never liked slavery but could
never figure out what might be done to end it in his lifetime. As the
carnage continued, Lincoln slowly developed a plan of limited
emancipation as a wartime executive order that he could wield to
do what was morally right, to undermine the vast pool of labor
within the Confederacy, and to slam the door on any possibility of
military intervention from England or France. He also hoped that
the prospect of ending the sin of slavery might reinvigorate the
Northern population both on the home front and among the troops,
although he still worried about the racism that permeated Northern society, his own included. Issues concerning race relations in a
postslavery United States were many and complex, but for now,
Lincoln had a war to fight and a country to reconstruct. He decided to leave as many of these details as possible until after the
fighting ended.

African Americans, of course, had resisted enslavement as tenaciously as they could over their nearly 250 years of bondage in America. When they thought they could get away with working slowly and inefficiently, breaking tools, uprooting crops, or running away, countless thousands had done so already. With secession and war many slaves sensed that their freedom might finally come. After all, for years their masters had bitterly and loudly complained about Yankees who hoped to end slavery. The war also resulted in fewer masters or patrols behind the lines of battle, and many slaves took advantage of that in attempting escape. Once Union soldiers began to penetrate into the Confederacy, many more slaves instinctively flocked toward them, whether or not they had heard of Lincoln's Emancipation Proclamation. Over 130,000 men who began the war as slaves, with Abraham Lincoln's vow to keep them enslaved, ended up serving in Lincoln's armies as troops. Certainly, these soldiers fought for themselves, their families, and their people. They also contributed significantly to the country's war effort, even while suffering abuse and discrimination from Northerners. The military assigned black troops to racially segregated units commanded by white officers. Blacks received less pay than whites. Black soldiers usually had the most demeaning duties behind the lines, and once they were sent into battle, they often received suicidal assignments.

Whatever the primary motives of black servicemen, they aided their country, and their commander in chief recognized it. Their communal service record forced Lincoln to confront his own racist assumptions. Before war's end, Lincoln offered tantalizing signals that he could accept black political equality (through voting and political office) and perhaps even something approximating social equality. But before Lincoln could focus more directly on Reconstruction, an assassin's bullet changed nearly everything. His successor, Andrew Johnson, detested black people.

The South suffered a defeat as complete and thorough as that of almost any nation since 1865. It lost its fledgling independence. Besides the devastating losses of men, war destroyed much of the South's infrastructure, including its agricultural and industrial capacity. With emancipation came an end to its primary system of controlling both labor and race, as well as the evaporation of almost one-third of the total physical wealth of the region—the money invested in slaves. Then came Union occupation troops and frightening uncertainty, and all of these plagues were visited upon a populace who generally believed they had been correct in their political, military, and racial decisions and had simply been overpowered.

For the former slaves, the defeat of the slave regime offered them their wildest dreams come true, but dreams turned quickly into living nightmares. They had no ally in the White House. Republicans in Congress struggled as much to take control of Reconstruction from Andrew Johnson as they did to address the urgent needs of former slaves. Unrepentant rebels formed political and terrorist organizations aimed at blacks and their few white allies. At whatever moment slaves became free and under whatever circumstances (through Lincoln's proclamation or through escape), at that moment they had "nothing but freedom": they had no legal claim to their homes, to land, to the clothes they wore, or even to their next meal.[4] Many white Southerners shuddered at Union occupation troops, officials from the Freedmen's Bureau, and "carpetbaggers" who came from the North to participate in shaping the new order of Southern life. But in fact, as African Americans knew too well, the North never sent enough people or resources to adequately protect the lives and liberties of the former slaves. And with even nominal voting rights granted to black men before any white women gained the elective franchise, many of the women political activists in the country who had joined the crusade for black rights, such as Susan B. Anthony, succumbed to their own racism and turned away from their former black friends and allies and the masses of precariously free people. Over time, the persistent racism of Northerners and the unflagging resistance of white Southerners resulted in the end of Reconstruction as a political program by 1877, which in turn resulted in an abandonment of African American rights throughout the nation. It would take the politics and political actors of a different day—of a different century—to deal with these issues in a meaningful way.

NOTES

1. Donald Fehrenbacher, ed., *Abraham Lincoln: A Documentary Portrait through His Speeches and Writings* (Stanford, CA: Stanford University Press, 1964), 142–43.

2. William Lowndes Yancey, *Speech of the Hon. William L. Yancey, of Alabama: Delivered in the National Democratic Convention, Charleston, April 28th, 1860* (Charleston, SC: Walker, Evans, & Co., 1860), 4, 13 ("master race").

3. Calculations drawn from Richard Current et al., eds., *Encyclopedia of the Confederacy* (New York: Simon & Schuster, 1993), 337–40. Using these same figures, casualties during the Civil War averaged out to about 772 per day, or 5,409 per week, for over four years.

4. Eric Foner, *Nothing but Freedom: Emancipation and Its Legacy* (Baton Rouge: Louisiana State University Press, 1983).

BIBLIOGRAPHICAL ESSAY

Anything close to a comprehensive bibliography of books, articles, and primary sources for this era would easily exceed the length of this book. This essay is highly selective and focuses primarily on monographs and other sources that helped shape my thinking about this work. The best, most comprehensive study of the politics of the United States prior to the Civil War remains the multivolume study by Allan Nevins, including *The Ordeal of the Union: The Fruits of Manifest Destiny, 1847–1852* (1947); *The Ordeal of the Union: A House Dividing, 1852–1857* (1947); *The Emergence of Lincoln: Douglas, Buchanan, and Party Chaos, 1857–1859* (1950); and *The Emergence of Lincoln: Prologue to Civil War, 1859–1861* (1950), while David M. Potter, *The Impending Crisis, 1848–1861* (1976), still stands out as the best monograph. The best subsequent monograph that approximates Potter's is Michael A. Morrison, *Slavery and the American West: The Eclipse of Manifest Destiny and the Coming of the Civil War* (1997). Other valuable surveys include Bruce C. Levine, *Half Slave and Half Free: The Roots of Civil War* (1992), which seamlessly integrates social and labor history with politics. Richard H. Sewell presents a more traditional survey of both the antebellum and Civil War eras in *A House Divided: Sectionalism and Civil War, 1848–1865* (1988). Michael F. Holt argued that the collapse of the second party system triggered secession and war in *The Political Crisis of the 1850s* (1978); George B. Forgie's highly controversial *Patricide in the House Divided: A Psychological Interpretation of Lincoln and his Age* (1979) nevertheless offers a fascinating alternative interpretation of the politicians of this time for those who are well read in the newspapers and correspondence of the era. James M. McPherson provides a superb analysis of the antebellum era in the first seven chapters of his prizewinning *Battle Cry of Freedom: The Civil War Era* (1988), and more than half of Roger L. Ransom's *Conflict and Compromise: The Political Economy of Slavery, Emancipation, and the American Civil War* (1989) deals with the antebellum period. Also valuable is *Essays on American Antebellum Politics, 1840–1860* (1982), edited by Stephen E. Maizlish and John J. Kushma.

Related to the role and impact of political parties, key works include Tyler Anbinder, *Nativism and Slavery: The Northern Know*

Nothings and the Politics of the 1850s (1992); Frederick J. Blue, *The Free Soilers: Third Party Politics, 1848–1854* (1973); William E. Gienapp, *The Origins of the Republican Party, 1852–1856* (1987); Daniel W. Howe, *The Political Culture of the American Whigs* (1979); and Michael F. Holt, *The Rise and Fall of the American Whig Party: Jacksonian Politics and the Onset of the Civil War* (1999).

To gain a better understanding of sectional politics and political culture, see Jean H. Baker, *Affairs of Party: The Political Culture of Northern Democrats in the Mid-Nineteenth Century* (1992); Susan-Mary Grant, *North over South: Northern Nationalism and American Identity in the Antebellum Era* (2000); and James A. Rawley, *The Politics of Union: Northern Politics during the Civil War* (1974), as well as Ronald P. Formisano, *The Transformation of Political Culture: Massachusetts Parties, 1790s–1840s* (1983), and Sean Wilentz, *Chants Democratic: New York City and the Rise of the American Working Class, 1788–1850* (1984). For the growing Northern obsession with the expansion of slavery in the country and in politics, see David Brion Davis, *The Slave Power Conspiracy and the Paranoid Style* (1969). The indispensable starting point for the South is William J. Cooper Jr., *The South and the Politics of Slavery, 1828–1856* (1978). Also see J. Mills Thornton III, *Politics and Power in a Slave Society: Alabama, 1800–1860* (1978), and William L. Barney, *The Road to Secession: A New Perspective on the Old South* (1972). Two quite different interpretations of the same state provide good insight into the region as well. The first, Bradley G. Bond's *Political Culture in the Nineteenth-Century South: Mississippi, 1830–1900* (1995), I find more persuasive regarding party institutions and members, although Christopher J. Olsen's *Political Culture and Secession in Mississippi: Masculinity, Honor, and the Antiparty Tradition, 1830–1860* (2000) more completely integrates social values and gender.

Few topics have enjoyed more attention, scrutiny, and reinterpretation than antislavery and abolitionism. Still useful are Thomas D. Morris, *Free Men All: The Personal Liberty Laws of the North, 1780–1861* (1974); Hans Trefousse, *The Radical Republicans: Lincoln's Vanguard for Racial Justice* (1969); Benjamin Quarles, *Black Abolitionists* (1969); and Richard Sewell, *Ballots for Freedom: Antislavery Politics in the United States, 1837–1860* (1976). To sample some of the breadth of more recent study, see Richard H. Abbott, *Cotton and Capital: Boston Businessmen and Antislavery Reform, 1854–1868* (1991); Edward Magdol, *The Antislavery Rank and File: A Social Profile of the Abolitionists' Constituency* (1986); John R. McKivigan and Stanley

Harrold, eds., *Antislavery Violence: Sectional, Racial, and Cultural Conflict in Antebellum America* (1999); Shirley J. Yee, *Black Women Abolitionists: A Study in Activism, 1828–1860* (1992); and John Stauffer's fascinating *The Black Hearts of Men: Radical Abolitionists and the Transformation of Race* (2002). A critical source of primary documents can be found in C. Peter Ripley et al., eds., *The Black Abolitionist Papers* (1985–1992), and Michael Meyer provides a good selection of documents from one of the most famous abolitionists in *The Narrative and Selected Writings: Frederick Douglass* (1984).

An organized women's rights movement did not exist in the South prior to the Civil War, but in the North that effort often intertwined itself with abolition. For two quite different glimpses into this intersection, see Jeanne Boydston, Mary Kelley, and Anne Margolis, eds., *The Limits of Sisterhood: The Beecher Sisters on Women's Rights and Woman's Sphere* (1988), and Stacey M. Robertson, *Parker Pillsbury: Radical Abolitionist, Male Feminist* (2000). Virginia Bernhard and Elizabeth Fox-Genovese make readily available scores of illustrative documents in their edition, *The Birth of American Feminism: The Seneca Falls Convention of 1848* (1995).

Political radicalism in the South—proslavery and prosecession—manifested itself in a variety of ways. John McCardell combines political, social, and cultural aspects of Southern extremism in *The Idea of a Southern Nation: Southern Nationalists and Southern Nationalism, 1830–1860* (1979). *The Ideology of Slavery: Proslavery Thought in the Antebellum South, 1830–1860* (1981), edited by Drew Gilpin Faust, provides the best overview of this critical topic as well as a good variety of samples that demonstrate the diversity of proslavery theory and argumentation. Focusing more narrowly on politics are Lacy K. Ford Jr., *Origins of Southern Radicalism: The South Carolina Upcountry, 1800–1860* (1988); Eric H. Walther, *The Fire-Eaters* (1992); and William W. Freehling, *The Road to Disunion: Secessionists at Bay, 1776–1854* (1990). One of the most important state studies is John C. Inscoe, *Mountain Masters, Slavery, and the Sectional Crisis in Western North Carolina* (1989). While Reginald Horsman provides a sharp analysis of American territorial expansionism in *Race and Manifest Destiny: The Origins of American Racial Anglo-Saxonism* (1981), Robert E. May supplies the best sectional explanation of this phenomenon in *The Southern Dream of a Caribbean Empire, 1854–1861* (1989). Also see Ronald T. Takaki, *A Pro-Slavery Crusade: The Agitation to Reopen the African Slave Trade* (1971).

For insight into various aspects of Southern society in general, some of the most noteworthy works include Eugene D. Genovese, *The Slaveholders' Dilemma: Freedom and Progress in Southern Conservative Thought, 1820–1860* (1992), and Kenneth S. Greenberg, *Masters and Statesmen: The Political Culture of American Slavery* (1985), as well as his controversial but very thoughtful *Honor and Slavery: Lies, Duels, Noses, Masks, Dressing As a Woman, Gifts, Strangers, Humanitarianism, Death, Slave Rebellions, the Proslavery Argument, Baseball, Hunting, and Gambling in the Old South* (1996). The best general study of Southern honor, however, is still Bertram Wyatt-Brown's *Southern Honor: Ethics and Behavior in the Old South* (1982). Clement Eaton's *The Mind of the Old South* (1964) also remains valuable. The following four studies sample current scholarship concerning ordinary whites in the Old South: Bill Cecil-Fronsman, *Common Whites: Class and Culture in Antebellum North Carolina* (1992); Stephanie McCurry, *Masters of Small Worlds: Yeoman Households, Gender Relations, and the Political Culture of the Antebellum South Carolina Low Country* (1995); Steven Hahn, *The Roots of Southern Populism: Yeomen Farmers and the Transformation of the Georgia Upcountry, 1850–1890* (1983); and J. William Harris, *Plain Folk and Gentry in a Slave Society: White Liberty and Black Slavery in Augusta's Hinterlands* (1985).

Religious zeal played a critical role in the growing intolerance that was part and parcel of the sectional crisis. The most useful works on this topic include Richard J. Carwardine, *Evangelicals and Politics in Antebellum America* (1993); Anne C. Loveland, *Southern Evangelicals and the Social Order, 1800–1860* (1980); and Mitchell Snay, *Gospel of Disunion: Religion and Separatism in the Antebellum South* (1993).

For African Americans, slave and free, North and South, some of the most important studies include Eugene D. Genovese, *Roll, Jordan, Roll: The World the Slaves Made* (1974); Charles Joyner, *Down by the Riverside: A South Carolina Slave Community* (1984); and Peter Kolchin, *American Slavery, 1619–1877* (1993), for the institution of slavery, the interplay between masters and slaves, and the dynamics of African American culture under the oppressive forces of bondage. For free blacks in the North, the key study is still Leon Litwack, *North of Slavery: The Negro in the Free States, 1790–1860* (1961); for free blacks in the South, see Ira Berlin, *Slaves without Masters: The Free Negro in the Antebellum South* (1974). Walter Johnson illuminates the experiences of black men and women involved in the Deep

South slave trade in his *Soul by Soul: Life inside the Antebellum Slave Market* (1999). John Hope Franklin and Loren Schweninger recount and analyze slave resistance in *Runaway Slaves: Rebels on the Plantation* (1999), and Clarence L. Mohr's *On the Threshold of Freedom: Masters and Slaves in Civil War Georgia* (1986) demonstrates how slaves themselves helped undermine the institution and worked for their own emancipation before Lincoln's proclamation. Melton McLaurin, *Celia, A Slave* (1991), offers a fascinating case study of one young woman's struggle for her safety as well as white reactions to slave resistance. Charles M. Christian provides a very useful, encyclopedic overview in *Black Saga: The African American Experience* (1999). A valuable and varied collection of primary sources is supplied by Steven Mintz, ed., *African American Voices: The Life Cycle of Slavery* (1995).

I relied quite heavily on the following works for several specific topics. See Nat Brandt, *The Town That Started the Civil War* (1990), for the Oberlin rescue; James L. Huston, *The Panic of 1857 and the Coming of the Civil War* (1987); Kenneth Stampp, *America in 1857: A Nation on the Brink* (1990); Mark W. Summers, *The Plundering Generation: Corruption and the Crisis of the Union, 1849–1861* (1987); Larry Gara, *The Presidency of Franklin Pierce* (1991); David Zarefsky, *Lincoln, Douglas, and Slavery: In the Crucible of Public Debate* (1990); Don Fehrenbacher, *The Dred Scott Case: Its Significance in American Law and Politics* (1978); Paul Finkelman, *An Imperfect Union: Slavery, Federalism, and Comity* (1981); and Peter B. Knupfer, *The Union As It Is: Constitutional Unionism and Sectional Compromise, 1787–1861* (1991).

The most important studies of the saga and impact of John Brown in Kansas and his raid on Harpers Ferry are Edward J. Renehan Jr., *The Secret Six: The True Tale of the Men Who Conspired with John Brown* (1996); Stephen B. Oates, *To Purge This Land with Blood: A Biography of John Brown* (1970); Paul Finkelman, ed., *His Soul Goes Marching On: Responses to John Brown and the Harpers Ferry Raid* (1995); and Jeffery S. Rossbach, *Ambivalent Conspirators: John Brown, the Secret Six, and a Theory of Slave Violence* (1982). A good source of contemporary newspaper reactions can be accessed through Furman University's "Secession Era Editorials Project" at http://history.furman.edu/~benson/docs/jbmenu.htm.

For the daunting task of exploring the roles of Abraham Lincoln and Jefferson Davis, I relied most heavily upon David Herbert Donald, *Lincoln* (1995); Robert W. Johannsen, *Lincoln, the South, and*

Slavery: The Political Dimension (1991); the multivolume collection of documents by Roy P. Basler et al., eds., *The Collected Works of Abraham Lincoln* (1953); and Donald Fehrenbacher's handy *Abraham Lincoln: A Documentary Portrait through His Speeches and Writings* (1964). For Jefferson Davis, current scholarship would not be possible without Haskell Monroe et al., eds., *The Papers of Jefferson Davis* (1971–). The best biographies are William C. Davis, *Jefferson Davis: The Man and His Hour* (1991), and William J. Cooper, *Jefferson Davis, American* (2000).

Other biographies that I have used extensively include David Herbert Donald, *Charles Sumner and the Coming of the Civil War* (1960); Frederick J. Blue, *Charles Sumner and the Conscience of the North* (1994); Drew Gilpin Faust, *James Henry Hammond and the Old South: A Design for Mastery* (1982); Craig M. Simpson, *A Good Southerner: The Life of Henry A. Wise of Virginia* (1985); David S. Reynolds, *Walt Whitman's America: A Cultural Biography* (1995); and William C. Davis, *Rhett: The Turbulent Life and Times of a Fire-Eater* (2001) as well as *The Union That Shaped the Confederacy: Robert Toombs and Alexander H. Stephens* (2001); H. Edward Richardson, *Cassius Marcellus Clay: Firebrand of Freedom* (1976); and David W. Blight, *Frederick Douglass' Civil War: Keeping Faith in Jubilee* (1989).

Index

Sacramento (California), 14, 78
Salt Lake City, 132
Sanborn, Franklin, 169, 172, 173, 180; and John Brown, 145
San Diego, 36
Sanford, Alexander, 119
Sanford, Eliza, 119
San Francisco, 13, 31, 35, 52, 74, 77, 78
San Salvador, 103
Santa Anna, Antonio López de, 29
Savannah (Georgia), 126, 156
Sayres, Edward, 15–16
Scott, Dred, 118–21. *See also Dred Scott v. Sandford*
Scott, Harriet, 121
Scott, Winfield, 2, 4–6, 17, 19; on slavery, 2–3
Secession, xi, 14, 17–19, 27, 59, 94, 98, 111–12, 142, 144, 147–49, 159, 166, 178, 181, 185–87; and Compromise of 1850, xix
Segregation, xxiv, 12, 23, 75–76, 115; African American support for, 75
Seward, William H., .xvii, xviii, 1, 2, 3, 6, 17, 42, 46, 80, 100, 108, 157–59, 163, 177, 179; on John Brown, 176; and election of 1860, 169, 186; and Harpers Ferry, 181; on homestead bill, 165; "irrepressible conflict," 158; on Kansas, 96
Shadd, Abraham, 107
Shadd, Mary Ann, 106–7
Shannon, Wilson, 69, 82, 102; and Wakarusa War, 83
Shawnee Mission (Kansas), 64, 66, 69, 82, 88, 90
Sherman, John, 181
Sherman, William Tecumseh, 181
Shields, James, 80
Sickles, Daniel E., 163–64
Sickles, Teresa, 163–64
Simms, William Gilmore, 8, 136
Slaughter, James, 149
Slave expansion, 27, 30, 36, 39, 44, 46–47, 51, 58, 59, 78–80, 105, 108, 117, 120, 122, 125–27, 139, 160, 165, 169

"Slave Power" conspiracy, 36, 43, 46, 48, 53, 69, 80, 105, 110, 149, 151, 152, 167, 175, 179, 187
Slaves and slavery, xvii, xix, xx, 47, 50, 51; attitudes toward, 8–9, 21–22; conditions, 22, 69; and the Constitution, 51; in Cuba, 79; domestic slave trade, xvii, xxii, 50, 72; slave resistance, 22, 70, 72, 110, 130, 145; sexual exploitation, 92; in territories, xxi–xxii, 3, 39–42, 117, 120–22, 165. *See also* Antislavery; Proslavery
Slidell, John, 116
Smith, Elizabeth Oakes, 18
Smith, Gerrit, xvii, 18, 41, 68, 89, 106, 169, 172, 179–80; and John Brown, 145
Smith, James McCune, 75
Smith, Joseph, 132
Soft Shell Democrats, 58
Sonora (Mexico), 31
Soulé, Pierre, 15, 27, 31–33, 52–53, 79, 103–5, 108
South America, and black colonization, 129
South Carolina, xviii, xx, 8, 13, 187
South Carolina Military Academy (The Citadel), 93
Southern Commercial Conventions, 125–27, 147–48, 165–66
Southern economy, xx, xxii–xxiii; on free labor, 95
Southern Literary Messenger, 7–8
Southern Quarterly Review, 8, 10
Southern Rights Associations, xviii
Southern Rights Convention (1852), 18
Southern Rights Party, 19
Southern society, xxi, 28, 58, 92; education, 93–94; fears of antislavery conspiracy, 194–95; Northern views of, 91–92; social classes, xx; yeomen, xix, xx
Spain, 27, 32–33, 52
Spratt, Leonidas W., 126
Springfield Republican, 110
Springfield State Register, 176
St. Catherines (Canada), 146, 150